Python Essentials

Modernize existing Python code and plan code migrations to Python using this definitive guide

Steven F. Lott

BIRMINGHAM - MUMBAI

Python Essentials

First published: June 2015

Production reference: 1250615

Published by Packt Publishing Ltd.
Livery Place
35 Livery Street
Birmingham B3 2PB, UK.

ISBN 978-1-78439-034-1

www.packtpub.com

Credits

Author
Steven F. Lott

Reviewers
Amoatey Harrison
Alessio Di Lorenzo
Dr. Philip Polstra

Commissioning Editor
Edward Gordon

Acquisition Editor
Subho Gupta

Content Development Editor
Adrian Raposo

Technical Editors
Dhiraj Chandanshive
Siddhi Rane

Copy Editors
Samantha Lyon
Kevin McGowan
Aditya Nair
Rashmi Sawant

Project Coordinator
Kinjal Bari

Proofreader
Safis Editing

Indexer
Priya Sane

Graphics
Sheetal Aute

Production Coordinator
Komal Ramchandani

Cover Work
Komal Ramchandani

About the Author

Steven F. Lott has been programming since the 70s, when computers were large, expensive, and rare. As a contract software developer and architect, he has worked on hundreds of projects, from very small to very large. He's been using Python to solve business problems for over 10 years.

He's particularly adept at struggling with thorny data representation problems.

He has also authored *Mastering Object-oriented Python* by Packt Publishing.

He is currently a technomad who lives in various places on the east coast of the US. His technology blog can be found at `http://slott-softwarearchitect.blogspot.com`.

About the Reviewers

Amoatey Harrison is a Python programmer with a passion for building software systems to solve problems. When he is not programming, he plays video games, swims, or simply hangs out with friends.

After graduating from the Kwame Nkrumah University of Science and Technology with a degree in computer engineering, he is currently doing his national service at the GCB Bank head office in Accra, Ghana. He also helped review a book on Python programming, *Functional Python Programming, Packt Publishing*, which was published in January 2015.

He would like to think of himself as a cool nerd.

Alessio Di Lorenzo is a marine biologist and has an MSc in geographical information systems (GIS) and remote sensing. Since 2006, he has been dealing with the analysis and development of GIS applications dedicated to the study and spread of environmental and epidemiological data. He is experienced in the use of the main proprietary and open source GIS software and programming languages.

He has coauthored *OpenLayers Starter* and reviewed *ArcPy and ArcGIS – Geospatial Analysis with Python*, both by Packt Publishing.

Dr. Philip Polstra (known as Dr. Phil to his friends) is an associate professor of digital forensics in the Department of Math and Digital Sciences at Bloomsburg University of Pennsylvania. He teaches forensics, information security, and penetration testing. His research over the last few years has been on the use of microcontrollers and small computer boards (such as the BeagleBone Black) for forensics and penetration testing.

He is an internationally recognized hardware hacker. His work has been presented at numerous conferences across the globe, including repeat performances at Black Hat, DEFCON, 44CON, B-sides, GrrCON, ForenSecure, and other top conferences. He has also provided training on forensics and security, both in person and online via http://www.pentesteracademy.com and other training sites.

He has published a number of books, including *Hacking and Penetration Testing with Low Power Devices*, *Syngress*, and *Linux Forensics from A to Z*, *PAP*. He has also been a technical editor or reviewer on numerous books.

When not teaching or speaking at a conference, he is known to build electronics with his children, fly airplanes, and also teach others how to fly and build airplanes. His latest happenings can be found on his blog at http://philpolstra.com.

www.PacktPub.com

Support files, eBooks, discount offers, and more

For support files and downloads related to your book, please visit www.PacktPub.com.

Did you know that Packt offers eBook versions of every book published, with PDF and ePub files available? You can upgrade to the eBook version at www.PacktPub. com and as a print book customer, you are entitled to a discount on the eBook copy. Get in touch with us at service@packtpub.com for more details.

At www.PacktPub.com, you can also read a collection of free technical articles, sign up for a range of free newsletters and receive exclusive discounts and offers on Packt books and eBooks.

https://www2.packtpub.com/books/subscription/packtlib

Do you need instant solutions to your IT questions? PacktLib is Packt's online digital book library. Here, you can search, access, and read Packt's entire library of books.

Why subscribe?

- Fully searchable across every book published by Packt
- Copy and paste, print, and bookmark content
- On demand and accessible via a web browser

Free access for Packt account holders

If you have an account with Packt at www.PacktPub.com, you can use this to access PacktLib today and view 9 entirely free books. Simply use your login credentials for immediate access.

Table of Contents

Preface

Python programming should be expressive and elegant. In order for this to be true, the language itself must be easy to learn and easy to use. Any practical language — and its associated libraries — can present a daunting volume of information. In order to help someone learn Python, we've identified and described those features that seem essential.

Learning a language can be a long voyage. We'll pass numerous islands, archipelagos, inlets, and estuaries along the route. Our objective is to point out the key features that will be passed during the initial stages of this journey.

The concepts of data structures and algorithms are ever-present considerations in programming. Our overall approach is to introduce the various Python data structures first. As part of working with a given class of objects, the language statements are introduced later. One of Python's significant advantages over other languages is the rich collection of built-in data types. Selecting an appropriate representation of data can lead to elegant, high-performance applications.

An essential aspect of Python is its overall simplicity. There are very few operators and very few different kinds of statements. Much of the code we write can be generic with respect to the underlying data type. This allows us to easily exchange different data structure implementations as part of making tradeoffs between storage, performance, accuracy, and other considerations.

Some subject areas could take us well beyond the basics. Python's object-oriented programming features are rich enough to easily fill several large volumes. If we're also interested in functional programming features, we can study these in far more depth elsewhere. We'll touch only briefly on these subjects.

What this book covers

Chapter 1, Getting Started, addresses installing or upgrading Python. We explore Python's Read-Evaluate-Print Loop (REPL) as a way to interact with the language. We'll use this interactive Python mode as a way to explore most of the language features.

Chapter 2, Simple Data Types, introduces a few features concerning numbers and some simple collections. We'll look at Python's Unicode strings as well as byte strings, including some of the conversions between strings and numbers.

Chapter 3, Expressions and Output, provides more details on Python expression syntax and how the various numeric types relate to each other. We'll look at the coercion rules and the numeric tower. We'll look at the print() function, which is a common tool for looking at output.

Chapter 4, Variables, Assignment and Scoping Rules, shows how we assign names to objects. We look at a number of different assignment statements available in Python. We also explore the input() function, which parallels the print() function.

Chapter 5, Logic, Comparisons, and Conditions, shows the logical operators and literals that Python uses. We'll look at the comparison operators and how we use them. We'll look closely at the if statement.

Chapter 6, More Complex Data Types, shows the core features of the list, set, and dict built-in types. We use the for statement to work with these collections. We also use functions such as sum(), map(), and filter().

Chapter 7, Basic Function Definitions, introduces the syntax for the def statement as well as the return statement. Python offers a wide variety of ways to provide argument values to functions; we show a few of the alternatives.

Chapter 8, More Advanced Functions, extends the basic function definitions to include the yield statement. This allows us to write generator functions that will iterate over a sequence of data values. We look at a few functional programming features available via built-in functions as well as the modules in the *Python Standard Library*.

Chapter 9, Exceptions, shows how we handle and raise exceptions. This allows us to write programs which are considerably more flexible. A simple "happy path" can handle the bulk of the processing, and exception clauses can handle rare or unexpected alternative paths.

Chapter 10, Files, Databases, Networks, and Contexts, will introduce a number of features related to persistent storage. We'll look at Python's use of files and file-like objects. We'll also extend the concept of persistence to include some database features available in the *Python Standard Library*. This chapter will also include a review of the `with` statement for context management.

Chapter 11, Class Definitions, demonstrates the `class` statement and the essentials of object-oriented programming. We look at the basics of inheritance and how to define class-level (static) methods.

Chapter 12, Scripts, Modules, Packages, Libraries, and Applications, shows different ways in which we can create Python code files. We'll look at the formal structures of script, module, and package. We'll also look at informal concepts such as application, library, and framework.

Chapter 13, Metaprogramming and Decorators, introduces two concepts that can help us write Python code that manipulates Python code. Python makes metaprogramming relatively simple; we can leverage this to simplify certain types of programming where a common aspect doesn't fit neatly into a class hierarchy or library of functions.

Chapter 14, Fit and Finish – Unit Testing, Packaging, and Documentation, moves beyond the Python language into the idea of creating a complete, polished product. Any well-written program should include test cases and documentation. We show common ways to make sure this is done properly.

Chapter 15, Next Steps, will demonstrate four simple kinds of applications. We'll look at the command-line interface (CLI), graphic user interface (GUI), simple Web frameworks, as well as MapReduce applications.

What you need for this book

We're going to focus on Python 3, exclusively. Many computers will have Python 2 already installed, which means an upgrade is required. Some computers don't have Python installed at all, which means that a fresh installation of Python 3 will be necessary. The details are the subject of *Chapter 1, Getting Started*.

It's important to note that Python 2 can't easily be used to run all of the examples. Python 2 may work for many of the examples, but it's not our focus.

In order to install software, you'll generally need administrative rights on the computer you intend to use. For a home computer, this is generally true. For computers supplied through work or school, administrative passwords may be required.

You may also want to have a proper programmer's text editor. Default text editing applications such as Windows Notepad or Mac OS X TextEdit can be used, but aren't ideal. There are numerous free text editors available: feel free to download several to locate the one that feels most comfortable for you.

Who this book is for

This book is for programmers who want to learn Python quickly. It shows key features of Python, assuming a background in programming. The focus is on essential features: the approach is broad but relatively shallow. We'll provide pointers and direction for additional study and research, assuming that the reader is willing and able to follow those pointers.

In many data-intensive industries, a great deal of big data analysis is done with Python and toolsets such as Apache Hadoop. In this case, the users of Python will be statisticians, data scientists, or analysts. Their interest isn't in Python itself, but in using Python to process collections of data. This book is designed to provide language fundamentals for data scientists.

This book can be used by students who are learning Python. Since this book doesn't cover the computer science foundations of programming, an additional text would be helpful.

Conventions

In this book, you will find a number of text styles that distinguish between different kinds of information. Here are some examples of these styles and an explanation of their meaning.

Code words in text, database table names, folder names, filenames, file extensions, pathnames, dummy URLs, user input, and Twitter handles are shown as follows: "We've built an `ArgumentParser` method using all of the default parameters."

A block of code is set as follows:

```
def prod(sequence):
    p= 1
    for item in sequence:
        p *= item
    return p
```

When we wish to draw your attention to a particular part of a code block, the relevant lines or items are set in bold:

```
def prod(sequence):
    p= 1
    for item in sequence:
        p *= item
    return
```

Any command-line input or output is written as follows:

```
MacBookPro-SLott:Code slott$ python3 -m test_all
```

New terms and **important words** are shown in bold. Words that you see on the screen, for example, in menus or dialog boxes, appear in the text like this: "Clicking on **Continue** will step through the **Read Me**, **License**, **Destination Select**, and **Installation Type** windows."

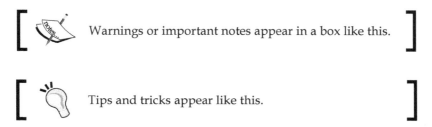

> Warnings or important notes appear in a box like this.

> Tips and tricks appear like this.

Reader feedback

Feedback from our readers is always welcome. Let us know what you think about this book—what you liked or disliked. Reader feedback is important for us as it helps us develop titles that you will really get the most out of.

To send us general feedback, simply e-mail feedback@packtpub.com, and mention the book's title in the subject of your message.

If there is a topic that you have expertise in and you are interested in either writing or contributing to a book, see our author guide at www.packtpub.com/authors.

Customer support

Now that you are the proud owner of a Packt book, we have a number of things to help you to get the most from your purchase.

Downloading the example code

You can download the example code files from your account at `http://www.packtpub.com` for all the Packt Publishing books you have purchased. If you purchased this book elsewhere, you can visit `http://www.packtpub.com/support` and register to have the files e-mailed directly to you.

Errata

Although we have taken every care to ensure the accuracy of our content, mistakes do happen. If you find a mistake in one of our books—maybe a mistake in the text or the code—we would be grateful if you could report this to us. By doing so, you can save other readers from frustration and help us improve subsequent versions of this book. If you find any errata, please report them by visiting `http://www.packtpub.com/submit-errata`, selecting your book, clicking on the **Errata Submission Form** link, and entering the details of your errata. Once your errata are verified, your submission will be accepted and the errata will be uploaded to our website or added to any list of existing errata under the Errata section of that title.

To view the previously submitted errata, go to `https://www.packtpub.com/books/content/support` and enter the name of the book in the search field. The required information will appear under the **Errata** section.

Piracy

Piracy of copyrighted material on the Internet is an ongoing problem across all media. At Packt, we take the protection of our copyright and licenses very seriously. If you come across any illegal copies of our works in any form on the Internet, please provide us with the location address or website name immediately so that we can pursue a remedy.

Please contact us at `copyright@packtpub.com` with a link to the suspected pirated material.

We appreciate your help in protecting our authors and our ability to bring you valuable content.

Questions

If you have a problem with any aspect of this book, you can contact us at `questions@packtpub.com`, and we will do our best to address the problem.

1
Getting Started

Python comes on some computers as part of the OS. On other computers, we'll need to add the Python program and related tools. The installation is pretty simple, but we'll review the details to be sure that everyone has a common foundation.

Once we have Python, we'll need to confirm that Python is present. In some cases, we'll have more than one version of Python available. We need to be sure that we're using Python 3.4 or newer. To confirm that Python's available, we'll do a few interactions at Python's >>> prompt.

To extend our foundation for the remaining chapters, we'll look at a few essential rules of Python syntax. This isn't complete, but it will help us write scripts and learn the language. After we've had more chances to work with simple and compound statements, the detailed syntax rules will make sense.

We'll also look at the Python "ecosystem", starting with the built-in standard library. We'll emphasize the standard library throughout this book for two reasons. First, it's immense—much of what we need is already on our computer. Second, and more important, studying this library is the best way to learn the finer points of Python programming.

Beyond the built-in library, we'll take a look at the **Python Package Index (PyPI)**. If we can't find the right module in the standard library, the second place to look for extensions is PyPI—https://pypi.python.org.

Installation or upgrade

To work with Python on Windows, we must install Python. For Mac OS X and Linux, a version of Python is already present; we'll often want to add a newer version to the preinstalled Python.

There are two significantly different flavors of Python available:

- Python 2.x
- Python 3.x

This book is about Python 3.4. We won't cover Python 2.x at all. There are several visible differences. What's important is that Python 2.x is a bit of a mess under the hood. Python 3 reflects some fundamental improvements. The improvements came at the cost of a few areas where the two versions of the language had to be made incompatible.

The Python community is continuing to keep Python 2.x around. Doing this is a help to people who are stuck with old software. For the most part, developers are moving forward with Python 3 because it's a clear improvement.

Before we get started, it's important to know if Python is already installed. The general test to see if Python is already installed is to get an OS command prompt. For Windows, use Command Prompt; for Mac OS X or Linux, use the Terminal tool. We'll show Mac OS X prompts from the Mac OS X Terminal. It looks like this:

```
MacBookPro-SLott:~ slott$ python3
Python 3.3.4 (v3.3.4:7ff62415e426, Feb  9 2014, 00:29:34)
[GCC 4.2.1 (Apple Inc. build 5666) (dot 3)] on darwin
Type "help", "copyright", "credits" or "license" for more information.
>>>
```

We've shown the OS prompt `MacBookPro-SLott:~ slott$`. We entered the `python3` command, which is typical for Linux and Mac OS X. In Windows, we'll often enter just `python`. The response was three lines of introduction followed by the `>>>` prompt. Enter `exit` and hit *return* to get some useful advice on how to leave Python. This example showed Python 3.3, which is a little out of date. An upgrade isn't required.

Some kind of "command not found" error from the OS means we don't have any Python, so we'll need to do an install.

If we get a Python message that starts with something like "Python 2.7.6", we'll need to do an upgrade.

The next section covers Windows installations. After that, we'll look at Mac OS X and then we will see Linux upgrades. In some cases, we may develop software on Windows desktop computers, but the ultimate destination is a large, centralized Linux server. The Python files can be the same between these two environments, so having Python on multiple platforms won't be very complex or confusing.

Installing Python on Windows

Python runs on many versions of Windows. There are some older, less-widely-used versions of Windows without an actively supported version of Python. For example, Windows 2000 is not supported.

The general procedure for installing Python is quite simple. We'll download an installer and do some preparation. Then we'll start the installer. Once that's finished, we'll be up and running.

To find the installer, start here:

```
https://www.python.org/downloads/
```

The web server should detect your OS and provide a big button with some variation of "Download Python 3.4.x" on it. Click on this button to start the download.

To look at the choices available, the `https://www.python.org/downloads/windows/` path provides all of the actively-supported versions of Python. This will show a long list of older versions. There are two installers available:

*   The Windows x86 MSI installer
*   The Windows x86-64 MSI installer

If we have a very old computer, we might need the 32-bit version. Most modern computers will have a 64-bit CPU. When in doubt, 64-bit is the assumption to make.

Double-click the `.msi` file to start running the installer. This starts with a question about installing Python for yourself or for all users. If you have appropriate privileges, the all users option is appropriate. On a shared computer, without appropriate privileges, you'll have to install it for yourself only.

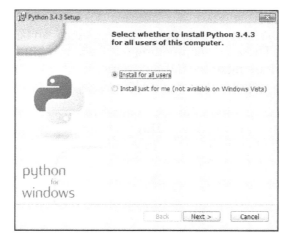

The second page will ask for an installation directory. Be careful about the path that you choose for the installation, and avoid spaces in filenames.

 Do not install Python into directories with spaces in their names. Avoid names such as "Program Files" and "My Documents". The space may cause problems that are difficult to diagnose.

Install Python into a simple directory with a short, space-free name like C:\python34.

Spaces in filenames is not a general problem, but it is awkward when first starting. There are many ways to cope with spaces in filenames. When learning a new programming language, however, it's important to minimize the awkward problems so that we can focus on the important topics.

The next page will also show a menu of components that can be installed; it's easiest to request everything. There's no compelling reason to turn off any of the optional components. We'll be looking at the IDLE development tool, which requires the **Tcl/Tk** package, so it's important to be sure that this is part of the installation.

In many cases, the final option on this list updates the system environment variables to include Python on the PATH variable. This isn't enabled by default, but it can be helpful if you're going to write BAT files in Windows.

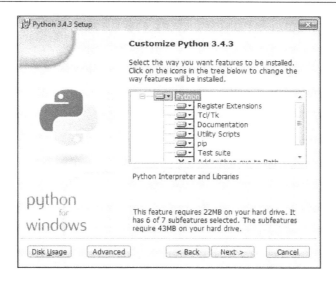

In addition to the basic Python interpreter, the Windows help installer is very helpful. This is a separate download and requires a quick installation. After we've installed this, we can use the *F1* key to bring up all of the Python documentation.

Once Python is installed, the *Using the Read-Evaluate-Print Loop (REPL)* section will show how to start interacting with Python.

Considering some alternatives

We'll focus on a particular implementation of Python called **CPython**. The distinction we're making here is that Python—the abstract language—can be processed by a variety of concrete Python runtimes or implementations. The CPython implementation is written in portable C and can be recompiled for many operating systems. This implementation tends to be extremely fast.

For Windows developers, there's an alternative implementation called **Iron Python**. This is tightly integrated with the Windows .NET development environment. It has the advantage of working with Visual Studio. It has the disadvantage of being based on the Python 2.7 language.

Another choice Windows users have is to use **Python Tools for Visual Studio (PTVS)**. This will allow you to use Python 3.4 from within Visual Studio. For developers who are used to Visual Studio, this might prove helpful.

Other Python implementations include Jython, Stackless Python, and PyPy. These alternatives are available for all operating systems, so we'll address these in the *Looking at other Python interpreters* section later.

Upgrading to Python 3.4 in Mac OS X

Python runs on all versions of Mac OS X. It turns out that Mac OS X relies on Python. However, it relies on Python 2.7, so we'll need to add Python 3.4.

The general procedure for installing Python on Mac OS X is quite simple. We'll download a disk image (`.dmg`) installer and do some preparation. Then we'll start the installer that's in the disk image. Once that's finished, we'll be up and running.

To find an installer, start here:

```
https://www.python.org/downloads/
```

The web server should detect your OS and provide a big button with some variation of "Download Python 3.4.x" on it. Click on this and download the `.dmg` file.

To look at the choices available, the `https://www.python.org/downloads/mac-osx/` path provides all of the actively-supported versions of Python for Mac OS X. This will show alternatives for older versions of Python.

When the `.dmg` device becomes available after the download, double-click on the `.mpkg` installer file to start running the installer.

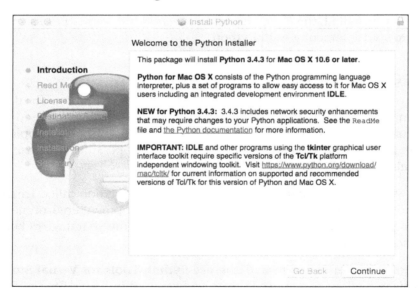

Clicking on **Continue** will step through the **Read Me**, **License**, **Destination Select**, and **Installation Type** windows. There's a **Customize** button that allows us to turn options on and off. We won't need to do this — the default installation is ideal.

We'll need to provide the username and password of a user who's authorized to administer this computer. This will not remove the existing Python that Mac OS X uses. It will add another version of Python. This means that we'll have at least two copies of Python. We'll focus on using Python 3, ignoring the built-in Python, which is Python 2.

To use Python 3, we have to enter `python3` at the OS prompt in the Terminal window. If we have *both* Python 3.3 and Python 3.4, we can enter the even more specific `python3.4` at the command prompt to specify which version of Python 3 we're using. Generally, the `python3` command will be the latest-and-greatest version of Python 3. The `python` command — unadorned with a version number — will be the Python 2.x that Mac OS X requires.

Adding the Tkinter package

Python relies on a library named Tkinter to provide support for writing programs with a GUI. This package relies on Tcl/Tk. The details can be found here:

`https://www.python.org/download/mac/tcltk/`

The summary of this is that we need to install version 8.5.17 or newer. See `https://www.python.org/download/mac/tcltk/#activetcl-8-5-17-0`. This will provide a graphic environment that Python will use. We must install Tcl/Tk in order for the `tkinter` package to work.

After we download the `.dmg` file and open the `.pkg` file, we'll see this window:

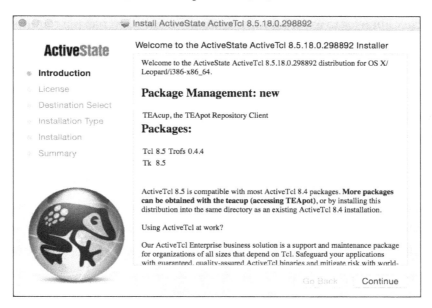

We'll be looking at the IDLE development tool, which requires `tkinter`. Consequently, this additional installation is essential.

We can avoid this extra download if we avoid using `tkinter`. Some developers prefer to use the Active State Komodo editor as their development tool; this does not require Tcl/Tk. Also, there are numerous add-on GUI frameworks that don't require `tkinter`.

Upgrading to Python 3.4 in Linux

For Linux, the latest Python may already be installed. When we enter `python3`, we may see that we already have a useful version available. In this case, we're ready to roll. In some cases, the OS will only have an older Python (perhaps older than 2.7) installed. In this case, we'll need to upgrade.

For Linux distributions, there are two paths for upgrading Python:

- Installing prebuilt packages: Many distributions have appropriate packages already available. We can use a package manager (such as `yum` or RPM) to locate and install the necessary Python package. In some cases, there will be additional dependencies, leading to a cascade of downloads and installs. Since Python 3.4 is relatively new, there may not be very many prebuilt packages for your particular Linux distribution. Details are available at `https://docs.python.org/3/using/unix.html#on-linux`.

- Building from source: Most Linux distributions include the GNU C compiler. We can download the Python source, configure the build script, and use `make` and `make install` to build Python. This may require upgrading some Linux libraries to assure that your Linux installation has the required support for Python 3.4. The installation steps are summarized as `./configure`, `make`, and `sudo make altinstall`. Details are available at `https://docs.python.org/3/using/unix.html#building-python`.

When we use `altinstall`, we'll end up with two Pythons installed. We'll have an older Python, which we can run using the `python` command. The `python3` command will, generally, be linked to the latest version of Python 3. If we need to be explicit, we can use the `python3.4` command to select a specific version.

As with the Mac OS X installation, adding the Python `tkinter` package is important. Sometimes, this is separate from the basic package. This may lead to upgrading Tcl/Tk, which may lead to some more downloads and installs. At other times, the Linux distribution has an up-to-date Tcl/Tk environment and nothing more needs to be done.

We can avoid the extra Tcl/Tk download if we avoid using `tkinter`. As mentioned earlier, many developers prefer to use the Active State Komodo editor as their development tool; this does not require `tkinter`. Also, there are numerous GUI frameworks that aren't based on `tkinter`.

Using the Read-Evaluate-Print Loop (REPL)

Once we have installed Python 3, we can do some minimal interaction with Python to assure ourselves that things are working. In the long run, we'll use a number of other tools to create Python programs. To start out, we'll interact directly on the command line.

Python's **Read-Evaluate-Print Loop (REPL)** is the foundation for Python programming. More sophisticated things—such as writing application scripts or web servers—are essentially the same as interaction with the REPL: the Python program reads statements from our application script file or web server script file and evaluates those statements.

This fundamental rule is one of the very appealing features of Python. We can write sophisticated scripts, or we can interact with the language in the REPL; the language is the same.

Confirming that things are working

To confirm that things are working, we'll start the Python interpreter from a command-line prompt. It might similar to like this:

```
MacBookPro-SLott:~ slott$ python3
Python 3.3.4 (v3.3.4:7ff62415e426, Feb  9 2014, 00:29:34)
[GCC 4.2.1 (Apple Inc. build 5666) (dot 3)] on darwin
Type "help", "copyright", "credits" or "license" for more information.
>>>
```

The details of getting to a command prompt vary from OS to OS. We've shown the Mac OS X Terminal tool in this example. We entered the `python3` command to be sure we ran our new version of Python, not the built-in Python 2.

The introductory message lists four special-purpose objects that are incorporated into the interactive Python environment. There are two more, `quit` and `exit`, which are also available. These are only present in the REPL interactive environment; they cannot be used in programs.

We'll look at how we get help later in a separate section, *Interacting with the help subsystem*. The other objects, however, produce useful tidbits of information and are the ideal way to be sure things are working. Enter `copyright`, `credits`, or `license` at the `>>>` prompt to confirm that Python is working.

Doing simple arithmetic

The REPL loop prints the results of each statement, allowing us to work with Python interactively. To be clear on what this means, we should define what constitutes a **statement** in the language. We'll avoid the strict formality of the Python language definition and provide a quick, informal definition of the relevant statement type.

The Python language has 20 or so kinds of statements. An expression—by itself—is a statement. Unless the value of the expression is `None`, the REPL will show the value of the expression. We'll often use an expression statement to evaluate functions that perform input and output.

This simple expression statement allows us to do things such as the following at the Python `>>>` prompt:

```
>>> 355/113
3.1415929203539825
```

We can enter any arithmetic expression. Python evaluates the expression, and if the result isn't `None`, we'll see the result. We've shown the true division operator, `/`, in this example.

We'll look at the various data types and operators in *Chapter 2, Simple Data Types*. For the moment, we'll identify a few features of Python. We have numbers in a variety of flavors, including integers, floating point, and complex values. Most values will be properly coerced to add precision. Have a look at these examples:

```
>>> 2 * 3.14 * 8j
50.24j
>>> _ **2
(-2524.0576+0j)
```

The first expression computed a value that includes an integer, `2`; a floating point value, `3.14`; and a complex value, `8j`. We used the `*` operator for multiplication. The result is complex, `50.24j`.

The second expression uses the `_` variable. This is a handy feature that's unique to the REPL. The result of each expression is implicitly assigned to this variable. We can use `_` in an expression to refer to the result of the previous expression. This only works in the REPL; it's never a part of a script.

When we computed _ **2, we squared 50.24j. This is -2524.0576. Since the source value was a complex number, the result is also a complex value even though the imaginary component of that complex value is zero. This is typical of Python—the data types of the operand values generally dictate the data types of the result of the operator. When there are different kinds of numbers, values are coerced according to the rules we'll look at in *Chapter 2, Simple Data Types*.

There's one notable exception to the rule that the types of the operands match the type of the result. The true division operator, /, produces floating point results from integer operands. The floor division operator, //, on the other hand, reflects the types of the operands. For example:

```
>>> 355 / 113
3.1415929203539825
>>> 355 // 113
3
```

We have these two division operators so that we can unambiguously specify what kind of division we'd like to perform. It saves us from having to write extra code to explicitly coerce results.

Assigning results to variables

The simple assignment statement produces no visible output:

```
>>> v = 23
```

This will create the variable v and assign the value of 23 to it. We can check this by using a very small expression statement. The expression is just the variable name:

```
>>> v
23
```

When we evaluate a very simple expression, such as v, we see the value of the variable.

Python's REPL has far-reaching consequences. Perhaps the most important consequence is that almost all examples of Python programming are provided as if we're entering the code at the >>> prompt. The documentation for very complex and sophisticated packages will be written as though we're going to use that package interactively. In most cases, we'll be writing application programs; we won't really do very much at the >>> prompt. But the idea of cutting through the complexity to arrive at something that can be done interactively is pervasive throughout the Python community.

Using import to add features

One significant part of Python is the presence of a vast library of additional features. Using an external library means that the core language can be kept quite simple. We can import any additional features we need, avoiding the clutter and complication of unused features.

The `import` statement is used to incorporate additional functions, classes, and objects into a program or the interactive environment. There are a number of variations of this statement. For example, we might want to use some of the more sophisticated math functions. We can search the Python documentation and discover that these are defined in the `math` library. We can include and use them like this:

```
>>> import math
>>> math.pi
3.141592653589793
>>> math.sin( math.pi/6 )
0.4999999999999994
```

In this example, we imported the `math` library. We evaluated `math.pi` to see one of the constants defined in this library. We evaluated $\sin\frac{\pi}{6}$. The result was almost (but not exactly) 1/2.

This also shows us an important thing about floating point numbers—they're just an approximation. This has nothing to do with Python specifically—it's a general feature of digital computing. It's very important to emphasize this fact about floating point numbers.

 Floating point numbers are only an approximation. They're not exact. They are not the abstract mathematical ideal of an irrational number with infinite precision.

We'll return to the topic of floating point numbers in *Chapter 2, Simple Data Types*. For now, we want to focus on external libraries.

One important library module that is part of Python is named `this`. To see the `this` module, enter `import this` at the `>>>` prompt, like so:

```
>>> import this
```

Another equally important module is `antigravity`.

```
>>> import antigravity
```

We'll leave the exploration of these modules as exercises for the reader. We don't want to spoil the fun! More handwaving explanation isn't as helpful as hands-on experience. See `http://xkcd.com/413/` for more on this topic.

We'll summarize by noting that the name "Python" has much to do with Monty Python and nothing to do with serpents.

Interacting with the help subsystem

Python's interactive help utility provides a great deal of useful information about modules, classes, functions, and objects. The help system is an environment that is distinct from Python's REPL; it provides distinct prompts to make this clear.

There are three help modes, each with its unique prompt:

- We'll see the `help>` prompt from the Python help environment. When we evaluate the `help()` function with no argument value, we'll enter Python's help environment. We can enter different subjects and read about various Python features. When we enter `quit` as a topic, we'll return to the REPL.

- Using Windows, we'll see the `-- More --` prompt: When we evaluate something like `help(int)` in a Windows environment, the output will be displayed using the MS-DOS **more** command. For more information, enter `?` for help on how to page through the `help()` output. At the Windows command line, entering `more /?` will provide additional information on how the **more** command helps you page through a long file.

- Using Mac OS X and Linux, we'll see the `:` prompt. When we evaluate the `help()` function with a specific argument value—for example, `help(float)`—in Mac OS X or Linux, we'll get output that's displayed using the **less** program. For more information on this, enter `h` for help while viewing the `help()` output. At the command prompt, enter `less -?` for more information on how the **less** program works.

There are additional ways to view the documentation available with Python modules. In IDLE, for example, there's a class browser and path browser that will show documentation about modules and files. This is based on the built-in `help()` function, but it's displayed in a separate window.

Using the pydoc program

Python includes the pydoc application that we use to view documentation. This application is something that we run from the OS command prompt. We do not use this from the Python >>> prompt; we use it from the OS prompt. While developing, we might want to leave a Terminal window open just to display module documentation.

The pydoc program has two operating modes:

- It can show some documentation about a specific package or module. This will use an appropriate program (**more** on Windows, but otherwise **less**) to display documentation for the given object. Here's how we can display documentation on the math module:

  ```
  MacBookPro-SLott:~ slott$ python3 -m pydoc math
  ```

- It can start a documentation web server. This will start a server (and also start a browser) to look at Python module documentation. When we use it, we'll have a session that looks like this:

  ```
  MacBookPro-SLott:~ slott$ python3 -m pydoc -b
  Server ready at http://localhost:50177/
  Server commands: [b]rowser, [q]uit
  server> q
  Server stopped
  ```

The second example will start a web server as well as a browser. The browser will show the pydoc-produced documentation. This is derived from the module and package structure as well as the documentation strings embedded in the Python code. When we were done reading the documentation, we entered q to quit the web server.

When we write Python packages, modules, classes, and functions, we can (and should) provide the content for pydoc/help() documentation. These documentation strings are part of our programming, and are as important as having programs that work correctly. We'll look at this embedded documentation in *Chapter 14, Fit and Finish – Unit Testing, Packaging, and Documentation*.

Creating simple script files

While we can use all of Python from the REPL, this is not a good way to produce a final application. Most of what we do with Python will be done via script files. We'll look at script files in detail in *Chapter 12, Scripts, Modules, Packages, Libraries, and Applications*. For now, we'll look at a few features.

A script file has to follow a few rules:

- The content must be plain text. While ASCII encoding is preferred by some, Python 3 can easily handle UTF-8 and most OS-specific variations such as Mac OS Roman or Windows CP-1252. A portable encoding like UTF-8 is strongly suggested.

- Python can cope with Mac OS X, Linux newline (\n), as well as Windows CR-LF (\r\n). Only a few Windows tools, such as Notepad, insist on CR-LF line endings; most other programming editors discern the line endings flexibly. Unless you really must use Notepad, it's often best to use Unix-style newline line endings.

- The filename should be a legal Python identifier. This is not a requirement, but it gives us considerable flexibility if we follow this suggestion. The Language Reference Manual, section 2.3, provides the details of what constitutes an identifier. A summary of these rules is that identifiers must begin with a letter (or a Unicode character that normalizes to a letter) or _. It continues with letters, digits, and the _ character. What's important is that we should avoid characters that are Python operators or delimiters in filenames. In particular, we should avoid the hyphen (-), which can become a problem in some Python contexts. OS filenames have much more flexible rules than Python identifiers, and the OS has ways to escape the meaning of OS-related punctuation; we are happiest when we limit our filenames to valid Python identifiers – letters, digits, and _.

- The filename extension should be .py. Again, this is not required, but it is very helpful to follow this rule.

For example, we'll try to focus on names such as test_1_2.py. We can't as easily use a file named test-1.2.py; the base name isn't a valid identifier — this name looks like a Python expression. While the second name is acceptable for a top-level script, it won't work as a module or package.

We'll look at some Python syntax rules in the next section. For now, we can create a simple script file named ex_1.py that has one line:

```
print("π≈", 355/113)
```

We can also use "\u03c0\u2248" instead of "π≈". The string "\N{GREEK SMALL LETTER PI}\N{ALMOST EQUAL TO}" will also work.

Once we have this file, we can have Python execute the file as follows:

```
MacBookPro-SLott:Chapter_1 slott$ python3 ex_1.py
π≈ 3.141592920353982
```

We've provided a filename, `ex_1.py`, as the positional argument to the `python3` program. Python reads the file and executes each line. The output that we see is the text printed to the console by the `print()` function.

The file is found by Python using ordinary OS rules for locating files, starting with the current working directory. This will work with any kind of filename.

If we followed the naming rules for our file—the filename is an identifier and the extension is `.py`—we can also use the following command to execute a Python module:

```
MacBookPro-SLott:Chapter_1 slott$ python3 -m ex_1
π≈ 3.1415929203539825
```

The `-m ex_1` option forces Python to search for a module named `ex_1`. The file associated with this module is named `ex_1.py`. Python has a search path that it uses to find the requested module. Unless special arrangements are made, Python will search the local directory first, and then will search the library directories. This allows us to run our scripts and Python's built-in applications with a simple, uniform syntax. It also allows us to add our own applications and modules by modifying the `PYTHONPATH` environment variable.

We'll look at the search path in *Chapter 12, Scripts, Modules, Packages, Libraries, and Applications*. The detailed documentation for the search path is part of the `site` package.

Simplified syntax rules

The syntax rules for Python are defined in section 2 of the *Python Language Reference* manual. We'll look at the rules in detail in *Chapter 3, Expressions and Output*.

Python has about 20 kinds of statements. Here's a quick summary of the rules:

- Almost all statements begin with a Python keyword such as `pass`, `if`, and `def`. The expression statement and the assignment statement are the exceptions.
- Python has two kinds of statements—one-line **simple** statements and multiline **compound** statements.
- Simple statements must be complete within a single line. An assignment statement is a simple statement. It begins with one or more user-provided identifiers and includes the = assignment symbol or an augmented variant like +=. An expression statement is also simple.

- Compound statements use indentation to show the suite of statements embedded within the overall statement. The standard indentation is four spaces. Most developers set their editor to replace tabs with four spaces. Inconsistent use of spaces and tabs will lead to syntax errors that can be hard to see because tabs and spaces are both invisible by default. Avoiding tab characters in general makes it easier to debug problems.

- Compound statements include class and function definitions — the body of the definition is indented. If statements and for and while loops are examples of compound statements that contain an indented suite of statements that are executed conditionally or repeatedly.

- The (and) characters must match. A single statement on a logical line may span multiple physical lines until the (and) characters match.

In effect, Python programs consist of one-statement-one-line. The end of a line is the statement terminator. We have a few techniques for extending a statement. The most common technique is based on Python's requirement that the (and) characters must balance.

We can, for example, write code like this:

```
print(
    "Hello world",
    "π≈",
    355/113
)
```

Downloading the example code

You can download the example code files from your account at http://www.packtpub.com for all the Packt Publishing books you have purchased. If you purchased this book elsewhere, you can visit http://www.packtpub.com/support and register to have the files e-mailed directly to you.

We've spread a single logical line to four physical lines using (and). One consequence of this is that a simple statement that we enter at the REPL must not be indented. A leading space will cause problems because leading spaces are used to show which statements are inside a compound statement.

Another consequence of this is less direct. Python executes a script file one statement at a time from start to finish. This means that complex Python programs will have a number of definitions first, and the "main" part of the processing will generally be last.

A Python comment starts with # and ends at the end of the line. This follows the same rules as the various Linux shells. Because of the way Python documentation strings are processed by `pydoc` and `help()`, most documentation is actually presented in separate string literals at the start of a package, module, class, or function definition. We'll look at these documentation strings in *Chapter 14, Fit and Finish – Unit Testing, Packaging, and Documentation*. The # comment is used sparingly.

The Python ecosystem

The Python programming environment has two broad subject areas:

- The language itself
- The extension packages. We can further subdivide the extension packages into:

  ° The standard library of packages
  ° The Python ecosystem of yet more extension packages

When we install Python, we install the language plus several hundred extension packages in the standard library. We'll return to the standard library in *Chapter 12, Scripts, Modules, Packages, Libraries, and Applications*. The Python ecosystem is potentially infinite. The good news is that PyPI makes it relatively easy to locate packages.

The idea of extensibility via add-ons

Python's design includes a small core language that can be extended by importing additional features. The Language Reference Manual describes 20 statements; there are only 19 operators. The idea is that we can have a great deal of confidence that a small language is correctly implemented, complete, and consistent.

The standard library documentation contains 37 chapters, and describes hundreds of extension packages. There are a lot of features available to help us solve our unique problem. It's typical to see Python programs that import numerous packages from the standard library.

We'll see two common variations of the `import` statement:

- `import math`
- `from math import sqrt, sin`

The first version imports the entire `math` module and creates the module as an object in the global namespace. The various classes and function names within that module must be properly qualified with the namespace to be used. A qualified name will look similar to `math.sqrt()` or `math.sin()`.

While the second version also imports the `math` module, it only introduces the given names into the global namespace. These names do not require qualifiers. We can use `sqrt()` and `sin()` as if they were built-in functions. The `math` module object, however, is not available, since it was not introduced into the global namespace.

An import happens exactly once. Python tracks the imported modules and will not import a module a second time. This allows us to freely import modules as needed without worrying about the order or other obscure dependencies among modules.

For confirmation of this one-time-only rule for imports, try the following:

```
>>> import this
>>> import this
```

The behavior the second time is different because the module has already been imported once.

Using the Python Package Index – PyPI

Many developers of Python modules will register their work with the PyPI. This is located at `http://pypi.python.org/`. This is the second place to look for a module that might help solve a particular problem.

The first place to look is always the standard library.

The PyPI web page has a handy search form as well as a browser that shows packages organized under nine different metadata variables. In many cases, a book or blog post may provide a direct path like this: `https://pypi.python.org/pypi/Sphinx/1.3b2`. This ensures that the proper version can be downloaded and installed.

There are three common ways to download and install software from the PyPI:

- Using `pip`
- Using `easy_install`
- Manually

Generally, we'll use tools such as `pip` or `easy_install` for almost all of our installations. Once in a while, however, we may need to resort to a manual installation.

Some modules may involve binary extensions to Python. These are generally C-language-sources, so they must be compiled to be useful. For Windows—where C compilers are rare—it's often necessary to find an `.msi` installer that includes prebuilt binaries. For Mac OS X and Linux, the C source may be compiled as part of the installation process.

In the case of large, complex numeric and scientific packages—specifically, `numpy` and `scipy`—the build process can become quite complex: generally, more complex than `pip` or `easy_install` can handle. There are many additional high-performance libraries for these packages; the builds include modules in FORTRAN as well as C. In this case, a prebuilt OS-specific distribution is used; `pip` isn't part of the process.

Installing additional packages will require administrator privileges. Consequently, we'll show the `sudo` command as a reminder that this is required for Mac OS X and Linux. Windows users can simply ignore the presence of the `sudo` command.

Using pip to gather modules

The `pip` program is part of Python 3.4. It's an add-on for Python3. To use `pip` to install a package, we generally use a command such as the following:

```
prompt$ sudo pip3.4 install some-package
```

For Mac OS X or Linux, we need to use the `sudo` command so that we have administrator privileges. Windows users will leave this off.

The `pip` program will search PyPI for the package named `some-package`. The installed Python version and OS information will be used to locate the latest-and-greatest version that's appropriate for the platform. The files will be downloaded, and the Python `setup.py` file that comes with the package will be run automatically to install it.

For Mac OS X and Linux users, it's helpful to note that the version of Python that is required by the OS doesn't usually have `pip` configured. A Mac OS X user with the built-in Python 2.7 and Python 3.4 can generally use the default `pip` command without any problems because there won't be a version of `pip` configured for Python 2.

In the case where someone has Python 3.3 and Python 3.4, and has installed `pip` for Python 3.3, they will have to choose which version they want to work with. Using the commands `pip3.3` or `pip3.4` will use one of the `pip` commands configured for the given version of Python. The default `pip` command may link to whichever version was installed last-something we shouldn't guess at.

The pip program has a number of additional features to uninstall packages and track which packages have been added to the initial Python installation. The pip program can also create installable packages of your new creation.

Using easy_install to add modules

The easy_install package is also part of Python 3.4. It's a part of the setuptools package. We use easy_install like this to install a package:

```
prompt$ sudo easy_install-3.3 some_package
```

For Mac OS X or Linux, we need to use the sudo command so that we have administrator privileges. Windows users will leave this off.

The easy_install program is similar to pip—it will search PyPI for the package named some-package. The installed Python version and OS information will be used to locate a version that's appropriate for the platform. The files will be downloaded. One of these files is the setup.py script; this will be run automatically to finish the installation.

Installing modules manually

In rare cases, we may have a package that isn't in the PyPI and can't be located by pip or easy_install. In this case, we generally have a two- or three-step installation process:

1. **Download**: We need to securely download the package. In many cases, we can use https or ftps so that secure sockets are used. In case we can't secure the connection, we may have to check md5 signatures on the files to be sure that our download is complete and unaltered.

2. **Unpack**: If the Python packages are compressed into a single ZIP or TAR file, we need to unzip or untar the downloaded file into a temporary directory.

3. **Set up**: Many Python packages designed for manual installation include a setup.py file that will do the final installation. We'll need to run a command like this:

    ```
    sudo python3 setup.py install
    ```

This sequence of steps, including the final command, is what is automated by pip and easy_install. We've shown the Mac OS X and Linux use of the sudo command to assure that administrator privileges are available. Windows users will simply leave this off.

The `setup.py` script uses Python's `distutils` package to define what must be installed into the Python library directory structure. The `install` option states what we want to do with the package we downloaded. Most of the time, we're going to install, so this is one of the most common options.

In rare exceptions, a package may consist of a single module file. There may not be a `setup.py` file. In this case, we will manually copy the file to our own `site-packages` directory.

Looking at other Python interpreters

This book will focus on a particular implementation of Python called the CPython. What this means is that Python — the abstract language — can be processed by a variety of concrete Python runtimes or implementations. The CPython implementation is written in portable C and can be recompiled for many operating systems.

Python can be embedded into an application. This means that a complex application can include the entire Python language as a way to write scripts that customize the given application. One example of this is the Ganglia monitoring system (`http://ganglia.sourceforge.net`). Python is part of the system; we can customize the behavior using Python scripts that will interact with Ganglia components. We won't be looking more deeply into these kinds of applications in this book; we'll focus on standalone implementations of Python.

There are several alternative Python implementations. In the *Installing Python on Windows* section in this chapter, we noted that Iron Python (`http://ironpython.net`) and PTVS (`http://pytools.codeplex.com`) are available. These provide tighter integration with the .NET framework.

There are still more implementations that we might encounter:

- **Jython**: This is a version of the Python interpreter that is written in Java and runs on the Java Virtual Machine (JVM). See `http://www.jython.org`. This project focuses on Python 2.7.

- **PyPy**: This is a version of the Python interpreter written in Python. See `http://pypy.org`. The circularity of "Python written in Python" is broken by the RPython translation toolchain, which creates a very sophisticated implementation of Python programs. This can provide significant performance improvements for a variety of long-running applications, such as web servers.

- **Stackless**: This version of Python has a different threading model from CPython. See `http://www.stackless.com`. This version can provide dramatic performance improvements for multithreaded servers.

Since the Python source is readily available, it's quite easy to look for optimization opportunities. The language is relatively simple, allowing experimentation to see what effect changes in implementation may have.

Summary

We've looked at installing or upgrading Python so that we can work with version 3.3 or 3.4, and we've looked briefly at the minor differences between Windows, Mac OS X, and Linux. The principle difference among the OS variants is that Windows lacks Python, whereas Mac OS X and Linux generally have a version of Python already installed. There are few other differences among the operating systems.

We've looked at some basic interactions using the REPL. We looked at some simple expressions and the built-in `help()` subsystem.

We've looked at some ways that the `import` statement extends the basic capabilities of our Python runtime environment, and we've also introduced the larger Python ecosystem. We can add to our Python library using the `pip` (and `easy_install`) tool. The PyPI is the central repository for most of the Python extension modules.

In the next chapter, we'll look at Python's numeric types in detail. Python numbers form a kind of "tower" that follows the mathematical notions of integer, rational, real, and complex numbers. We'll look at the mathematical operators and some of the standard libraries for working with numbers.

We'll also look at some of the more complex data types available, including/alongside specific tuples, strings, and frozensets. These are relatively simple because they are immutable. As is the case with ordinary numbers, the values of these more complex objects don't change either.

2
Simple Data Types

Now we'll look at a number of data types that are built-in as well as some that are part of Python's standard library. We'll start with Python's numeric types. These include three built-in types: `int`, `float`, and `complex`, plus the standard library types `Fraction` and `Decimal`.

We'll also look at strings, `str`, and simple collections, `tuple`. These are more complex than numbers because they contain multiple items. Since their behavior is less complex than the kinds of objects we'll see in later chapters, they serve as a good introduction to the general concept of sequences in Python.

Note the capitalization of the names of `Fraction` and `Decimal`. The built-in type names start with a lowercase letter. Types that we must import have a module name that starts with a lowercase letter, but the type name starts with a capital letter. This convention is widespread, but not universal.

All of the types we'll look at in this chapter have the common feature of immutability. This concept applies to the two collections we'll look at: once built, a string or a tuple cannot be changed. Rather than change it, we create a new object. In *Chapter 6, More Complex Data Types*, we'll look at collections which can be updated without creating a new object.

In this chapter, we'll look at the built-in functions for converting to and from string representations. This will help us when displaying output or converting input from a string to a useful Python object.

Note that we're continuing to play fast and loose with formal Python syntax. We'll defer a detailed examination of the syntax rules until *Chapter 3, Expressions and Output*. For now, the kinds of simple expression statements we're focusing on must be restricted to a single line.

Introducing the built-in operators

Before looking at the various kinds of numbers available, we'll introduce the Python operators. The operators fall into three broad groups:

Group	Operators
Arithmetic	+, -, *, **, /, //, %
Bit-oriented	<<, >>, &, |, ^, ~
Comparison	<, >, <=, >=, ==, !=

The differences between these groups are partly subjective. There's only a small technical difference in the way the comparison operators work. Most of the operators are binary, only one (~) is unary, and a few (+, -, *, **) can be used in either context.

The +, -, *, /, and % operators have meanings similar to those used other programming languages. There is an arithmetic meaning for - and +. Python adds the ** operator when raising a number to a power. The ** operator takes higher precedence than the unary form -; this means that -2**4 is -16.

Bit-oriented operators apply only to integers. They also apply to sets. These are emphatically not logical operators. The actual logical operators are described in *Chapter 5, Logic, Comparisons, and Conditions.*

Making comparisons

The comparison operators (<, >, ==, !=, <=, >=) have meanings similar to those used in other programming languages. The coercion rules apply to comparisons between numbers. If the objects are of mixed types, one of them will be coerced "up" the numeric tower from integer to float, or float to complex. The result of a comparison is a Boolean (True or False) irrespective of the types of the two operands.

The various coercion rules do not apply to strings or other objects. Strings are not implicitly converted to numbers. 2 != '2' is true because the integer 2 is not a string '2'.

Some popular languages (for example, Java, C++) have primitive types such as int or long which are not proper objects—they're not instances of a class—and the rules that apply to objects do not apply to them. Java allows the == comparison for int objects, but using the same comparison operator with string objects doesn't compare the characters of the two strings, it only compares the references. This is emphatically not the case with Python. All Python objects are proper instances of a class: the == comparison in Python strings compares the two strings character by character.

We'll look at comparisons in more detail in *Chapter 5*, *Logic, Comparisons, and Conditions*.

Using integers

Python integers are objects of the class `int`. These objects have the largest number of operators, including all of the arithmetic, bit-oriented, and comparison operators.

Integer values are limited by available memory. This means they can be quite large. We can easily compute 1,000!, a number with over 2,500 digits. We'll save the details for *Chapter 8*, *More Advanced Functions*. A number of similarly gargantuan size is:

```
>>> 2**8530
610749...581824
```

This is a very large number. We've elided most of it. It's easily represented in Python.

Generally, we provide integer literals in decimal, base 10. We can also write literals in three other bases: hexadecimal, octal, and binary.

The prefix of `0x` is the prefix for base 16 values: `0x10` is `16`. We can use the letters `a-f`, as is typical in many other programming languages; `0xdeadbeef` is valid. The prefix `0o` (zero and the letter o) is used for base eight; try to avoid using the maliciously confusing `0O` (zero and capital O) for octal values, for example, `0o33653337357`. We can write base two literal values using the `0b` prefix: `0b10` is `2`. The most common use case for non-decimal numbers is providing hexadecimal values for an array of bytes, and this is relatively rare.

Using the bit-oriented operators

Bit-oriented operators are defined for integers. They're not defined for complex or floating-point objects.

The `<<` and `>>` operators perform bit shifting. `1 << 8`, for example, is 256. We've shifted the value 1 to the left 8 bit positions.

The `&`, `|`, and `^` operators compute the bitwise "and", bitwise "or", and bitwise "xor" of two integer values. Here are some examples:

```
>>> 9 & 5
1
>>> 9 | 5
13
>>> 9 ^ 3
10
```

To visualize these operators, we can use the `bin()` function to see the binary values involved.

```
>>> bin(9)
'0b1001'
>>> bin(5)
'0b101'
```

Using the `bin()` function can clarify how the bits of 9 | 5 combine to create the bits of 13. The ~ operator is the bitwise two's complement of an integer value. ~14, for example, is -15. These are emphatically not logical operators. Logical operators are described in *Chapter 5, Logic, Comparisons, and Conditions*.

Do not confuse a `&` b with a `and` b:
- a `&` b computes a bitwise "and" of the bits in the integers *a* and *b*.
- a `and` b computes the Boolean "and" based on the truth values of *a* and *b*.

Using rational numbers

Rational numbers are fractions composed of two integer values. Python doesn't have a built-in rational number type. We must import the `Fraction` class using this:

```
>>> from fractions import Fraction
```

This will introduce the `Fraction` class definition to our global environment. Once we have this, we can create objects of the class `Fraction` as follows:

```
>>> Fraction(355,113)
Fraction(355, 113)
```

Arithmetic and comparison operators apply to fractions. When doing mixed-type expressions, fractions fit into the numeric tower above integers and below floating-point values. Here's an example of an integer coerced to a fraction:

```
>>> Fraction(4,2)*3
Fraction(6, 1)
```

Performing an operation that involves a `Fraction` value and an `int` value requires that the `int` object is coerced up to the `Fraction` class.

We can extract the numerator and denominator of a fraction using their attribute names. Here's an example:

```
>>> a= Fraction(355,113)*5
```

```
>>> a.numerator
1775
>>> a.denominator
113
```

We've created a `Fraction` object, `a`, from an expression involving a `Fraction` object and an integer. We've then extracted the `numerator` and `denominator` attributes of the variable `a`.

Using decimal numbers

For currency calculations, we generally use `Decimal` numbers. Python doesn't have a built-in decimal number type. We import the `Decimal` class using this:

```
>>> from decimal import Decimal
```

This will introduce the `Decimal` class definition to our global environment. We can now create `Decimal` objects. It's important to avoid accidentally mixing `Decimal` and `float` values, because `float` values are only an approximation. To be sure that `Decimal` values are exact, we must use only integers or strings.

```
>>> Decimal("2.72")
Decimal('2.72')
```

We've created a `Decimal` value from a string. The resulting `Decimal` object will represent this exactly, carefully preserving the appropriate decimal places and rounding up or down as required. For common financial calculations, `Decimal` is required. Here's an example:

```
>>> (Decimal('512.97')+Decimal('5.97'))*Decimal('0.075')
Decimal('38.92050')
```

We've added two prices, $512.97 and $5.97 and computed a sales tax of 7.5%. The tax is $38.92050, to be precise. This is generally rounded to $38.92.

If we try this kind of financial calculation with floating-point values, we have a bit of a problem:

```
>>> (512.97+5.97)*0.075
38.920500000000004
```

The floating-point approximations don't produce an exact answer.

Python coercion rules work well with `Decimal` and `int` values. We can calculate `Decimal('3.99')*3` and get `Decimal('11.97')` as the answer.

The coercion rules aren't implemented by the `Decimal` and `float` classes. It might make some sense for `Decimal` values to be coerced up to `float` values. On the other hand, this might indicate a profound programming error when mixing exact currency values and floating-point approximations. Since this is ambiguous, and debatable, the general approach followed by Python is summarized by this line from Tim Peters' *The Zen of Python*:

> *In the face of ambiguity, refuse the temptation to guess.*

Consequently, mixing `Decimal` and `float` leads to `TypeError` exceptions instead of following coercion up the numeric tower and switching from exact to approximate values. We must explicitly convert `Decimal` to `float` to do mixed-type expressions.

Using floating-point numbers

Floating-point values are instances of the class `float`. These objects work with arithmetic and comparison operators. They don't participate in the bit-oriented operators.

The details of Python floating-point implementations can vary. CPython depends on the standard C libraries, which should provide reasonably consistent results on a wide variety of hardware and OS platforms. C libraries generally use IEEE 754 floating-point values; Python's `float` type is the C language `double`. This means that a float will be a 64-bit value with (effectively) a 53-bit fraction and an 11-bit exponent. The exponent range is from 2^{-1022} to 2^{1023}.

We can write floating-point numbers two ways: as digits with a decimal point, as well as in "scientific" notation:

```
>>> 6335.437
6335.437
>>> 6.335437E3
6335.437
```

The E notation shows a power of 10. That means 6.335437E3 is 6.335437×10^3.

It's very important to note that floating-point values are an approximation. We can't emphasize enough that they're not exact and should not be used for currency calculations. Here's an example of what happens when working with floating-point approximations:

```
>>> (5**6) ** (1/6)
4.999999999999999
```

This should not be surprising in any way. Mathematically, $(5^6)^{\frac{1}{6}} = 5$. Since values like 1/6 don't have exact binary representations, this kind of expression reveals the consequences of working with approximations.

The fact that floating-point numbers use a binary representation leads to interesting complications. A number such as 1/6 has no exact decimal representation; we can use .1666... to indicate that the decimal positions repeat infinitely. However, a number such as 1/5 has an exact decimal representation, 0.2. Neither of these numbers has an exact binary representation. Since we must use a finite number of bits, we'll notice slight discrepancies between idealized values and the finite values produced on a digital computer.

Note that exact equality comparisons between floating-point numbers, while permitted, is generally not a good idea. In *Chapter 5, Logic, Comparisons, and Conditions*, we'll address how to use a narrow range instead of exact equality. Instead of a == b, we need to focus on abs(a-b) < ε.

Using complex numbers

The top of Python's number tower is of the complex type. It can be thought of as expressions built from a pair of floating-point numbers: one is a real value, the other is an imaginary value. The imaginary value is multiplied by $j = \sqrt{-1}$. We write (2+3j) to mean $2 + 3\sqrt{-1}$.

When working with complex numbers, we often import the cmath library instead of the math library. The math.sqrt() function is constrained to work only with float values, and will raise an exception rather than provide an imaginary value. The cmath.sqrt() function will provide a proper imaginary value, if required.

This library shows us that $e^{\pi j} + 1 = 0$ is essentially true:

```
>>> cmath.e**(cmath.pi*1j)+1
1.2246467991473532e-16j
```

Note that we used 1j to represent $j = \sqrt{-1}$. If we try to use the identifier j (without a number in front of it) it is seen as a simple variable. The value 1j is a complex literal because it starts with a digit and ends with j.

Since floating-point values have about 53 bits, which is about 16 decimal digits, we can expect float approximations of irrational values like π and e to be off by about 10^{-16}.

The numeric tower

We've seen Python's three built-in numeric types: int, float, complex, plus two more types—Fraction and Decimal—imported from the standard library. The numbers module in the standard library provides four base class definitions for the numeric types. We rarely need to use this module explicitly; it's a convention that we need when we have to implement our own numeric types.

The numeric types form a kind of "tower" that parallels the various kinds of numbers seen in conventional mathematics. The foundation of the tower is integers. Rational numbers are above integers. Floating-point values are still further up, and complex numbers are at the top of the tower.

A common expectation is that a language will automatically coerce numeric values to permit expressions such as 2*2.718 to work properly and produce a useful result. When multiplying an integer by a float value, we expect integers to be coerced to a floating-point value.

In order for this to work, there are two general rules applied to the result of a binary arithmetic operation:

- If both operands are of the same type, the result has that type. For example, 2 ** 1024 does not produce a floating-point result. It produces an immense integer.
- If the operands are mixed, one of them will be coerced "up" the numeric tower from integer → rational → floating-point → complex.

There is one notable exception to the preceding rules. The / and // operators define two different kinds of division. The / operator provides true division: even integer operands will yield a floating-point result. For example:

```
>>> 355/113
3.1415929203539825
```

The // operator provides floor division: the result will be truncated as if it were an integer-only division. The resulting type won't be coerced, but the answer will be truncated. For example:

```
>>> 355./113.
3.1415929203539825
>>> 355.//113.
3.0
```

The presence of the // operator means that an expression which is designed with integers in mind will also work correctly with floating-point values. Similarly, we may write an expression with an informal expectation of floating-point values; by using /, it will also work with integers.

Note that these coercion rules for numeric types do not apply to strings or other objects. Strings are not implicitly converted to numbers. The expression '2'+2 results in a TypeError exception. We'll look at explicit conversions later, in the *Using the built-in conversion functions* section.

The tower metaphor provides a handy way to remember the coercion rules. Given two values from different levels, the lower-level value is coerced up the tower to the higher-level values.

The math libraries

The Python library has six modules relevant to mathematical work. These are described in *Chapter 9, Numeric and Mathematical Modules,* of the *Python Standard Library* document. Beyond this, we have external libraries such as NumPy (http://www.numpy.org) and SciPy (http://www.scipy.org). These libraries include vast collections of sophisticated algorithms. For an even more sophisticated toolset, the Anaconda project (https://store.continuum.io/cshop/anaconda/) combines NumPy, SciPy, and 18 more packages.

These are the relevant built-in numeric packages:

- numbers: This module defines the essential numeric abstractions. We rarely need this unless we're going to invent an entirely new kind of number.

- math: This module has a large collection of functions. It includes basic sqrt(), the various trigonometric functions (sine, cosine, and so on) and the various log-related functions. It has functions for working with the internals of floating-point numbers. It also has the gamma function and the error function.

- cmath: This module is the complex version of the math library. We use the cmath library so that we can seamlessly move between float and complex values.

- decimal: Import the Decimal class from this module to work with currency values accurately.

- fractions: Import the Fraction class to work with a precise rational fraction value.

- `random`: This module contains the essential random number generator. It has a number of other functions to produce random values in various ranges or with various constraints. For example `random.gauss()` produces a Gaussian, normal distribution of floating-point values.

The three main ways of importing from these libraries are as follows:

- `import random`: We use this when we want to be perfectly explicit about the origin of a name elsewhere in our code. We'll be writing code similar to `random.gauss()` and `random.randint()` using the module name as an explicit qualifier.

- `from random import gauss, randint`: This introduces two selected names from the `random` module into the global namespace. We can use `gauss()` and `randint()` without a qualifying module name.

- `from random import *`: This will introduce all of the available names in the `random` module as globals in our application. This is helpful for exploring and experimenting at the `>>>` prompt. This may not be appropriate in a larger program because it can introduce a large number of irrelevant names.

A less-commonly used feature allows us to rename objects brought in via the `import` statement. We might want to use `from cmath import sqrt as csqrt` to rename the `cmath.sqrt()` function to `csqrt()`. We have to be careful to avoid ambiguity and confusion when using this `import-as` renaming feature.

Using bits and Boolean values

As noted earlier, the bit-oriented operators &, |, ^, and ~ have nothing to do with Python's actual Boolean operators and, or, not, and if-else. We'll look at Boolean values, logic operators, and related programming in *Chapter 5, Logic, Comparisons, and Conditions*.

If we misuse the bit-oriented operators & or | in place of a logical and or or, things may appear very peculiar:

```
>>> 5 > 6 & 3 > 1
True
>>> (5 > 6) & (3 > 1)
False
```

The first example is clearly wrong. Why? This is because the & operator has relatively high priority. It's not a logical connective, it's more like an arithmetic operator. The & operator is performed first: 6&3 evaluates to 2. Given this, the resulting expression, 5 > 2 > 1, is True.

When we group the comparisons to perform them first, we'll get a False for 5>6, and a True for 3>1. When we apply the & operator the result will be False, which is what we expected. Using bit operators inappropriately as logical connectives can work if we use parentheses to be sure that the bit operators are performed last. It's a very bad idea, however.

It's easier, clearer, and altogether better to use the proper Boolean operators shown in *Chapter 5, Logic, Comparisons, and Conditions*.

Working with sequences

In this chapter, we'll introduce Python sequence collections. We'll look at strings and tuples as the first two examples of this class. Python offers a number of other sequence collections; we'll look at them in *Chapter 6, More Complex Data Types*. All of these sequences have common features.

Python sequences identify the individual elements by position. Position numbers start with zero. Here's a `tuple` collection with five elements:

```
>>> t=("hello", 3.14, 23, None, True)
>>> t[0]
'hello'
>>> t[4]
True
```

In addition to the expected ascending numbers, Python also offers reverse numbering. Position -1 is the end of the sequence:

```
>>> t[-1]
True
>>> t[-2]
>>> t[-5]
'hello'
```

Note that position 3 (or -2) has a value of None. The REPL doesn't display the None object, so the value of t[-2] appears to be missing. For more visible evidence that this value is None, use this:

```
>>> t[3] is None
True
```

The sequences use an extra comparison operator, in. We can ask if a given value occurs in a collection:

```
>>> "hello" in t
True
>>> 2.718 in t
False
```

Slicing and dicing a sequence

We can extract a subsequence, called a **slice**, from a sequence using more complex subscript expressions. Here's a substring of a longer string:

```
>>> "multifaceted"[5:10]
'facet'
```

The [5:10] expression is a slice which starts at position 5 and extends to the position before 10. Python generally relies on "half-open" intervals. The starting position of a slice is included whereas the stop position is excluded.

We can omit the starting position from a slice, writing [:pos]. If the start value of a slice is omitted, it's 0. We can omit the ending, also, writing it as [pos:]. If the stop value of a slice is omitted, it's the length of the sequence, given by the len() function.

The way that Python uses these half-open intervals means that we can partition a string with very tidy syntax:

```
>>> "multifaceted"[:5]
'multi'
>>> "multifaceted"[5:]
'faceted'
```

In this example, we've taken the first five characters in the first slice. We've taken everything after the first five characters in the second slice. Since the numbers are both five, we can be completely sure that the entire string is accounted for.

And yes, we can omit both values from the slice: "word"[:] will create a copy of the entire string. This is an odd but sometimes useful construct for duplicating an object.

There's a third parameter to a slice. We generally call the positions **start**, **stop**, and **step**. The step size is 1 by default. We can use a form such as "abcdefg"[::2] to provide an explicit step, and pick characters in positions 0, 2, 4, and 6. The form "abcdefg"[1::2] will pick the odd positions: 1, 3, and 5.

The step size can also be negative. This will enumerate the index values in reverse order. The value of "word"[::-1] is 'drow'.

Using string and bytes values

Python string values are similar — in some respects — to simple numeric types. There are a few arithmetic-like operators available and all of the comparisons are defined. Strings are immutable: we cannot change a string. We can, however, easily build new strings from existing strings, making the mutability question as irrelevant for string objects as it is for number objects. Python has two kinds of string values:

- **Unicode**: These strings use the entire Unicode character set. These are the default strings Python uses. The input-output libraries are all capable of a wide variety of Unicode encoding and decoding. The name for this type is `str`. It's a built-in type, so it starts with a lowercase letter.

- **Bytes**: Many file formats and network protocols are defined over bytes, not Unicode characters. Python uses ASCII encoding for bytes. Special arrangements must be made to process bytes. The internal type name is `bytes`.

We can easily encode Unicode into a sequence of bytes. We can just as easily decode a sequence of bytes to see the Unicode characters. We'll show these two methods in the *Converting between Unicode and bytes* section, after we've looked at literals and operators.

Writing string literals

String literals are characters surrounded by string delimiters. Python offers a variety of string delimiters to solve a variety of problems. The most common literals create Unicode strings:

- **Short string**: Use either `"` or `'` to surround the string. For example: `"Don't Touch"` has an embedded apostrophe. `'Speak "friend" and enter'` has embedded quotes. In the rare cases where we have both, we can use `\` to avoid a quote: `'"Don\'t touch," he said.'` uses apostrophes as delimiters, and an escaped apostrophe within the string. While a string literal must be complete on a single line, a `'\n'` will expand into a proper newline character internally.

- **Long string**: Use either `"""` or `'''` to surround a multi-line string. The string can span as many lines as necessary. A long string can include any characters except for the terminating triple-quote or triple-apostrophe.

Python has a moderate number of `\` escape sequences to allow us to enter characters that aren't possible from a keyboard. If we use ordinary `str` literals, Python replaces all the escape sequences with proper Unicode characters. In an ordinary `bytes` literal, each escape sequence becomes a one-byte ASCII character.

Many Python programs are saved as pure ASCII text, but this is not a requirement. When saving a file in ASCII, escapes will be required for non-ASCII Unicode characters. When saving files in Unicode, then relatively few escapes are required, since any Unicode character available on our keyboard can be entered directly. Here are two examples of the same string:

```
>>> "String with π×r²"
>>> "String with \u03c0\u00d7r\N{superscript two}"
```

The first string uses Unicode characters; the file must be saved in the appropriate encoding, such as UTF-8, for this to work. The second string uses escape sequences to describe the Unicode characters. The \u sequence is followed by a four-digit hex value. The \N{...} escape allows the name of the character. A \U escape—not shown in the example—requires an 8-digit hex value. The second example can be saved in any encoding, including ASCII.

The most commonly-used escape sequences are \", \', \n, \t, and \\ to create a quote inside a quoted string, an apostrophe inside an apostrophe delimited string, a newline, a tab, and a \ character. There are a few others, but their meanings are so obscure that numeric codes usually make more sense. For example, \v, should probably be written as \x0b or \u000b; the original meaning behind \v is largely lost to history.

Note that '\u000b' is replaced by the actual Unicode character. We also have '\u240b' which is a Unicode glyph, 'V_T', that symbolizes that vertical tab character. Most of the non-printing ASCII control characters also have these symbolic glyphs.

Using raw string literals

Sometimes, we need to provide strings in which the \ character is not an escape character. When preparing regular expressions, for example, we prefer not be forced to write \\ to represent a single \ character. Similarly, when working with Windows filenames, we don't want "C:\temp" to have an ASCII horizontal tab character ('\u0008') replace the '\t' sequence of characters in the middle of the string literal. We could write "C:\\temp" but it seems error-prone.

To avoid this escape processing, Python offers the **raw string**. We can prefix any of the previous four flavors of delimiters with the letter r or R. For example, r'\b[a-zA-Z_]\w+\b', is a raw string. The \ characters will be left intact by Python: the '\b' sequences are not translated to '\u0008' characters.

If we do this *without* using the r" character as the raw string delimiter, we'll create a string literal equivalent to this: '\x08[a-zA-Z_]\\w+\x08'. This shows how a '\b' characters are transformed to '\x08' in a non-raw string. Omitting the leading r' leads to a string that does not represent the regular expression we intended.

Using byte string literals

We may need to include byte strings in our programs as well as Unicode strings. In order to do this, we use a prefix of b or B in front of the string delimiter. A byte string is limited to ASCII characters and escape sequences that produce single-byte ASCII characters.

Generally, byte strings focus on the hexadecimal escape, \xhh, with two hex digits for byte strings. We can also use the octal escape, \odd, with octal digits.

We can also prepare raw byte strings using any combination of r or R paired with b or B as a prefix to the string. Here's a regular expression in ASCII bytes:

```
>>> rb"\\x[0-9a-fA-F]+"
b'\\\\x[0-9a-fA-F]+'
```

The output is in Python's canonical notation using lengthy escapes for the '\\' regular expression pattern.

To be fastidious, we are also able to use a u" prefix to indicate that a given string is explicitly Unicode. This is relatively rare because it restates the default assumption. It can come in handy in a program where byte strings predominate; the use of u"some string" can make the Unicode literal stand out from numerous b"bytes" literals.

Using the string operators

Two of the arithmetic operators, + and *, are defined for both classes of string objects, str and bytes. We can use the + operator to concatenate two string objects, creating a longer string. Interestingly, we can use the * operator to multiply a string and an integer to create a longer string: "="*3 is '==='.

Additionally, adjacent string literals are combined into a larger string during code parsing. Here's an example:

```
>>> "adjacent " 'literals'
'adjacent literals'
```

Since this happens at parse time, it only works for string literals. For variables or other expressions, there must be a proper + operator.

All of the comparison operators work for strings. The comparison operators compare two strings, character by character. We'll look at this in detail in *Chapter 5, Logic, Comparisons, and Conditions*.

We cannot use string operators with mixed types of operands. Using `"hello" +`
`b"world"` will raise a `TypeError` exception. We must either encode the Unicode `str`
into `bytes`, or decode the `bytes` into a Unicode `str` object.

Strings are sequence collections. We can extract characters and slices from them.
Strings also work with the `in` operator. We can ask if a particular character or a
substring occurs in a string like this:

```
>>> "i" in "bankrupted"
False
>>> "bank" in "bankrupted"
True
```

The first example shows the typical use for the `in` operator: checking to see if a given
item is in the collection. This use of `in` applies to many other kinds of collections. The
second example shows a feature that is unique to strings: we're looking for a given
substring in a longer string.

Converting between Unicode and bytes

Most of the Python I/O libraries are aware of OS file encodings. When working
with text files, we rarely need to explicitly provide encoding. We'll examine the
details of Python's input-output capabilities in *Chapter 10, Files, Databases, Networks,
and Contexts.*

When we need to encode Unicode characters as a string of bytes, we use the
`encode()` method of a string. Here's an example:

```
>>> 'String with πxr²'.encode("utf-8")
b'String with \xcf\x80\xc3\x97r\xc2\xb2'
```

We've provided a literal Unicode string, and encoded this into UTF-8 bytes.
Python has numerous encoding schemes, all defined in the `codecs` module.

To decode the Unicode string represented by a string of bytes, we use the `decode()`
method of the bytes. Here's an example:

```
>>> b'very \xe2\x98\xba\xef\xb8\x8e'.decode('utf-8')
'very ☺'
```

We've provided a byte string with eleven individually hex-encoded bytes.
We decoded this to include six Unicode characters.

Note that there are several aliases for the supported encodings. We've used
`"utf-8"` and `"UTF-8"`. There are still more explained in the `codecs` chapter of
the *Python Standard Library*.

The ASCII codec is the most commonly used of these. In addition to ASCII, many strings and text files are encoded in UTF-8. When downloading data from the Internet, there's often a header or other indicator that provides the encoding, in the rare case that it's not UTF-8.

In some cases, we have a document which in bytes, written in traditional ASCII. To work with ASCII files, we convert the bytes from the ASCII encoding to Unicode characters. Similarly, we can encode a subset of Unicode characters using the ASCII encoding instead of UTF-8.

It's possible that a given sequences of bytes does not properly encode Unicode characters. This may be because the wrong encoding was used to decode the bytes. Or it could be because the bytes are incorrect. The decode() method has additional parameters to define what to do when the bytes cannot be decoded. The values for the errors argument are strings:

- "strict" means that exceptions are raised. This is the default.
- "ignore" means that invalid bytes will be skipped.
- "replace" means that a default character will be inserted. This is defined in the codecs module. The '\ufffd' character is the default replacement.

The choice of error handling is highly application-specific.

Using string methods

A string object has a large number of method functions. Most of these apply both to str and bytes objects. These can be separated into four groups:

- **Transformers**: which create new strings from old strings
- **Creators**: which create a string from a non-string object(s)
- **Accessors**: which access a string and return a fact about that string
- **Parsers**: which examine a string and decompose the string, or create new data objects from the string

The transformer group of method functions includes capitalize(), center(), expandtabs(), ljust(), lower(), rjust(), swapcase(), title(), upper(), and zfill(). These methods all make general changes to the characters of a string to create a transformed result. Methods such as lower() and upper() are used frequently to normalize case for comparisons:

```
>>> "WoRd".lower()
'word'
```

Using this technique allows us to write programs which are more tolerant of character strings with minor errors.

Additional transformers include functions such as `strip()`, `rstrip()`, `lstrip()`, and `replace()`. The functions in the strip family remove whitespace. It's common to use `rstrip()` on input lines to remove any trailing spaces and the trailing newline character which might be present.

The `replace()` function replaces any substring with another substring. If we want to do multiple independent replacements, we can do something like this.

```
>>> "$12,345.00".replace("$","").replace(",","")
'12345.00'
```

This will create an intermediate string with the "$" removed. It will create a second intermediate string from that with the , character removed. This kind of processing is handy for cleaning up raw data.

Accessing the details of a string

We use accessor methods to determine facts about the string; the results may be Boolean or integer values. For example, the `count()` method returns a count of the number of places an argument substring or character was found in the object string.

Some widely-used methods include the `find()`, `rfind()`, `index()`, and `rindex()` methods which will find the position of a substring in the object string. The `find()` methods return a special value of `-1` if the substring isn't found. The `index()` methods raise a `ValueError` exception if the substring isn't found. The "r" versions find the right-most occurrence of the target substring. All of these methods are available for both `str` and `bytes` objects.

The `endswith()` and `startswith()` methods are Boolean functions; they examine the beginning or ending of a string. Here are some examples:

```
>>> "pleonastic".endswith("tic")
True
>>> "rediscount".find("disc")
2
>>> "postlaunch".find("not")
-1
```

The first example shows how we can check the ending of a string with the `endswith()` method. The second example shows how the `find()` method locates the offset of a given substring in a longer string. The third example shows show the `find()` method returns a signal value of -1 if the substring can't be found.

Additionally, there are seven Boolean pattern-matching functions. These are `isalnum()`, `isalpha()`, `isdigit()`, `islower()`, `isspace()`, `istitle()`, and `isupper()`. These will return `True` if the function matches a given pattern. For example, `"13210".isdigit()` is `True`.

Parsing strings into substrings

There are a few method functions which we can use to decompose a string into substrings. We'll hold off on looking at `split()`, `join()`, and `partition()` in detail until *Chapter 3, Expressions and Output*.

As a quick overview, we'll note that `split()` splits a string into a sequence of strings based on locating a possibly repeating separator substring. We might use an expression such as `'01.03.05.15'.split('.')` to create the sequence `['01', '03', '05', '15']` from the longer string, by splitting on the `'.'` character. The `join()` method is the inverse of `split()`. That means that `"-".join(['01', '03', '05', '15'])` will create a new string from the individual strings and the separator; the result is `'01-03-05-15'`. The partition can be viewed as a single-item split to separate the head of a string from the tail.

Python's assignment statement deals very gracefully with such a method that returns more than one value. In *Chapter 4, Variables, Assignment and Scoping Rules*, we'll look at multiple assignment more closely.

The `split()` method should not be used to parse filenames, nor should the `join()` method be used to build filenames. There's a separate module, `os.path`, which handles this properly by applying OS-specific rules.

Using the tuple collection

The `tuple` is one of the simplest collections available in Python. It is one of the many kinds of Python sequences. A tuple has a fixed number of items. For example, we might work with (x, y) coordinates or (r, g, b) colors. In these cases, the number of elements in each tuple is fixed by the problem domain. We don't want the flexibility of a collection that can vary in length.

Generally, we'll include `()` around a `tuple` to set it apart from the surrounding syntax. This isn't *always* required; Python creates `tuple` objects implicitly in some common contexts. However, it is always a good idea. If we write an assignment statement like this:

```
a = 2, 3
```

This statement will implicitly create a 2-tuple, `(2, 3)`, and assign the object to the variable `a`.

The `tuple` class is part of Python's family of `Sequence` classes; we can extract the items of a `tuple` using their positional indices. The `str` and `byte` classes are also examples of Sequence. In addition to simple index values, we can use slice notation to pick items from a `tuple`.

The value `()` is a zero-length tuple. To create a singleton tuple, we must use `()` and include a `,` character: this means that `(12,)` is a singleton tuple. If we omit the `,` character we've written an expression, not a singleton tuple.

A trailing comma is *required* for a singleton tuple. An extra comma at the end of a tuple is quietly ignored everywhere else: `(1, 1, 2)` is equal to `(1, 1, 2,)`.

The `tuple` class offers only two method functions: `count()` and `index()`. We can count the number of occurrences of a given item in a `tuple`, and we can locate the position of an item in a `tuple`.

The None object

One very simple kind of Python object is the `None` object. It has few methods, and there's only a single instance of this object available. It is a handy way to identify something as missing or not applicable. It's often used as a default value for optional parameters to a function.

The `None` object is a singleton; there can be only one. This object is immutable: we can't change it in any way.

With the interactive use of Python, the REPL doesn't print the `None` object. For example, when we evaluate the `print()` function, the proper result of this function is always `None`. The side-effect of this function is to print things on our console. Looking forward to *Chapter 3, Expressions and Output*, we'll give this quick example of a function that returns `None`:

```
>>> a = print("hello world")
hello world
>>> a
>>> a is None
True
```

We've evaluated the `print()` function and saved the result of the print function in the `a` variable. The visible side-effect of printing is to see the string value displayed on the console. The result is the `None` object, which is not printed. We can, however, use the `is` comparison operator to see that the value of `a` really is the `None` object.

The consequences of immutability

Python has two broad flavors of objects: mutable and immutable. A mutable object has an internal state that can be updated by using operators or method functions. An immutable object's state cannot be changed.

The canonical examples of immutable objects are the numbers. The number 2 must always have a single, immutable value midway between 1 and 3. We can't change the state of 2 to make it 3 without making a mockery of the idea of mathematical truth.

In *Chapter 6, More Complex Data Types*, we'll look at a number of mutable data structures. The most important three mutable collections are `set`, `list`, and `dict`. These objects can have items added, and removed; we can change the state of the object.

In addition to numbers being immutable, three other common structures are also immutable: `str`, `bytes`, and `tuple`. Because strings and bytes are immutable, the string manipulation methods will always create a new string object from one or more existing string objects.

This means we cannot mutate characters or substrings within a longer string. We might think we need to attempt something like this:

```
>>> word="vokalizers"
>>> word[2]= "c"
```

But this can't work because a string object is immutable. We always build new strings from the old string's parts. We do it like this:

```
>>> word= word[:2]+"c"+word[3:]
```

This works by extracting pieces of the original string and including new characters mixed with the old.

Using the built-in conversion functions

We have a number of conversion functions in the various types of data we've seen in this chapter. Each of the built-in numeric types has a proper constructor function. As with many Python functions, each of these has a number of different kinds of arguments it can handle:

- `int()`: Creates an `int` from a wide variety of other objects
    - `int(3.718)` for another number
    - `int('48879')` for a string in base 10
    - `int('beef', 16)` for a string in the given base – 16 in this example
    - The `int()` function can ignore the extra prefix characters on numbers written in Python literal syntax: `int('0b1010',2)`, `int('0xbeef',16)`, and `int('0o123',8)`

- `float()`: Creates a `float` from other objects
    - `float(7331)` for another number
    - `float('4.8879e5')` for a decimal string

- `complex()`: Creates `complex` values from a variety of objects
    - `complex(23)` creates `(23+0j)`
    - `complex(23, 3)` creates `(23+3j)`
    - `complex('23+2j')` creates `(23+2j)`

We can convert single numbers, pairs of numbers, and even some strings into `Fraction` objects:

- `Fraction(2,3)`: This is the most common way to create `Fraction` objects.
- `Fraction(2.718)`: This creates a value `Fraction(765048986699563, 281474976710656)`. This shows how floating-point values are actually approximations. If we wanted a more accurate value, we should do a meaningful conversion ourselves, using `Fraction(2718,1000)`, which would avoid the error bits present in many floating-point values.
- `Fraction("3/4")`: This also works very nicely to create a proper `Fraction` object.

When we convert a `float` value to a `Fraction`, the results look unusual. However, considering that float values are an approximation, the `Fraction` value reveals the nature of the approximation.

We can also convert integers, strings, and floats to `Decimal` objects:

- `Decimal(2)`: Interestingly, this produces `Decimal('2')` as the result. This shows us that the preferred format for `Decimal` values is strings.

- `Decimal('2.718')`: This will produce the expected value. This is generally how we create `Decimal` objects.

- `Decimal(2.718)`: This will produce a value that reflects floating-point approximations: `Decimal('2.717999999999999971578290569595992565155029296875')`. Because of this, we generally avoid creating `Decimal` objects from `float` objects.

We have a number of additional conversions from numbers to various kinds of strings: `bin()`, `oct()`, `hex()`, and `str()` produce strings in base 2, 8, 16, and 10 respectively. We can also use various formatting features of numbers using `"{0:b}".format(x)` for binary, `"{0:o}".format(x)` for octal, and `"{0:x}".format(x)` for hexadecimal. If we include the "#" modifier in the format string, we have considerable flexibility in the strings produced. For example:

```
>>> "{0:x}".format(12)
'c'
>>> "{0:#x}".format(12)
'0xc'
```

These functions show many different ways to create numbers from strings and create formatted strings from numbers.

Summary

We've looked at some core data types available in Python. We've looked at five different kinds of numbers, including integers, floating-point, complex, `Fraction` and `Decimal`. Each fills a different niche. Three of these are built-in, the other two must be imported from the standard library.

We've also looked at three different kinds of collections. The `tuple` is a simple sequence of items with relatively few methods. `str` is a Unicode string, which has several methods for creating new strings as transformations of existing strings. `bytes` is a byte string, which also has a variety of methods. We can decode bytes to create Unicode strings. We can encode Unicode strings into bytes.

We've touched on how the `import` statement is used to introduce new types and new modules. This will add features from the standard library.

We've also looked at a number of functions to convert various numeric types. Many of these functions also convert strings to numbers. We'll make heavy use of `int()` and `float()` to convert strings to numbers. The reverse—converting numbers to strings—can be done with the `str()` function. It can be done better, however, with the formatting tools we'll look at in the next chapter.

In *Chapter 3, Expressions and Output*, we'll build on these basic concepts. We'll look in more depth at Python language syntax. We'll also look at functions for creating nicely formatted output. This will allow us to write simple programs. In *Chapter 4, Variables, Assignment and Scoping Rules*, we'll add even more essential language features so that we can write more sophisticated programs.

3
Expressions and Output

Expressions are central to Python programming. As noted in *Chapter 1, Getting Started*, Python has a rich collection of operators and built-in functions. In this chapter, we'll summarize the relationship between data types and the operators they support.

Perhaps the most fundamental program possible is one that performs a calculation and displays output. To demonstrate this, we'll look at the `print()` function in this chapter. We'll expand on the basics by looking at a number of ways to produce nicely-formatted text output.

We'll need to look in detail at the Python syntax rules. This will be essential for writing scripts with more complex sequences of statements. It will also set the stage for looking at compound statements in *Chapter 5, Logic, Comparisons, and Conditions*.

This chapter will also demonstrate some additional string processing techniques. We'll summarize some of the standard library modules that are focused on string processing. We'll look closely at the `re` module; we use this to build regular expressions that help parse string input. Between the built-in methods of the `str` class, and the `re` module, we can handle a wide variety of text input conversion.

Expressions, operators, and data types

Python expressions are built from operators and operands. In *Chapter 2, Simple Data Types*, we introduced some of the basics of number and string operands, and looked at the variety of operators. We'll summarize the details here so that we can address some additional operator features.

Our numeric operands form a "tower", with types including:

Type	Cardinality	Number of operators
complex	Ideally, the most distinct values built from a pair of irrational numbers, $\infty \times \infty$. Actually (float × float) or about 2^{128} values.	The fewest operators; only arithmetic, some built-in functions, and the cmath module.
float	Ideally this is a rational number union with irrational numbers ($\infty + \infty$). Actually closer to 2^{64} distinct values.	Arithmetic operators, comparisons. Many additional math modules and built-in functions.
fractions.Fraction	Ideally, these are rational numbers ($\infty \times \infty$). Actually only limited by available memory to represent two integers.	Arithmetic operators, comparisons, built-in functions.
decimal.Decimal	Ideally, rational numbers. Actually only limited by memory	Arithmetic operators, comparisons, built-in functions.
int	Ideally, natural numbers, ∞. Actually limited only by memory.	Arithmetic operators, comparisons, plus bit-handling operators, libraries and built-in functions.

The Fraction and Decimal class definitions must be imported, the other three classes are built-in. We typically use a statement such as from fractions import Fraction.

The idea behind the tower is that many arithmetic operators coerce operands up the tower from integer to float to complex. Most of the time, this fits with our implicit mathematical expectations. We would be unhappy if we had to write explicit conversions to compute 2.333*3. Python's arithmetic rules assure us that we'll get the expected floating-point result.

The Decimal class doesn't fit well with the implicit coercion rules: in the rare case of trying to do arithmetic between float and Decimal, it's unclear how to go about it. An attempt to make a Decimal value from a float value will expose tiny errors because float values are an approximation. An attempt to make a float value from a Decimal value subverts the Decimal objective of yielding exact results. In the face of this ambiguity, an exception will be raised. This means that we'll need to write explicit conversions.

String objects are not implicitly coerced into numeric values. We must explicitly convert a string to a number. The int(), float(), complex(), Fraction(), and Decimal() functions convert a string to a number object of the appropriate class.

We can group operators into a number of categories.

- **Arithmetic**: +, -, *, **, /, //, %
- **Bit-oriented**: <<, >>, &, |, ^, ~
- **Comparison**: <, >, <=, >=, ==, !=

The bit-oriented operators are supported by operands of the int class. The other number classes don't have useful implementations of these operators. The bit-oriented operators are also defined for sets, something we'll look at in *Chapter 6, More Complex Data Types*.

Using operators on non-numeric data

We can apply some of the arithmetic operators to strings, bytes, and tuples. The results are focused on creating larger strings or larger tuples from smaller pieces. Here are some examples of this:

```
>>> "Hello " + "world"
'Hello world'
>>> "<+>"*4
'<+><+><+><+>'
>>> "<+>"*-2
''
```

In the first example, we applied + to two strings. In the second example, we applied * between a str and an int. Interestingly, Python produces a string result by concatenating several copies of the original string object. Multiplying by any negative number creates a zero-length string.

The print() function

When working with Python's REPL, we can enter an expression and Python prints the result. In other contexts, we must use the `print()` function to see results. The `print()` function implicitly writes to `sys.stdout`, so the results will be visible on the console where we ran the Python script.

We can provide any number of expressions to the `print()` function. Each value is converted to a string using the `repr()` function. The strings are combined with a default separator of `' '` and printed with a default line ending of `'\n'`. We can change the separator and line ending characters. Here are some examples of this:

```
>>> print("value", 355/113)
value 3.1415929203539825
>>> print("value", 355/113, sep='=')
value=3.1415929203539825
>>> print("value", 355/113, sep='=', end='!\n')
value=3.1415929203539825!
```

We've printed a string and the floating-point result of an expression. In the second example, we changed the separator string from a space to `'='`. In the third example, we changed the separator string to `'='` and the end-of-line string to `'!\n'`.

Note that the `sep` and `end` parameters must be provided by name; these are called **keyword arguments**. Python syntax rules require that keyword argument values are provided after all of the positional arguments. We'll examine the rules in detail in *Chapter 7, Basic Function Definitions*.

We can use `,` as a separator to create simple **comma-separated values (CSV)** files. We can also use `\t` to create a kind of CSV file with a tab character as the column separator. The `csv` library module does an even more complete job of CSV formatting, specifically including proper escapes or quoting for data items which contain the separator character.

To write to the standard error file, we'll need to import the `sys` module, where that object is defined. For example:

```
import sys
print("Error Message", file=sys.stderr)
```

We've imported the `sys` module. This contains definitions of `sys.stderr` and `sys.stdout` for the standard output files. By using the `file=` keyword parameter, we can direct a specific line of output to the `stderr` file instead of the default of `stdout`.

This can work well in a script file. Using the standard error file doesn't look very interesting at the REPL prompt since, by default, both standard output and standard error go to the console. Some IDE's will color-code the standard error output. We'll look at many ways to open and write to other files in *Chapter 10, Files, Databases, Networks, and Contexts.*

Examining syntax rules

There are nine fundamental syntax rules in section 2.1 of the *Python Language Reference*. We'll summarize those rules here:

1. There are two species of statements: simple and compound. Simple statements must be complete on a single logical line. A compound statement starts with a single logical line and must contain indented statements. The initial clause of a compound statement ends with a : character. It's possible, using rules 5 and 6, to join a number of physical lines together to create a single logical line.

   ° Here's a typical simple statement, complete in a single logical line:

   ```
   from decimal import Decimal
   ```

   ° Here's a typical compound statement with a nested simple statement, spread across two logical lines:

   ```
   if a > b:
       print(a, "is larger")
   ```

2. A **physical line** ends with \n. In Windows, \r\n is also accepted.

3. A **comment** starts with # and continues to the end of the physical line. It will end the logical line.

   ° Here's an example of a comment:

   ```
   from fractions import Fraction # We'll use this to improve
   accuracy
   ```

4. A special comment can be used to annotate the file encoding. This is generally not needed, since most IDE's and text editors handle the file encoding politely. We should generally save Python files in UTF-8 encoding. Older files may be saved in ASCII.

5. Physical lines can be joined explicitly into a logical line using the \ as an escape character in front of the physical end-of-line character. This is rarely used and generally discouraged.

6. Physical lines can be joined implicitly into a logical line using (), [], or {}; these must pair properly for the logical line to be complete. An expression beginning with (can span multiple physical lines until there is a matching). This is used frequently and is strongly encouraged.

   ° Here's an example of a statement that relies on () to join four physical lines into one logical line:

   ```
   print (
       "big number",
       2 ** 2048
   )
   ```

7. Blank lines contain only spaces, tabs and newlines. The interactive REPL uses a blank line to end a compound statement; the REPL is the only context in which a blank line is meaningful.

8. Leading whitespace is **required** to properly group statements inside the clauses of compound statements. Either spaces or tabs can be used to indent. Consistency is essential. A four space indent is widely used and strongly encouraged.

9. Except at the beginning of the line, — where it determines nesting of compound statements — whitespace can be used freely between tokens. Note that there are some preferences regarding precisely how spaces are used within a statement; the **Python Enhancement Proposal (PEP)** number 8 provides some advice. See https://www.python.org/dev/peps/pep-0008/ for fodder for endless disputes.

Perhaps the most important two rules are rule 6 and rule 8. Rule 6 means that it is very common to use (), [], and {} to force multiple physical lines to be joined into a single logical line.

Rule 8 requires that our indentation is done consistently: indents and outdents must be matched. While it's legal to use tabs, spaces, and any haphazard — but consistent — mix of tabs and spaces, four spaces is highly recommended. Tabs are discouraged because they're hard to distinguish from spaces. Most editors can be set to replace the tab key with four spaces. A good text editor can recognize the basics of Python syntax and can handle indents and outdents gracefully.

Use () to allow a statement to span multiple physical lines; avoid \ at end-of-line.

Use a four space indent.

Also note that Python will merge adjacent strings when parsing the source. We can have code that looks like this:

```
>>> message = ("Hello"
... "world")
>>> message
'Helloworld'
```

This assignment statement used a gratuitous () pair to allow the logical line to span multiple physical lines. The expression is simply two adjacent strings, "Hello" and "world". When Python parses the source text, these two adjacent strings are merged; only a single string is used when evaluating the statement.

Additionally, note that the REPL prompt changed from >>> to ... because the REPL recognized the first physical line as a partial statement. This is a handy reminder that our statement isn't complete. When the final) was parsed, the statement was complete and the prompt switched back to >>>.

Splitting, partitioning, and joining strings

In *Chapter 2, Simple Data Types*, we looked at different processing methods for a string object. We can transform a string into a new string, create strings from non-string data, access a string to determine properties or locations within the string, and parse a string to decompose it.

In many cases, we need to extract elements of a string. The split() method is used to locate repeating list-like structures within a string. The partition() method is used to separate the head and tail of a string.

For example, given a string of the form "numerator=355,denominator=115" we can use these two methods to locate the various names and values. Here's how we can decompose this complex string into pieces:

```
>>> text="numerator=355,denominator=115"
>>> text.split(",")
['numerator=355', 'denominator=115']
>>> items= _
>>> items[0].partition("=")
('numerator', '=', '355')
>>> items[1].partition("=")
('denominator', '=', '115')
```

We've used the `split(",")` method to break the longer string on each `,` character, creating a list object which has two substrings. The REPL automatically assigns all expression results to a variable named `_`. We assigned the object to the `items` variable because the value of `_` gets overwritten by each expression statement.

We used the `partition("=")` method on each item in the `items` variable to break the assignment down into name, `=`, and value. A more complex application would probably perform more complex processing on the names and values.

The `join()` method is the inverse of the `split()` method. This works with a sequence of string objects to create a single long string from many smaller strings. Here's an example of using a tuple of strings to create a longer string:

```
>>> options = ("x", "y", "z")
>>> "|".join(options)
'x|y|z'
```

We've created a sequence of three strings and assigned it to a variable named `options`. We then used the string `"|"` to join the items in the `options` sequence. The result is a longer string with the items separated by the given string.

The `split()` and `join()` methods work well with singletons. If we try to split a single item with no punctuation, we get a sequence with a single item. If we join a singleton item, the separator will not be used.

Python's string methods give us the tools to handle a variety of string parsing and decomposition. For a more general solution, we'll have to resort to even more powerful tools. We'll look at the regular expression module, `re`, later.

If we want to create complex strings, we use the `format()` method. We'll look at this next.

Using the format() method to make more readable output

Sophisticated string creation can be done with the `format()` method. We create a template string and values which can be plugged into the template. Here's an example of how this works:

```
>>> c=42
>>> "{0:d}°C is {1:.1f}°F".format(c, 32+9*c/5)
'42°C is 107.6°F'
```

We've created a variable, c, with a value of 42. We've used a template, `"{0:d}°C is {1:.1f}°F"`, to format two values. The argument value with an index of 0 is c, the argument value with an index of 1 is the value of the expression `32+9*c/5`.

The template string includes literal characters, plus replacement fields. Each replacement field is surrounded by `{}`. The replacement field has two components with a syntax of `{index:specification}`. The *index* component identifies which item is taken from the positional arguments to the `format()` method. The *specification* component shows us how to format the selected object.

The example gives two specifications. One specification is the character d, which is the decimal integer conversion. The other is the slightly more complex `.1f`, which is a floating-point conversion with one digit to the right of the decimal point.

There is considerable sophistication available in the format specifications. There are eight fields to a format specification. The syntax gloss looks like this:

```
[[fill]align] [sign] [#] [0] [width] [,] [.precision] [type]
```

We've surrounded each field with `[]` to group the names visually. Note that all the fields are actually optional and have default values.

We'll summarize the fields from right to left in order of importance.

- **Type**: This specifies the overall type of conversion. Depending on the kind of Python object, there are a number of type codes available:
  - For string values, the type code of s is used.
  - For integer values, type codes of d, n, b, o, x, or X can be used. These provide decimal, locale-aware numbers, binary, octal, or hexadecimal output.
  - For float values, type codes are e, E, f, F, g, G, n, or %. The e formats provide explicit exponents. The f codes show `float` values with no exponent. The g values are called **general** and choose e or f, depending on the size of the number. The n code is locale-aware, using the locale settings for floating-point presentation. The % multiplies by 100 and includes the % symbol.

- **Precision**: The `.precision` value is only used for floating-point formats. It's the number of positions to the right of the decimal point.

- **The , separator**: If a , character is used, then US-style , as 1,000's separators are included. This isn't locale-aware, so it can't be overridden by the OS and the Python locale module.

- **Width**: If omitted, the number is formatted as wide as necessary. If provided, the number is filled out to this width. By default, the fill uses leading spaces, but this can be changed by providing values for the *fill* and *align* fields.

- **0**: This forces filling to the required width with leading zeroes. This is the same as a fill and align of 0=.

- **#**: This is used with b, o, and x formatting to include a prefix of 0b, 0o, or 0x in front of the number.

- **Sign**: By default, positive numbers have no sign and negative numbers have a leading -. Providing a *sign* field of + means that all signs are shown explicitly. Providing a *sign* field of - means that an extra space is included for positive numbers, assuring that positive and negative numbers will align in columns when printed using a fixed-width font.

- **Fill and align**: This fills up the space to the value of the *width* field. If we provide *align* without a specific *fill* character, the default character is a space. We can't provide a *fill* character on its own, though. There are four codes we can use:

  - < or *fill*< will push the data to the left, and the filling will be on the right.

  - > or *fill*> will push the data to the right, the fill character will be used on the left.

  - ^ or *fill*^ will center the data, filling both left and right.

  - = or *fill*= will put the sign first, and the fill character will be used after the sign. This will make the signs more prominent in a column of numbers.

Here's an example that uses a fairly complex format specification:

```
>>> amount=Decimal("234.56")
>>> "Pay: ${0:*>10n} dollars".format(amount)
'Pay: $****234.56 dollars'
```

We've created an object, amount, with a Decimal value. We then used a format specification of *>10n on this number. This used leading * characters to fill out the number to 10 characters.

Summary of the standard string libraries

Python's standard library offers a number of modules with additional string processing features.

- `string`: The string module contains constants that decompose the ASCII characters into letters, numbers, whitespace, and so on. It contains the full definition of the formatter that is used by the `str.format()` method. We'll look at this in the next section. It also contains the `Template` class which defines a string template into which values can be interpolated.

- `re`: The regular expression library allows us to define a pattern that can be used to parse input strings. We'll look at this in the next section.

- `difflib`: The `difflib` module is used to compare sequences of strings, typically from text files. There are a number of comparison algorithms available in this module.

- `textwrap`: We can use the `textwrap` module to format large blocks of text.

- `unicodedata`: The `unicodedata` module provides functions for determining what kind of Unicode character is present. Unicode Standard Annex 44 defines a collection of properties that apply to the Unicode characters. One commonly-used function is the general category of a character; this includes simple Latin rules like "Lu" for uppercase letter or "Nd" for decimal number. The general category codes also include "Sk" which is for non-letter like modifier symbols.

- `stringprep`: This is an implementation of RFC 3454, which prepares Unicode text strings in order to support sensible string comparisons.

Using the re module to parse strings

Regular expressions give us a simple way to specify a set of related strings by describing the pattern they have in common. A regular expression is an element of set theory that could (in theory) define the set of all possible related strings. The theoretical matching process would be a quick check to see if a given string in this set of all possible strings is generated by the expression. Since the set of all possible strings generated from a pattern could potentially be infinite, this isn't how things work in practice.

When we use the `re` module, we generally do three things. Firstly, we specify the pattern string. Secondly, we compile the pattern into an object that efficiently determines if and where a given string matches the pattern. Finally, we repeatedly use the `pattern` object to efficiently match, search, or parse the given input strings.

As a concrete example, we need to process input which contains lines like this: `Birth Date: 3/8/1987` or `Birth Date: 1/18/59`. Note that the number of digits in each date and the amount of whitespace is allowed to vary.

We may perform any of the following three common kinds of processing:

- A **matching** regular expression might be `Birth Date:\s+\d+/\d+/\d+`. The `\s+` subexpression means one or more spaces. The `\d+` subexpression of this means one or more digits. A match pattern is usually designed to match the whole string.

- A **searching** regular expression might be `\d+/\d+/\d+`. This search pattern includes one or more digits, `\d+`, and literal punctuation, `/`. This expression describes a substring that can be found somewhere within the given string.

- A **parsing** pattern separates the various digit groups from the surrounding context. This is a slight modification to one of the previous examples to include `()`, that specifies what to capture. We might use `(\d+)/(\d+)/(\d+)` to show that the digit groups should be extracted for further processing.

We can accomplish these matching, searching, and parsing operations with the `re` module in Python.

Using regular expressions

The general recipe for using regular expressions in a Python program has three essential steps. Of course, we must use import re to include the required module. The three steps are:

1. Define the pattern string. This will almost always be a raw string, starting with `r"`, because the regular expression string will be full of `\` characters that we don't want to be treated as escapes by Python. Because `\` begins a Python language escape, if we want to write a standalone `\` character, we have to double them up in a non-raw string. It is better to use a raw string to write `r"\d+/\d+/\d+"` than `\\d+/\\d+/\\d+`.

2. Evaluate the `re.compile()` function to create a `pattern` object. The resulting object will do the real work of matching a given target string against the regular expression `pattern` object.

   We can combine the pattern and the compile in one statement like this:

   ```
   >>> date_pattern = re.compile(r"Birth Date:\s+(.*)")
   ```

3. Use the compiled `pattern` object to match or search the candidate strings. The result of a successful match or search will be a `Match` object. We can then use the match object, where necessary, to extract fields. For example:

```
>>> match = date_pattern.match("Should Not Match")
>>> match
>>> match = date_pattern.match("Birth Date: 3/8/87")
>>> match
<_sre.SRE_Match object at 0X82e60>
```

In the first example, the `date_pattern.match()` expression returned `None` because the given string didn't match the regular expression. In the second example, the given string did match the regular expression pattern, and a `Match` object was created. If our regular expression is used for parsing, we'll interrogate the `Match` object to get the various substrings.

When we have a `Match` object, it can have captured substrings that match parts of the overall pattern. We'll usually make use of the various `group()` methods to get substrings. Here are some examples:

```
>>> match.group()
'Birth Date: 3/8/87'
>>> match.group(1)
'3/8/87'
>>> match.groups()
('3/8/87',)
```

In the first example, we saw all of the matching content. In the second example, we saw the value of group number one, the first portion of the regular expression wrapped in `()`. In the final example, we saw all `()`-wrapped groups in the regular expression. Since there was only one such group, the value of `groups()` is a single-item `tuple` with matching text.

Creating a regular expression string

There are numerous rules for creating regular expression patterns, and we'll look at a few of them here. The definitive list is in the *Python Standard Library* documentation for the `re` module, in section 6.2.1. For more information on this topic, see *Mastering Python Regular Expressions* from Packt Books. See https://www.packtpub.com/application-development/mastering-python-regular-expressions.

First we'll look at the "atomic" regular expressions. Then we'll look at the rules for combining regular expressions into a larger regular expression. Here are some simple, atomic regular expressions:

- Any single character. With a few exceptions, this means just about any printable character. The exceptions are the characters which have special meaning in the regular expression language, including ., *, ?, (,), [,], | among others.

- A . matches any character. To match a period, the \ escape character is used: \. matches a period.

- Some escape sequences match whole classes of characters.

    ◦ \d matches any digit. \D matches any non-digit character.

    ◦ \s matches any whitespace character. \S matches any non-space character.

    ◦ \w matches any word character. \W matches any non-word character. By default, these follow the Unicode rules. We can override this to follow a considerably simpler set of ASCII-only rules.

There are some suffixes that we can put after a regular expression.

- A * suffix means the previous expression can be matched zero or more times. This has the effect of making the previous RE pattern optional as well as eligible for repetition.

- A + suffix means the previous expression can be matched one or more times. This means that the previous pattern is mandatory and can also be repeated.

- A ? suffix means the previous expression is optional; it can be matched zero times or just one time.

- To actually match a suffix character, use the \ escape. For example, * matches an asterisk.

We can combine individual expressions into larger patterns. Here are some common techniques for doing this:

- A sequence of regular expressions is a regular expression. We simply put the expressions one after another inside the pattern string. When we write an expression like Birth it's a sequence of five atomic expressions which match each individual character.

- A sequence of characters in [] matches any one of the given characters. This is generally used with single-character expressions; often we'll see constructs like [a-zA-Z0-9_] to match any letter or digit or _. To match multiple-character strings we use a suffix after the []. We can use r"[0-9a-fA-F]+" to match one or more hexadecimal digits. To make - one of the alternative characters, it must be first or last within the list of characters inside the [].

- Two regular expressions separated by | is a regular expression. Either one can match. We might be looking at a pattern like true|false. We must match one of the two regular expressions: either true or false. To match the pipe character, |, it must be escaped like this \|.

- A regular expression surrounded by ()'s is a regular expression. It's also preserved as a group, so that we can use the matching characters while parsing. To match parentheses, they must be escaped, \(matches a (. Substrings captured via () are available via the group() method of the match object.

These rules help us examine the details of a specific pattern. Here's a pattern we might use to parse some input:

    r"(\w+)\s*[=:]\s*(.*)"

This is a regular expression which is a sequence of 5 regular expressions.

- The characters (\w+) make a regular expression, \w, with a + suffix enclosed in (). This matches any sequence of one or more word characters.

- \s* is a regular expression. It's a simple expression \s with a suffix of *. It matches zero or more whitespace characters. This means that spaces are optional after the initial word. If spaces are present, any number may be used.

- [=:] is a regular expression built from two single-character expressions, = and :. It matches either one of the two characters.

- \s* is used a second time to permit any number of whitespace characters between the = or : and the value.

- The final regular expression is (.*) which matches any sequence of characters.

When we use this regular expression, if a Match object is created, it will have two groups. We can then extract the name and value matched by the patterns within this regular expression.

Working with Unicode, ASCII, and bytes

The re module works with bytes as well as Unicode strings. We must provide proper pattern literals depending on which kind of string we're working with. With Unicode, we use pattern literals with the r prefix: r"\w+". With bytes, we use the rb prefix, rb"\w+"; the rb means raw bytes instead of raw Unicode characters.

The rules for the character classes are, of course, different. A Unicode string that matches the "\w+" pattern can have any of a wide variety of Unicode "word" characters. A bytes object that uses the "\w+" pattern will match ASCII characters from the set a-z, A-Z, 0-9 and _.

We must explicitly use bytes for the pattern literals when parsing, searching, or matching with bytes.

We can use an option in the re.compile() to force a Unicode pattern to follow the simplified ASCII rules. If we write re.compile(r"\w+", re.ASCII) we've replaced the default Unicode assumption for \w with the ASCII rule for \w even though we're doing Unicode string matching.

Using the locale module for personalization

When looking at the str.format() method, we saw that the n format type produced a number with formatting based on the user's locale. This means that the formatting varies according to the OS locale settings. Users in different countries will see that their personal locale settings are used properly.

Here's an example of using the locale module to get locale-specific formatting:

```
>>> import locale
>>> locale.setlocale(locale.LC_ALL,'')
'en_US.UTF-8'
>>> "{0:n}".format(23.456)
'23.456'
>>> locale.setlocale(locale.LC_ALL,'sv_SE')
'sv_SE'
>>> "{0:n}".format(23.456)
'23,456'
```

This script used the locale module to set the Python locale to match the prevailing OS locale. The locale is reported to be English as used in the US (en_US) and the preferred Unicode encoding is shown as UTF-8.

The formatted value of 23.456 showed up with a US English decimal point. This fits the expectations of users in the US.

We then switched the locale to Sweden. The language was reported as sv_SE, which means the Swedish language, as used in Sweden. The formatted value switched to 23,456 with a decimal comma, which is appropriate for users in Sweden.

Let's continue this example, and use the locale.currency() formatting function:

```
>>> locale.currency(23.54)
'23,54 kr'
```

The amount was formatted using , for the decimal separator and kr as the local currency in Sweden. The locale module includes the currency names.

Note that we provided the numeric value, 23.54, in Python syntax, which does not vary by locale. Python floating-point literals always use decimal points. Only the output string from the currency() function uses the , character as a decimal place separator.

Summary

In this chapter, we've reviewed the essential numeric types and the operators available on Python. We've looked at some expressions that involve a mixture of string and numeric data.

In order to view the output from our scripts, we've looked at the print() function. This is used widely to produce output. The print() function is a very handy tool for debugging particularly complex functions or classes.

Additionally, we've looked at how we can use the str.format() method to produce elaborately formatted data. This gives us a wide variety of techniques for converting Python objects to strings that can be displayed. We've also looked at some ways that we can parse strings using string method functions such as split() and partition().

Beyond the basics of string processing, we've looked at how we can use the re module to match, search, and parse strings. This module is sophisticated and has a large number of features for extracting useful information from input strings.

In *Chapter 4, Variables, Assignment and Scoping Rules*, we'll expand on our script-writing by using variables to store intermediate results. We'll also look at how objects are created and removed. These rules will lead to an understanding of which variables are visible in which portions of a complex program.

4
Variables, Assignment and Scoping Rules

An expression creates objects; we can assign objects to variables to preserve them for future use. Python offers a number of variations on the theme of assignment. In addition to simply assigning a single variable, we can assign items from a tuple to multiple variables. We can also combine an operator with assignment, which updates a mutable object.

In this chapter, we'll also look at the `input()` function as a way to introduce new objects into a running script. This is limited—it doesn't compare with a proper **graphical user interface (GUI)**. It will, however, help us learn more Python programming techniques before we introduce how to read data from files and the filesystem in *Chapter 10*, *Files, Databases, Networks, and Contexts*.

We'll also look at some important Python language concepts. We'll look at the way Python programs are always written generically, without specific bindings to data types or classes. We'll also look at the general concept of a namespace, and how this is applied widely in various Python language constructs. It defines the scope in which an identifier is visible; something that will become increasingly important as our programs become more complex.

Simple assignment and variables

We've seen a few examples of the essential Python assignment statement in previous chapters. The statement includes a variable, =, and an expression. Since a single object is an expression, we can write:

```
>>> pi = 3.14
```

This will create the floating-point literal 3.14 and assign this object to a variable named pi.

Variable names must follow the rules in section 2.3, *Identifiers and Keywords*, of the *Python Language Reference*. The reference manual uses the Unicode character class definitions provided in the unicodedata module.

Interesting background information on the problem of programming language identifiers is available in Unicode Standard Annex 31, *Unicode Identifier and Pattern Syntax*. This shows how the Python problem of how "what is an identifier?" fits into the larger context of other programming languages and the variety of natural languages used around the world.

In Python, identifiers have a small set of start characters; these are chosen to allow a lexical scanner to determine what kinds of characters can follow. If identifiers began with digits, it would be rather complex to distinguish identifiers from numbers. Consequently, identifiers must begin with a letter or _. After the initial character, Python allows an identifier to continue with characters that may come from a larger set of characters: letters, digits, and _.

What do we really mean by "letter" or "digit"? In earlier versions of Python, these terms were defined by the Latin-based ASCII alphabet. Using Unicode means that the terms now have more inclusive definitions.

Python defines the identifier starting character as belonging to the following Unicode categories: uppercase letters (Lu), lowercase letters (Ll), title case letters (Lt), modifier letters (Lm), other letters (Lo), and letter numbers (Nl). Python also includes the small set of characters in the Other_ID_Start category. The set of characters defined by these categories is large. Latin letters in the ranges a-z and A-Z, for example, are in this set. When writing more mathematically-oriented programs, the Greek letters α-ω and Α-Ω can also be used as identifier start characters. We can write this:

```
>>> π = 355/113
```

This assigns the result of the expression to the variable, π. Some programmers find that their OS keyboard interface makes letters outside a single national alphabet awkward to use; consequently, they suggest focusing on Latin letters for programming.

Identifiers can continue with any of the letters defined in the previous paragraph, the _ character, and characters from the following categories: nonspacing marks (Mn), spacing combining marks (Mc), decimal numbers (Nd), and connector punctuations (Pc). This allows us to include ordinary decimal digits as well as other "combining" marks that modify the previous character. For example:

```
>>> π̂=p_2+0.5*p_1
```

This shows the character **GREEK SMALL LETTER PI** followed by the **COMBINING DIACRITICAL CIRCUMFLEX** to create a "pi-hat" variable, $\hat{\pi}$. It may be awkward to type for some developers, but it also may fit nicely with a population genomics formulae which use this symbol combination. The Inheritance By Descent estimator, for example, uses $\hat{\pi}$. The expression shown earlier involves two other variables, p_2 and p_1, which use more common Latin letters, _, and digits.

Note that variable names that begin and end with __ (two underscores) are reserved by Python for special purposes. For example, we have global variables such as __name__, __debug__, and __file__ which are set when our script starts running.

There's no reason for our application to ever create new names which begin and end with __. We're not prohibited from creating such variables, but any name that we might adopt could be used by some internal feature of Python.

It's best to assume that at all names beginning and ending with __ (double underscore) are reserved by Python and do something special. Even if the name is not used in the current release, that doesn't mean it won't be used in a future release.

Multiple assignment

We looked at tuples in *Chapter 2, Simple Data Types*. One of the important reasons for using a tuple is that it has a fixed number of items. Since a tuple is a kind of sequence, we can refer to items within a tuple using numeric indices.

Consider the following RGB triple:

```
>>> brick_red = (203, 65, 84)
```

We can use brick_red[0] to get the red element of this triple.

We can also do this:

```
>>> r, g, b = brick_red
>>> r
203
```

We've used multiple assignment to decompose the RGB three-tuple into three individual variables.

This works when the number of variables on the left side of the = matches the number of items in the collection on the right side. When working with fixed-sized tuples, this is an easy condition to guarantee.

When working with mutable collections such as `list`, `set`, or `dict`, this kind of assignment may not work out well. If we can't guarantee the number of elements in a mutable collection, we may wind up with a `ValueError` exception because our collection doesn't match the number of variables.

Note that Python's syntax flexibility means that we can also do things like this:

```
>>> n, d = 355, 113
```

It isn't absolutely necessary to wrap a tuple in `()`. It's generally a best practice to use `()` around a tuple. However, in a few cases, the statement is perfectly clear without the additional parentheses.

Using repeated assignment

Python allows us to write statements like this: `a = b = 0`. This must be used carefully, because a single object is now shared by two variables. When working with immutable objects like numbers, strings, and tuples, multiple variables share a reference to a common object.

When we look at mutable objects in *Chapter 6, More Complex Data Types*, we'll see that this kind of repeated assignment can become a source of confusion. While this assignment is legal, it must be used only with immutable objects like numbers, strings, or tuples.

Using the head, *tail assignment

When working with sequences, there are some algorithms which work by separating the head of the sequence from the rest of the sequence. We can do this with a variation on the assignment statement. We like to call this the `head, *tail =` assignment statement.

Let's say that we have an input string with a list of values, something like this:

```
>>> line = "255  73 108 Radical Red"
>>> line.split()
['255', '73', '108', 'Radical', 'Red']
```

We have split the string into space-delimited words with `line.split()`. In this case, the head of the list is the first three fields of the red, green, and blue elements of a color. The tail is all the remaining fields, which is the name parsed into separate words.

We can use `head, *tail =` assignment to split the first three fields from the remaining files.

It looks like this:

```
>>> r, g, b, *name = line.split()
>>> g
'73'
>>> name
['Radical', 'Red']
```

We've assigned the first three items to three separate variables, r, g, and b. The *
means that all of the remaining items will be collected into a single variable, name.

We can reconstruct the original name with the join() method, with a space as the
separator string:

```
>>> " ".join(name)
'Radical Red'
```

We've used a space to join the elements of the sequence named name. This will
reconstruct the original color name as a single string instead of a list of words.

Augmented assignment

The augmented assignment statement combines an operator with assignment.
A common example is this:

```
a += 1
```

This is equivalent to

```
a = a + 1
```

When working with immutable objects (numbers, strings, and tuples) the idea of an
augmented assignment is syntactic sugar. It allows us to write the updated variable
just once. The statement a += 1 always creates a fresh new number object, and
replaces the value of *a* with the new number object.

Any of the operators can be combined with assignment. The means that +=, -=, *=,
/=, //=, %=, **=, >>=, <<=, &=,^=, and |= are all assignment operators. We can see
obvious parallels between sums using +=, and products using *=.

In the case of mutable objects, this augmented assignment can take on special
significance. When we look at list objects in *Chapter 6, More Complex Data Types*, we'll
see how we can append an item to a list object. Here's a forward-looking example:

```
>>> some_list = [1, 1, 2, 3]
```

This assigns a `list` object, a variable-length sequence of items, to the variable `some_list`.

We can update this `list` object with an augmented assignment statement:

```
>>> some_list += [5]
>>> some_list
[1, 1, 2, 3, 5]
```

In this case, we're actually mutating a single `list` object, changing its internal state by extending it with items from another `list` instance. The existing object was updated; this does not create a new object. It is equivalent to using the `extend()` method:

```
>>> some_list.extend( [8] )
>>> some_list
[1, 1, 2, 3, 5, 8]
```

We've mutated the `list` object a second time, extending it with items from another single-item `list` object.

This optimization of a `list` object is something that we'll look at in *Chapter 6, More Complex Data Types*.

The input() function

For simple applications, the `input()` function can be used to gather input from a user. This function writes a prompt and accepts input. The returned value is a string. We might use this in a script file as follows:

```
c= float(input("Temperature, C: "))
print("f =", 32+9*c/5)
```

This will write a simple prompt on the console, and accept a string as input. The string value will be converted to a floating-point number, if possible. If the string is not a valid number, the `float()` function will raise an exception. This will then print a line of output.

Here's how it looks when we run it:

```
MacBookPro-SLott:Code slott$ python3 Chapter_4/ex_1.py
Temperature, C: 11
f = 51.8
```

We've highlighted the command, which is entered after the OS shell prompt. The statements in the script file, named as part of the command, are executed in order.

Our input to Python, 11, is also highlighted, to show how the `input()` function supports simple interaction.

The `input()` function only returns a Unicode string. Our script is responsible for any further parsing, validation, or conversion.

When working on simple console applications, there are some additional libraries which may prove helpful. There is a `getpass` module which helps to get passwords by suppressing the character echo that's a default feature of console input. This is highly recommended as an alternative to plain passwords in a parameter file or the passwords provided on the command line.

We can include the `readline` module to provide a comprehensive history of input that makes it easier for interactive users to recover previous inputs. Additionally, the `rlcompleter` module can be used to provide auto-complete features so that users only need to enter partial commands.

Beyond this, Python can include an implementation of the Linux `curses` library for building richly interactive **character user interface** (**CUI**) applications. This is sometimes used to provide colored output on the console, something that can make a complex log easier to read.

Python is used in a wide variety of application contexts. When building a web server, for example, the idea of console or command-line input is utterly out of place. Similarly, the `input()` function isn't going to be part of a GUI application.

Python language concepts

We'll introduce a few central concepts of the Python language before looking at more complex examples in later chapters. The first of the central concepts is that everything in Python is an object. Several popular languages have **primitive** types which escape the object-oriented nature of the language. Python doesn't have this feature. Even simple integers are objects, with defined methods.

Because everything is an object, we're assured of consistent behavior with no special cases. In some languages, the `==` operator works in one way for primitive types and in another way for objects. Python lacks this divergent behavior. All built-in classes implement the `==` operator consistently; unless we make specific (and pathological) implementation choices, our own classes will also behave consistently.

This consistency is particularly pleasant when working with strings. In Python, we always compare strings for equality using something like `txt.lower() = "hours"`. This will make the expected character-by-character comparison between the value of `txt.lower()` and the literal `"hours"`.

Less commonly, we can see if two variables are references to the same underlying object using the is comparison operator. This is generally used to compare a variable with the None object. We use is None because the None object is a proper singleton; there can be only one instance of None. We'll look at this again in *Chapter 5, Logic, Comparisons, and Conditions.*

Object types versus variable declarations

In Python, we specify the processing generically with respect to type. We may write a sequence of statements with the implicit understanding that floating-point values should be used. We can formalize this to an extent using an explicit float() conversion function.

In some languages, each variable has a statically defined type. Only objects of the named type can be assigned to the variable.

In contrast to languages with statically defined variables, a Python variable can be understood as a name which is attached to an object. We can attach a name to any object of any class. We don't statically declare a narrow range of allowed types for a variable.

Python allows us to assign multiple names to the same object by assigning the object to several variables. For example, when we evaluate a function, the function parameter variable names are assigned to the argument objects. (We'll look at this in more depth in *Chapter 7, Basic Function Definitions.*) This means that each object may have two variables referring to it: one parameter variable inside the function and another variable outside the function.

We can use the internal id() function to see if two variables refer to the same underlying object:

```
>>> a = "string"
>>> b = a
>>> id(a)
4301974472
>>> id(b)
4301974472
```

From this, we can see that Python variables a and b have references to the underlying object, not copies of the object.

In the rare cases that object copying is necessary, we must do it explicitly. Details vary, based on the general kind of class. For example, sequences are trivially cloned by creating a slice that includes the entire sequence. Some classes offer a copy() method. Objects can also be cloned via functions in the copy library.

The lack of a fixed type declaration for a variable has several consequences:

- It's trivial to introduce a variable to decompose a complex expression. Here's a complex expression:

```
a = some_function( some_complex_function( another_function( b ) ) )
```

- We can trivially rewrite this by pulling out subexpressions and assigning them to variables:

```
af = another_function(b)
scf = some_complex_function(af)
a = some_function(scf)
```

    We've extracted each subexpression and assigned them to separate variables. We never need to know what the intermediate result types are.

- All algorithms are written generically. When we run a script, we apply our generic Python code to concrete objects. Our canonical example of this binding is based on the numeric tower. We can apply the same expression, `32+9*c/5`, to objects of the classes `complex`, `float`, `int`, `Decimal`, and `Fraction`. All of these classes provide the necessary implementations of the various operators. However, a string object won't implement all of the arithmetic operations required, and won't work. Similarly, we can execute statements like `head`, `*tail = sequence` for a wide variety of sequence-like classes, including `list`, `str`, `bytes`, and `tuple`. However, if we assign a numeric value to the variable named `sequence`, the statement won't work.

Avoiding the declaration of variables with static types is a great simplification. We can introduce variables as needed. We can write clear, simple, generic software and leave it to the Python runtime processing to determine if the runtime objects have the required implementations for operators and methods.

Avoiding confusion when naming variables

Without variable declarations, there's a small possibility of creating programs which are confusing if we use vague, generic variables. A variable with a vague name like `list_of_items` might get used more than once in a longish sequence of statements. Worse, of course, are variables with names like `t` or `temp`.

 Name variables as specifically as possible. Avoid vague, generic names.

The other aspect of overusing variable names is the idea of a "longish" sequence of statements. If the body of a function is so long that generically-named variables could get reused accidentally, the size of the function has become a problem. No stretch of Python code should be so long that the variables used within it are confusing.

 Keep sequences of code short and focused. Avoid long sequences of code where variables might get reused incorrectly.

It's import to name variables simply and clearly. In Python, the use of *Hungarian notation* to decorate a variable name with type information is considered deplorable. The original concept of Hungarian notation was to place a few characters as a prefix on a variable to indicate the type. In Python, we do not name a variable `lst_str_names` using a prefix to indicate that the variable refers to a list of string values.

Because Python code is written generically, a well-written function can apply to many different data types. If we try to encode data type information in variable names, we may actually be sowing confusion: the algorithm may work for types not explicitly stated in the variable name.

In some situations, we need to distinguish between a collection of items and an individual item. We might have a `name_list` and an individual `name`. Or we might have a `name_iter`, when working with generator functions, and an individual `name`. A small, clear naming convention like this is better than elaborately misleading Hungarian notation.

 Avoid complex Hungarian notation in variable names.

In a more complex program, we might have a dictionary that maps integer keys to sets associated with those keys; each set may have a collection of individual strings. It's difficult to summarize this with a Hungarian prefix or suffix. Would we want to try and call this `map_int_set_str_something`?

Looking ahead to *Chapter 7*, *Basic Function Definitions* and *Chapter 11*, *Class Definitions*, we'll often use `docstring` comments in functions, classes, and modules to capture the details of what kind of structure is appropriate for a function. We may even include test cases in the `docstring` comments; test cases are perhaps the clearest and most precise way to describe data.

Write `docstring` comments in every context that allows them: function, class, module, and package.

One consequence of Python's use of variables is that we rely on unit test cases to ensure that results are of the expected types as well as being correct. Programmers who work in languages with statically-typed variables are very aware that unit test cases are essential for correctness, even when a compiler does type checking of all variable declarations. In Python, the test cases are just as important as in languages that have static type checking. If it is necessary to clarify the intent of a function or class, we can include type checking in the test cases.

Write unit tests; use the `unittest` module, the `doctest` module, or both.

Garbage collection via reference counting

We've seen how expressions create new objects. Even something as simple as `2**2024` creates a new integer object. What happens to these objects? When will we run out of memory?

Python uses reference counting to determine how many times an object is being used when we do something like this:

```
>>> 2**2024
192624...497216
```

The resulting object is a very large integer; it is assigned to the variable _ automatically. The object, shown as `192624...497216`, has a single reference; this keeps it alive in memory.

When we do this, next:

```
>>> 2**2025
385248...994432
```

We get a new object, and it is assigned to the variable _. The large integer value formerly assigned to _ has no more references. Since it's no longer being used, it's garbage, and the memory it occupied can be reused.

Each time we assign an object to a variable, the reference count goes up by one. Each time the variable's value is reassigned, the previous object that is no longer in use has its reference count decreased by one.

When a variable is no longer required, the variable is removed, and the objects referred to by the variable also have their reference counts reduced by one.

Variables belong to namespaces. Most of our early examples used the global namespace. In *Chapter 7, Basic Function Definitions*, we'll see local namespaces. To summarize: when a namespace is removed, all of the variables in that namespace are removed, and all of the object references are decremented by one.

 When the number of references to an object reaches zero, the object is no longer needed. The memory occupied by that object can be reclaimed.

We can easily create two complex objects which refer to each other. In the presence of these kinds of circular references, of course, the counts can never reach zero. The objects may never get removed from memory. We can use the gc module to discover more about this.

In the case where we must have objects with mutual references, we need to leverage the weakref module. This module provides references among objects that do not interfere with reference counting, allowing a large data structure of multiple objects to gracefully vanish from memory when no longer in use.

The little-used del statement

We can remove variables manually with the del statement. Here's an example:

```
>>> a = 2**2024
>>> del a
```

We've created an integer object, and assigned it to the variable a. When we remove the variable, this will reduce the reference count on the integer object. The memory occupied by the big integer is now eligible to be reclaimed.

This kind of thing is done very rarely. Python's ordinary reference counting does almost everything we need. It's generally best not to waste brain calories tying to micro-manage memory allocation.

The Python namespace concept

We've already seen two applications of the Python namespace. When we assign variables at the >>> prompt, we're introducing the variable into the global namespace. When we import a module, the module creates its own namespace within the global namespace.

That's why we can then use qualified names like `math.sqrt()` to refer to objects inside the module's namespace.

When we look at functions and class definitions, we'll see additional use, of namespaces. In particular, when evaluating a function or a class method, a local namespace is created, and all variables are part of that local namespace. When the function evaluation finishes (because of an explicit `return` statement or the end of the indented block,) the local namespace is dropped, removing all local variables and reducing the reference count on all objects assigned to those local variables.

Additionally, the `types` module includes the `SimpleNamespace` class. An instance of this class allows us to build a complex object without a formal class definition. Here's an example:

```
>>> from types import SimpleNamespace
>>> red_violet= SimpleNamespace(red=192, green=68, blue=143)
>>> red_violet
namespace(blue=143, green=68, red=192)
>>> red_violet.blue
143
```

We've imported the `SimpleNamespace` class. We created an instance of that class, assigning three local variables, `red`, `green`, and `blue`, that are part of the new `SimpleNamespace` object. When we examine the object as a whole, we see that it has three internal variables.

We can use syntax like `red_violet.blue` to see the `blue` variable inside the `red_violet` namespace.

The `argparse` module is used by command-line programs to parse the command-line arguments. This module also contains a `Namespace` class definition. An instance of `Namespace` is used to collect the various arguments parsed from the command line. An application can set additional variables in the `Namespace` object to handle particularly complex parsing and configuration issues.

Globals and locals

When we use a variable name in an expression, Python searches two namespaces to resolve the name and locate the object to which it refers. First, it checks the local namespace. If the name is not found, it will check the global namespace. This two-step search will ensure that local variables used inside a function or class method are used before global variables with the same name.

When working from the >>> prompt using the REPL, we can only create and use global variables. Further examples will have to wait until *Chapter 7, Basic Function Definitions*.

When we use the locals() and globals() functions at the >>> prompt, we can see that they have the same results. At the >>> prompt, and at the top-level of a script file, the local namespace is the global namespace. When evaluating a function, however, the function works in a separate, local namespace.

Summary

We've looked at how we assign objects to variables. We've looked at the simple assignment statement, as well as multiple assignment and augmented assignment. With augmented assignment, we can update a variable by applying an operator and an operand. This is a handy syntactic shortcut.

We've also addressed the input() function, which is a way to create new objects based on user input. It's very handy for simple command-line scripts. More sophisticated GUIs, of course, will have considerably more sophisticated input mechanisms.

The concept of a namespace, and how variables are tracked via a namespace, is central to Python. When a namespace is no longer needed, it's discarded, removing all of the variables. This will also reduce the reference count on all of the objects referred to by the variables. Once an object's reference count is reduced to zero, the object can be removed from memory. This is a tidy and simple way to handle variables.

In *Chapter 5, Logic, Comparisons, and Conditions*, we'll look at another fundamental data type: Boolean. We'll look at Python's approach to Boolean values and the logical operators of and, or, not, and if-else. We'll also look at the various comparison operators.

We'll look at several kinds of Python statements, include the if-elif-else statement, the pass statement, and the assert statement. This will allow us to write somewhat more sophisticated scripts.

5
Logic, Comparisons, and Conditions

Our exploration of the Python language started with expression statements and the assignment statement. We can view output using the `print()` function as a simple statement. We can gather input using the `input()` function in an assignment statement. In order to process data conditionally, we need the `if` statement.

In order to look at the `if` statement, we'll need to look at Boolean data and Boolean operators. The `and`, `or`, `not`, and `if-else` Boolean operators have a "short-circuit" behavior: if the result is defined by just the left-hand operand, the right-hand side is not evaluated. This is an important feature of these logic operators. (The `if-else` operator is formally called the **Boolean expression**, but it behaves like the Boolean operators.)

We'll also look at the comparison operators. A comparison is a common way to create the Boolean values used to choose between suites of statements within an `if` statement.

We'll introduce the `pass` statement here. This statement does nothing. It's a place-holder to use when an empty suite of statements is all we need.

The `assert` statement can be used to demonstrate that a particular logical condition is true at some point in the program's execution. This can clarify a potentially confusing algorithm. It can also serve as a handy debugging tool to make a program crash when something has gone awry.

Boolean data and the bool() function

All objects can have a mapping to the Boolean domain of values: `True` and `False`. All of the built-in classes have this mapping defined. When we define our own classes, we need to consider this Boolean mapping as a design feature.

The built-in classes operate on a simple principle: if there's clearly no data, the object should map to `False`. Otherwise, it should map to `True`. Here are some detailed examples:

- The `None` object maps to `False`.
- For all of the various kinds of numbers, a zero value maps to `False`. All non-zero values are `True`.
- For all of the collections (including `str`, `bytes`, `tuple`, `list`, `dict`, `set`, and so on) an empty collection is `False`. A non-empty collection is `True`.

We can use the `bool()` function to see this mapping between object and a Boolean:

```
>>> red_violet= (192, 68, 143)
>>> bool(red_violet)
True
>>> empty = ()
>>> type(empty)
<class 'tuple'>
>>> bool(empty)
False
```

We've created a simple sequence, a `tuple` of three values, and assigned it to the `red_violet` variable. Since this is non-empty, it maps to `True`. On the other hand, the empty tuple, assigned to the `empty` variable, maps to `False`.

One important consequence of this built-in mapping is that any object can be used in a Boolean construct. Looking ahead, we'll often see programs with constructs that echo this idiomatic pattern:

```
for input from some_file:
    if not input.strip(): continue
```

Some details of this example will have to wait for *Chapter 10, Files, Databases, Networks, and Contexts*. What's important about this example is that we can read a line from a file, strip whitespace with the `strip()` method, and use a simple Boolean expression to see if the result is an empty string. If it is an empty string, we can easily ignore it by using the `continue` statement.

This construct works because strings map to Boolean values. An empty string maps to `False`, allowing us to check for the absence of content with a very simple and elegant expression.

Comparison operators

In *Chapter 2*, *Simple Data Types*, we looked at the six essential comparison operators: `<, >, ==, !=, <=,` and `>=`. The minimum of `==` and `!=` are defined by default for all classes, so that we can always compare objects for simple equality. For the numeric types, the ordering operators are also defined. Furthermore, Python's type coercion rules are implemented by the numeric types so that the expression `2 < 3.0` will have the `int` coerced to `float`.

For sequences, including `str, bytes, tuple,` and `list`, the two operands are compared item-by-item. This tends to put strings into alphabetical order. This works well for words. It also usually puts tuples into the expected order. However, for number-like strings, the sorting may seem a little odd. Here's the example:

```
>>> "11" < "2"
True
```

The strings `"11"` and `"2"` are not numbers. They're only characters. It's a common confusion to imagine these values as numbers and hope that `"11"` comes after `"2"`. If this is the desired behavior, we'll need to convert these number-like strings to proper numbers using the `int()` function.

For `set` objects, the comparison operators map to the superset and subset relationships. Python's `<` operator is implemented as the proper subset relationship. The `<=` operator is implemented as the subset relationship. We'll look at this in detail in *Chapter 6*, *More Complex Data Types*.

For other types, comparisons become less meaningful. Orderings between mappings is not a simple concept. How do we order two mappings: do we compare keys only, values only, or some combination of both? If we try to compare both keys and values, what are the rules for missing keys? Since there's no simple answer, Python doesn't define the ordering operators for mappings.

For types outside the numeric tower, there are no coercion rules. The equality comparisons simply compare the object IDs to see if the two operands are references to same object.

In general, ordering operators are not implemented by default and will raise `TypeError` exceptions. This is a common expectation for many classes.

If we try to compare two file objects, what attribute of the file should we be comparing? Size? Creation date? Rather than create confusion, comparison operators are simply not implemented for many classes.

Combining comparisons to simplify the logic

In some cases, we may need to see if a value lies within a given range. One handy syntax simplification is to combine ordering comparisons into a simplified expression. We can meaningfully write expressions like this:

```
5 > a >= 0
```

In this kind of expression, Python interprets the combined operators to mean `5 > a` and `a >= 0`. We aren't forced to repeat the middle expression, `a`, to decompose the ordering test into two binary comparisons.

Testing float values

One important feature of float values is that they are only approximations. We can easily write calculations which seem mathematically exact, but produce odd-looking results. Specific examples vary a bit from implementation to implementation. Here's one example:

```
>>> a=1
>>> b=(a/105)*3*5*7
>>> a == b
False
>>> abs(a-b)
2.220446049250313e-16
```

In an abstract mathematical sense, `(a/105)*3*5*7`, must equal the original value of the `a` variable. We can see, however, that the floating-point approximation created by the true division operator has a small error. In this case, the error value is approximately `2.22e-16`, which is `2**-52`: the least significant bit of a 52-bit value is incorrect after this chain of floating-point operations.

Because of the presence of these small error terms, we should avoid trivial `==` tests with floating-point values. A simple equality test can often turn out to be false when the two values differ by a tiny amount.

Generally, we should use `abs(a-b) < ε` instead of `a == b`. We can set the ε value to be small enough to detect what is equal. If, for example, we're going to display a value with three decimal places, there's little reason to compute anything past the 5th decimal place. In that case, `ε=10e-5` can be used to define the acceptable tolerance for floating-point equality.

Avoid `float == float` comparisons; use `abs(float-float) < ε` instead.

Comparing object IDs with the is operator

To determine if two variables are actually referencing the same object, we have a special comparison operator: `is`. This is different from the somewhat more complex equality test. The `is` operator is a very simple test comparing the internal identifiers for two objects.

If `a is b`, then `a == b` must also be true, as the two variables refer to the same underlying object. However, if `a == b`, then `a is b` may not necessarily be true. Two distinct objects can have the same value. Here's an example using floating-point values:

```
>>> a = 3.14
>>> b = 3.14
>>> a == b
True
>>> a is b
False
```

This example works nicely for floating-point objects. We can see that two seemingly-equal objects are actually distinct instances which represent the same numeric value.

An example like this doesn't work for small integer values, however. For a narrow range of integer values, Python tends to reuse a small pool of internal objects. This avoids the proliferation of copies of ubiquitous values. If we try to set `a=1` and `b=1`, we'll see that `a is b`: Python reused the same object.

With a little experimentation, we can see that the reuse of small integers is true for numbers between -5 and 256. Implementation details will vary. What's important is that some immutable objects are implicitly allocated from a pool.

Object identity is revealed with the `id()` function. This shows the unique, internal object identifier. For example:

```
>>> id(a)
4298491200
>>> id(b)
4298491224
```

We can see that these are two distinct objects which happen to be equal in value.

Equality and object hash values

An important part of equality comparison in Python is the hash value comparison. A hash is a small integer value that summarizes a larger, more complex value. A hash should not change; mutable objects should not provide a hash value.

Any object that we're going to collect into a set or use as a key to a mapping must provide both a hash value and a proper equality comparison. All of the built-in immutable types we've seen—numbers, `tuple`, `str`, and `bytes`—offer the necessary implementations of these methods. The built-in mutable types that we'll look at in *Chapter 6, More Complex Data Types*, such as `list`, `set`, and `dict`, don't provide a hash value and can't be used as keys in a mapping.

A hash function reduces a complex value to a small number. In Python, hash values generally use 61 bits. For a complex object, the hash value summarizes the object as a whole. It might be a sum of all the individual bytes, computed $(m2^{61})$. It might be a sum of hash values for other internal objects. Comparing hash values makes for significantly less work than comparing each individual item in a complex object.

For immutable objects, the hash value is computed once and will be as immutable as the object itself. For mutable objects, a hash value could be computed. However, if the hash value changes, then the object won't behave well as an item in a set or as a key to a mapping. A changing hash value for a mutable object is not a very good idea.

When putting items into a set, for example, Python does a quick equality check using the hash values. If the hash values are different, the underlying objects must be different, and no more comparison needs to be done. If the hash values match, however, then the detailed equality test must be used to see if the objects really are equal or only happen to have the same hash value.

In some implementations of Python, you can use this kind of test to see if two different numbers happen to have the same hash value:

```
>>> hash(12)
12
>>> hash(12*2**61)
12
```

 Implementations vary; this was Mac OS X, v3.3.4:7ff62415e426, your results may be different.

If we tried to put these two values into a set, Python would do a hash check to see that they are *potentially* equal, followed by a detailed comparison to see that they're not equal.

Logic operators – and, or, not, if-else

Python offers us four logical operators: and, or, not, and if-else. These work with Boolean values to create Boolean results. They're entirely distinct from the bit-wise operators of &, |, ^, and ~, that we looked at in *Chapter 2*, *Simple Data Types*.

The and, or, and not operators are common in all programming languages. They fit the widely-used definitions from Boolean algebra.

The if-else Boolean expression has three operands. In the middle, it uses a Boolean condition, but the other two operands can be objects of any types. Here's an example:

```
selection = "yankee" if wind < 15 else "stays'l"
```

The if-else operator has a Boolean condition in the middle. In this example, it's the comparison, wind < 15. If the condition is True, then the left-most expression is the result, the string "yankee". If the condition is False, then the right-most expression is the result; here, it's "stays'l".

The logical operators implicitly apply the bool() function to their operands. This means that we can do things like the following

```
valid= line and line[0] != "#"
```

The and expression involves two Boolean operands. When Python implicitly evaluates bool(line), a non-empty line will be True; a zero-length line will be False. The valid variable will be False for empty lines; it will also be False for non-empty lines where line[0] is not the "#" character.

This implicit use of bool() also means this is true:

```
>>> not 12
False
```

The value of not 12 is evaluated as not bool(12). The bool() value of a non-zero numeric value is True; the final result of this expression is therefore False.

Short-circuit (or non-strict) evaluation

Consider the following:

```
>>> total= 0
>>> count= 0
>>> average = total != 0 and total/count
>>> average
False
```

What just happened? Or, more precisely, what didn't happen? Why doesn't this raise a ZeroDivisionError exception? The first two assignment statements are unsurprising; they assign zero to two variables, total and count. The logical expression, however, has a number of interesting features. Firstly, Python evaluates expressions left-to-right. This means that the total != 0 subexpression is evaluated first. The result of this comparison is False.

Secondly, and perhaps more importantly, the and operator breaks the strict evaluation rules. If the left side value is equivalent to False, the overall result is False. The right side is not evaluated at all. If the left side value is equivalent to True, the result is simply the right side value.

This is sometimes called a short-circuit evaluation rule. There's no reason to evaluate the right side if the result is known from the left side.

The result is not necessarily a Boolean; it's simply one of the operands given to the and operator. Here are some examples:

```
>>> 0 and 12
0
>>> () and "non-false"
()
>>> 12 and ()
()
```

In the first example, 0 is equivalent to False, and that object is the entire result of the and operator. In the second example, the empty tuple, (), is equivalent to False; it is the result of the operator.

In the third example, the left hand side, 12, is non-zero, and therefore, equivalent to True. This means that the right side must be evaluated. The right side is the result of the and operator; in this case, it is an empty tuple, ().

The or operator is similar; if the left side is equivalent to True, there's no reason to evaluate the right side. We can use this feature to apply default values.

We can write expressions like the following.

```
x = parameter or 42
```

If the value of the parameter variable is a True value, the value of the or operator will be that equivalent-to-true value. If the value of the parameter variable is not a True value (for example, it might be None), then the result will be the literal value 42.

We can, of course, also use the `if-else` operator for this. Here's an example:

```
x = 42 if parameter is None else parameter
```

If the value of the `parameter` variable is the `None` object, the left side operand — the literal 42 — is the result. If the value of the `parameter` variable is not the `None` object, then the right side operator — the value of the `parameter` variable — is the result.

The if-elif-else statement

Our central tool for conditional processing is the `if` statement. This is a compound statement which is built from a number of clauses. The initial clause starts with the `if` keyword. Any number of `elif` (short for "else if") clauses can be used. Each of these clauses has a conditional expression and an indented suite of statements. We can also add a single catch-all `else` clause at the end; this doesn't have a condition, but does have a suite of statements.

The minimal `if` statement, with a single clause, might look like this:

```
if abs(a-b) < ε:
    print("{a} \N{ALMOST EQUAL TO} {b}".format(a=a, b=b))
```

The `if` statement contains a single expression. If the expression is `True`, the suite of statements is executed. In this case, the suite is a single expression statement, using the `print()` function.

The `else` clause can be used in simple `if` statements.

```
if count == 0:
    print("Insufficient Data")
else:
    print("Mean = {0:.2f}".format(total/count))
```

In this case, we have two conditions. We've formally stated the `count == 0` condition for one `print()` function. We have an unstated condition for the other `print()` function. It's relatively easy — in this simple case — to deduce the implied condition.

Adding elif clauses

In some cases, we can decompose complex situations into a list of cases. For example, we might have some conditions like this:

```
if y % 400 == 0:
    leap = True
elif y % 100 == 0:
```

```
        leap = False
    elif y % 4 == 0:
        leap = True
    else:
        leap = False
```

We've written a rather complex chain of logic here. We've specified four distinct conditions:

- y is a multiple of 400, in which case, the `leap` variable will be set to `True`. For example, the year 2000 was a leap year.

- y is a multiple of 100 (and not a multiple of 400), in which case, the `leap` variable will be set to `False`. The year 2100 will not be a leap year.

- y is a multiple of 4 (and neither a multiple of 100 nor of 400), which sets the `leap` variable to `True`. The year 2016 will be a leap year.

- y is not a multiple of 4, 100, or 400, the `leap` variable is set to `False`. The year 2015 is not a leap year.

Since Python evaluates the clauses in a strict order, each `elif` clause has an implicit "and not any of the previous clauses". This means that the conditions in each `elif` can be written very succinctly, but they also need the previous clauses as part of their context.

As the number of `elif` clauses grows, the possibility of introducing a subtle logic bug also grows. This can create the situation where the implied condition for the `else` clause is very hard to deduce correctly. Consequently, some programs include logic that looks like this:

```
if y % 400 == 0:
    leap = True
elif y % 400 != 0 and y % 100 == 0:
    leap = False
elif y % 400 != 0 and y % 100 != 0 and y % 4 == 0:
    leap = True
elif y % 400 != 0 and y % 100 != 0 and y % 4 != 0:
    leap = False
else:
    raise Exception("Logic Error")
```

This example shows each implied condition written out fully. It also shows the `else` clause used to raise an exception in the unlikely case that a condition was overlooked or misstated. Some developers argue that this is simply a waste of time. Others recognize that anything which is merely implied is a possible source of errors, and prefer to state conditions explicitly.

For simple sets of conditions, this may be needless over-engineering. In other cases, this long-winded variation is more reliable because it removes all assumptions and implicit conditions.

The pass statement as a placeholder

In some algorithms, an `else` clause may be more important than an `if` clause. This happens when an algorithm is designed to handle a certain set of conditions — the happy path — by default. All of the other non-happy-path conditions require some exceptional processing.

When the default condition is relatively clear and easy to write, but there's no processing required for the condition, we have a syntax issue in Python. The interesting processing belongs to an `else` clause, but we have no real code for the initial `if` clause. Here's a typical pattern shown with invalid syntax:

```
if happy_path(x):
    # nothing special required
else:
    some_special_processing(x)
# Processing Continues
```

The `happy_path()` condition confirms that the default processing will work. There's no actual processing do be done when this is true. Since we don't want to do anything, what do we write in the `if` clause?

The preceding code is invalid Python. We can't have an empty suite in the `if` clause. Since we can't write the code that's shown, we have to find alternative syntax that works.

One obvious choice is to negate the logic of the `happy_path()` condition. We can simply use the `not` operator.

```
if not happy_path(x):
    some_special_processing(x)
```

This has the desired effect. However, the `not` operator may be hard to see. When the `happy_path()` condition is a complex logic expression, the extra `not` can be confusing.

This is where the Python `pass` statement might be clearer than the `not` operator. It would look like this:

```
if happy_path(x):
    pass # nothing special required
```

```
else:
    some_special_processing(x)
# Processing Continues
```

We've filled the syntactic void in the `if` clause with a "do nothing" statement. We have used `pass` to create a proper suite in the `if` clause. We left the comment in place because that kind of information might be helpful.

There are a few other uses for the `pass` statement. We'll look at them in *Chapter 11, Class Definitions*.

The assert statement

The `assert` statement is a highly specialized form of `if` statement. This statement confirms that a given condition is true. If the condition is not true, the `assert` statement raises an exception. In the simplest case, the script stops running because the exception is not handled in our programming.

It looks like this:

```
assert a > b >= 0
```

We have used an `assert` statement to provide documentation of a relationship between variables that must be true at a given point in our Python script, function, or method. If the condition, `a > b >= 0`, is false, then the `AssertionError` exception is raised.

We can customize the exception which is raised by providing a second argument to the `assert` statement:

```
assert a > b >= 0, "a={0} and b={1}".format(a, b)
```

We've provided a string which includes information about the assertion. This string will be an argument to the exception object which is created.

An exception has two interesting features. Firstly, it's an object with arguments that we can set when we raise it. Secondly, and more importantly, it interrupts the normal sequential execution of statements. A `try`/`except` statement can be written to handle exceptions: the execution stops in the `try` clause and begins in an `except` clause that matches the exception. Without a `try` statement that matches the exception, raising an exception stops the program. We'll look at exceptions in detail in *Chapter 9, Exceptions*.

Note that the `assert` statement can be disabled. When we run Python3 with the `-O`, optimize, command-line option, then the `assert` statements are not included in the internal Python byte code.

The logic of the None object

In *Chapter 2, Simple Data Types*, we introduced the None object. It is a unique, immutable object, often used to indicate that a parameter should have a default value or that an input is not available. Some languages have a special null object or null pointer that have similar semantics to the Python None object.

The None object has no arithmetic operators defined. It's equivalent to False. The == and != operators are generally defined for None. However, these operators aren't always appropriate because other objects might exhibit similar behavior.

Generally, we'll use the is comparison when trying to determine if a variable is set to None. The == test can be redefined by a class that implements the __eq__ special method; the is test cannot be overridden.

 Because == can be reimplemented, always use is None instead of == None.

Since bool(None) == False, we can use a variable which may be None in an if condition. Nevertheless, we should generally use is None or is not None to be clearer.

Here's an example:

```
if not a:
    print("a could be None")
```

This relies on the way Python implicitly evaluates bool(a) to see if the value of the a variable is equivalent to True. It's often better to be perfectly explicit:

```
if a is None:
    print("a is None")
```

This shows that we're matching the value of the a variable against the None object.

Summary

We've looked closely at Python's Boolean data type, which only has two values (True and False) and four operators: and, or, not, and if-else. The Boolean operators and the if statement will both implicitly coerce values to a Boolean. This means that non-empty strings will behave in the same as the True value.

We've looked at the comparison operators. These work with other objects and create Boolean results.

In the case of numeric comparisons, the numeric coercion rules are used to allow us to compare `float` against `int` values without having to write explicit conversions. For string or tuple values, we've seen that items are compared in order.

We've also seen how the logical operators of `or` and `and` are not strict about evaluating their operands. If the left-hand side of `and` is `False`, the right-hand side isn't evaluated. Similarly, if the left-hand side of `or` is `True`, the right-hand side isn't evaluated.

We looked at several kinds of Python statements, including the `if-elif-else` statement, the `pass` statement, and the `assert` statement. These statements allow us to write somewhat more sophisticated scripts.

In *Chapter 6, More Complex Data Types*, we'll look at the `list`, `set`, and `dict` collections. We'll see how we can use the `for` statement to process all items in a given collection. This will give us the ability to write scripts of considerable sophistication.

6
More Complex Data Types

We'll look at a number of built-in and standard library collection types. These collections offer more features than the simple tuple collection. We'll look at the `for` and `while` statements which allow us to process the individual items of a collection.

We'll look at some functions which we can use to work with collections of data; these include the `map()`, `filter()`, and `functools.reduce()` functions. By using these, we don't need to write an explicit `for` statement to process a collection. We'll also look at more specific kinds of reductions such as `max()`, `min()`, `len()`, and `sum()`.

We'll also look at the `break` and `continue` statements; these modify a `for` or `while` loop to allow skipping items or exiting before the loop has processed all items. This is a fundamental change in the semantics of a collection-processing statement.

The concepts of mutability and immutability are part of understanding how an object behaves. The built-in types in this chapter are all mutable. This is quite different from the way that immutable objects like strings and tuples behave.

The mutability and immutability distinction

In *Chapter 2, Simple Data Types*, we looked at the immutability issue. This is an important characteristic of Python objects. We'll need to look at some more aspects of mutability in *Chapter 7, Basic Function Definitions*. We'll look at how we can create our own mutable classes in *Chapter 11, Class Definitions*.

We've seen that Python's various classes include those which create mutable objects and those which create immutable objects. The immutable classes include all of the number classes, strings, bytes, and tuples. The tuple `(247, 83, 148)` object cannot be changed: we cannot assign a new value to an item with an index of 1.

A `tuple` object has the structure of `Sequence`: we can extract items based on their position. However, we cannot change the internal state of a `tuple` object.

A `list` is also a subclass of the `Sequence` class. We can, however, change the state of a `list` object without creating a new `list` instance.

The abstract base class definitions for `Sequence` and `MutableSequence` are in the `collections.abc` module. The documentation for this module shows how the various complex types relate to each other.

While some of the features of `list` and `tuple` are similar, they address different use cases. The benefits of immutability are simplicity, reduced storage demands, and higher-performance for some kinds of processing. The benefit mutability is that a single object can undergo an internal state change.

Using the list collection

Python's `list` collection is its built-in mutable sequence. We can create list objects easily using a literal display that simply provides expressions enclosed in `[]`. It looks like this:

```
fib_list = [1, 1, 3, 5, 8]
```

As with tuples, the items are identified by their position in the `list` collection. Positions are numbered from the left starting from zero. Positions are also numbered from the right, using negative numbers. The last value in a list is at position -1, the next-to-last value at position -2.

 Index values begin with zero. Index position 0 is the first item. Index values can be done in reverse with negative numbers. Index position -1 is the last item.

We can also create lists using the `list()` function. This will convert many kinds of collections into `list` objects. Used without arguments, `list()` creates an empty `list` just like `[]`. Since the `list()` function is so versatile at converting collections into `list` objects, we'll use it much more in later chapters.

We can update a `list` collection using methods like `append()`:

```
fib_list.append(fib_list[-2] + fib_list[-1])
```

In this example, the value of `fib_list[-1]` is the last element in the list, and `fib_list[-2]` is the penultimate value. The expression creates a new number, which can be appended to the `fib_list` object.

We can manipulate a single element in a list using a subscription, such as those shown in the previous example. The value in the `[]` must be a single integer, which identifies an item in the list. It looks like this:

```
>>> fib_list[2]
3
```

The item in position two (the third item in the list) has a value of 3.

We can extract a sublist using slicing notation. A slicing uses a multi-part value in the `[]`. The result of a slicing is always a list built from the original list object. There are several ways to specify slicings, we'll show a number of examples:

```
>>> fib_list[2:5]
[3, 5, 8]
>>> fib_list[2:]
[3, 5, 8, 13]
>>> fib_list[:-1]
[1, 1, 3, 5, 8]
```

The first slicing, `[2:5]`, starts at the index of 2 and stops just before the index of 5. This means that the index values of 2, 3, and 4 are sliced out of the original list. Since lists are indexed from zero, an index of 2 is the third position in the list. It's essential to think of a slicing as a "half-open" interval.

Most of Python uses "half-open" intervals.

When we write the slice expression `[a:b]`, position a is included while position b is not included. This slice specifies all index values, i, such that $a \leq i < b$. There are $b - a$ values in the slice.

The second slicing, `[2:]`, omits the ending, which means that it starts at an index of 2 and includes all items to the end of the list.

The third slicing, `[:-1]`, omits the starting position, which means that it starts at an index of 0. The ending is given as -1, the last item in the list. Since slicings stop short of the given final position, this slicing will omit the last item from the list.

We can use `[:]` as a degenerate case where the start and end are both omitted. This works very well when making a shallow copy of an entire `list` object.

Slicings can be extended to include a third parameter. This allows us to specify a *start*, *stop*, and a *step* value. We can do things like this:

```
>>> fib_list[::2]
[1, 3, 8]
>>> fib_list[1::2]
[1, 5, 13]
```

In the first example, the start and stop are omitted, so we'll use the entire list. The step value is 2, so we'll extract a new list using the even-numbered indexes: 0, 2, 4, …, and so on.

In the second example, we provided a start and a step value. This will begin with index 1, and increment by 2. It will extract a list built from the odd-numbered indices: 1, 3, 5, …, and so on.

We can use a negative step value to visit a list in reverse order. This can be confusing, but it works very nicely.

List objects have a few operators, including + and *. We'll also look at the various kinds of list assignment statements we can use that involve slicing expressions on the left side of the assignment statement. These can mutate a list by changing some of the values.

Using list operators

We can use the + operator to concatenate two list objects: [1, 1] + [2, 3, 5] for example. If we want to extend a list, we can use this augmented assignment statement:

```
>>> fib_list += [ fib_list[-2] + fib_list[-1] ]
```

Note that we had to create a singleton list collection so that the + operator would concatenate the new list to an existing list.

Since a list object is mutable, this += assignment will update a list object; it is extended with the new list collection. Contrast this with a tuple, where a new tuple must be created from the two original tuples, and assigned to the variable.

In *Chapter 5, Logic, Comparisons, and Conditions*, we noted that sequences like list and tuple are compared item-by-item. This means that [1, 1, 2] < [1, 2] will be True.

Lists and other sequences also support the in operator. We can ask if a specific value is in a list collection. We can also confirm that a given value is not in a list collection. These are simple Boolean expressions that look like this:

```
>>> 13 in fib_list
True
>>> 12 not in fib_list
True
```

We've used the `in` operator to confirm that the value 13 is in the `fib_list` variable and the value 12 is not in that `list` object.

Mutating a list with subscripts

We can change an item in a `list` collection using a subscription or slicing on the left side of an assignment statement. A subscription uses `[]` and a single integer value to identify an item within a `list`. We can replace an item like this:

```
fib_list[0]= 1
```

We will replace the item at index 0 (the first item) with a value of 1. If we mention an index value which is not in the list, an `IndexError` will be raised.

We can replace any simple slice of a list with a different list. The replacement list does not have to be the same size. Indeed, it can be an empty list, which will effectively remove items from the list. Here's an example where we mutate a long slice by providing a shorter replacement:

```
fib_list[2:5]= [3]
```

We've specified a slicing which contains three items—index values of 2, 3, and 4— and replaced these items with a list that has only a single item. The resulting list will look like this:

```
[1, 1, 3, 13]
```

Positions 0 and 1 remain untouched. Also positions from 5 to the end of the original list are also left untouched.

We can replace an extended slicing—one that includes a step value—but the replacement must be the same size. If we don't provide the proper number of replacement values, we'll get a `ValueError` exception.

Mutating a list with method functions

We can mutate a `list` object with any of a large number of method functions. The mutator methods of a list almost always return a value of `None`. With the exception of the `pop()` method, mutators don't return a meaningful value.

There are also method functions which provide information about a list; these must return a value. We'll look at access-only method functions.

The mutator methods of a list include `append()`, `clear()`, `extend()`, `insert()`, `pop()`, `remove()`, `reverse()`, and `sort()`. Here are some examples:

```
>>> fib_list
[1, 1, 3, 5, 8, 13]
>>> fib_list.extend( [21, 34] )
>>> fib_list
[1, 1, 3, 5, 8, 13, 21, 34]
>>> fib_list.insert(0, 0)
>>> fib_list
[0, 1, 1, 3, 5, 8, 13, 21, 34]
>>> fib_list.remove(34)
>>> fib_list
[0, 1, 1, 3, 5, 8, 13, 21]
>>> fib_list.pop()
21
>>> fib_list.pop(0)
0
```

We've shown our initial list with six items. We extended the list with a second list that has two more items, `[21, 34]`. The result is a single list composed of the two original lists.

The `insert()` method has a value and a position. In this example, both were zero. When we use `help(list.insert)` we see that the index position is the first argument value. The value to be inserted before that position is provided as the second argument value.

When we remove an item from a list, we provide the item value to remove. For very large lists, this may involve a significant amount of time searching for the required item.

The `pop()` method does two things. It removes an item by position, and returns that item as the result value. The default position is the last item, -1. We can also remove items from the beginning of a list, using index position 0.

We can also use the `del` statement to remove items from a list. The statement `del fib_list[0]` will remove the first item from a list.

We haven't shown the `reverse()` and `sort()` methods which change the order of the items in the list. The `sort()` method can be quite a bit more sophisticated than these methods. We'll look into sorting in *Chapter 8, More Advanced Functions*.

We didn't give an example of the `clear()` method. This removes all of the items from the list.

Note that, with the exception of `pop()`, we must explicitly request a display of the `fib_list` object to see any output from Python's REPL. These mutator methods only return a value of `None`. It's too common a mistake to see `a = a.append(x)`; this statement always sets the variable `a` to `None`.

Accessing a list

As shown previously, we can access a list using a subscription as well as a slicing. A subscription gives us a single item. A slicing, on the other hand, makes a shallow copy of the items in the original list.

The method functions for accessing a list include `count()`, `index()`, and `copy()`. Here are some examples to show how these functions work:

```
>>> fib_list.count(1)
2
>>> fib_list.index(5)
3
```

The `count()` method counts all the items which are equal to the given value. In this case, there were two items equal to 1 in the list. If the given value is not found in the list, the count will be zero.

The `index()` method locates the given item value, and returns the index position of that value in the list. If the value does not exist, a `ValueError` exception is raised.

The `copy()` method of a list object does the same thing as the empty slicing. The expressions, `fib_list[:]` and `fib_list.copy()`, are both copies of the original list.

Using collection functions

Python offers a number of functions which work with any kind of collection. These include `sorted()`, `max()`, `min()`, and `sum()`. We also have some higher-order functions, `map()`, `filter()`, and the entire `itertools` module. We'll address additional higher-order functions in *Chapter 8, More Advanced Functions*.

The `sorted()` function returns a sorted list from a collection. It transforms the given collection into a `list` collection as part of the sorting process. If the collection doesn't define the proper iterator methods, it can't be easily sorted by using this function.

The `max()` and `min()` functions reduce a collection to a single value: either the largest or the smallest value in the collection. This reduction presumes that the items can be meaningfully compared. Consider a `tuple` that has mixed values in it:

```
((255, 73, 108), 'Radical Red')
```

We can't meaningfully evaluate `max()` or `min()` on a collection of mixed values like this. The functions will be forced to compare a tuple of numbers against a string. This will raise a `TypeError` exception.

The `sum()` function reduces a collection of numbers to a single value. It can be used on almost any kind of object that implements the + operator; we can amalgamate a list of lists to create a very long list. Here's an example of using these collection functions with a simple `set` object:

```
>>> some_set = {7, 2, 3, 5}
>>> sorted(some_set)
[2, 3, 5, 7]
>>> max(some_set)
7
>>> min(some_set)
2
>>> sum(some_set)
17
```

We've created a set with four integers in it. When we evaluate the `sorted()` function, we get a `list` object which contains the items sorted into ascending order. When we evaluate `max()` or `min()` functions, we get the largest or smallest value in the collection. The `sum()` function adds up the values in the set collection.

Using the set collection

All of the collections we've looked at previously have been sequences: `str`, `bytes`, `tuple`, and `list` have items which can be accessed by their position within the collection. A `set` collection is an unordered collection where items are present or absent.

Items in a `set` collection must be immutable; they must provide a proper hash value as well as an equality test. This means that we can create sets of numbers, strings, and tuples. We can't easily create a set of lists or a set of sets.

The syntax of a `set` display is a sequence of expressions wrapped in { }.

Here's an example `set` built using numbers:

```
>>> fib_set = {1, 1, 3, 5, 8}
>>> fib_set
{8, 1, 3, 5}
```

We've created a `set` object by enclosing the values in { }. This syntax looks very similar to the syntax for creating `list` or `tuple`. Note that the elements in the `set` collection are displayed in a different order. There's no guarantee what the order will be; different implementations may show different orders.

It's important to note that we tried to include two instances of the integer 1 in the `set` collection. Since an item is either present in the `set` collection or absent, the item cannot be included a second time. Duplicate items are silently ignored.

We can also create a `set` collection by applying the `set()` function to a collection of values. We can create a `set` collection from a `list` or `tuple` collection. We can also create a `set` collection from a simple string: each individual character will become an item in the resulting set. We can use `set([1, 1, 3, 5, 8])` to apply the `set()` function to a literal list object.

The syntax { }, interestingly, does not create an empty `set`. This actually creates an empty `dict` class. To create an empty `set`, we must use the `set()` function.

We have a fairly large number of operators for set objects. In addition to the operators, we also have a large number of method functions. These can be categorized as follows:

- **Mutators**: These modify a `set` object
- **Accessors**: These access a list and return a fact about that `set` object.

The mutator methods of a `set` collection almost always return a value of `None`. With the exception of the `pop()` method, mutators don't return a value. The accessors, which provide information about a list, must return a value. We'll look at the operators first.

Using set operators

Sets have a large number of operators which closely parallel mathematical operators for sets. The mapping leverages the bit-oriented operators; it interprets them to mean set membership instead of bits in an integer value.

We have the following operators: |, &, -, and ^, which stand for union ($a \cup b$), intersection ($a \cap b$), difference ($a \setminus b$), and symmetric difference ($a \Delta b$).

Examples of these two sets are:

```
>>> words = set("How I wish".split())
{'How', 'I', 'wish'}
>>> more = set("I could recollect pi".split())
{'recollect', 'pi', 'I', 'could'}
```

Each set is built by splitting a string into individual space-separated words. The results contain the proper elements; the order, however, may vary. Here are examples of each of the operators:

```
>>> words | more
{'wish', 'could', 'pi', 'I', 'How', 'recollect'}
>>> words & more
{'I'}
>>> words - more
{'How', 'wish'}
>>> words ^ more
{'recollect', 'wish', 'pi', 'How', 'could'}
```

The union operator creates a new set with elements that are drawn from both sets. We could say that the union of a | b creates a set of elements, {x}, where each element is either an element of *a* **or** an element of *b*. There's a tidy parallel between the concept of the Boolean **or** operator and the set union.

The intersection operator, a & b, finds the items which are an element of *a* **and** an element of *b*. Again, there's a close parallel between the Boolean **and** operator and set intersection.

The set difference operator will remove items from the left set which are in the right set. We could say that the resulting elements are elements of *a* and not elements of *b*. There's no commonly-used Boolean operator which parallels the definition of set difference.

The symmetric difference operators are the items unique to both sets; the common items have been removed. This corresponds to the **exclusive or** Boolean operation. We could say that the result is members of *a* or members of *b* but not members of both sets.

Mutating a set with method functions

Sets have some mutators which parallel those of a `list` collection. These methods include `add()`, `remove()`, `discard()`, and `clear()`. Since the methods are mutators, they do not return a useful value. The `add()` method parallels `list.append()`: it adds a single item to the set.

The `remove()` and `discard()` methods will remove an item from a set; the `remove()` method will raise an exception if the item is not in the set, the `discard()` method always succeeds, even if the item is not in the set. The `clear()` method discards all items from the set.

We can, for example, update our `fib_set` variable like this:

```
f_n = max(fib_set)
f_n1 = max(fib_set-{f_n})
fib_set.add(f_n+f_n1)
```

We've located the largest value in the set, and assigned this to the `f_n` variable. We used the set difference operator to create a new set without the maximum value. When we evaluate `max()` on this new set, we'll get the next-to-largest value. Finally, we mutated the set with the `add()` method to insert a value into the set.

The set difference operator, `-`, does not mutate the set: like all arithmetic operators, it creates a new object from the operands. The `add()` method, however, does mutate the given set.

Note that Fibonacci numbers aren't the best use of a `set` collection. The first two Fibonacci numbers are both one.

The `pop()` method is unique; it is a mutator which also returns a value. The value popped from the set will be selected arbitrarily. There's no easy way to predict which item will be removed and returned.

Each of the operators has a method function that matches the operator. The following operators: `|`, `&`, `-`, and `^` correspond to the `update()`, `intersection()`, `difference()`, and `symmetric_difference()` methods. We can write `a | b` or we can write `a.update(b)`. Both have the same results.

Using augmented assignment with sets

The augmented assignment statements also work well with sets. We can use `|=`, `&=`, `-=`, and `^=`, to update a set based on elements from another set. For example, consider this statement:

```
words |= more
```

The `words` set will be mutated to include all the items from the `more` set.

Each of the augmented assignment statements also has a corresponding update method. The method names for these mutators are `update()`, `intersection_update()`, `difference_update()`, and `symmetric_difference_update()`. These methods are mutators which match the augmented assignment statements.

Accessing a set with operators and method functions

There are a few operators which count as set accessors. Perhaps the most fundamental method for accessing a set is the `in` operator; this will check to see if a particular element exists in a set.

```
>>> 'I' in words
True
```

The comparison operators for sets implement basic set theory operations. When we use `<`, `<=`, `>`, or `>=` between two sets, we're doing subset and superset comparisons. For example:

```
>>> {'I'} < words
True
>>> {'How', 'I', 'wish'} <= words
True
```

In the first case, the set `{'I'}` is a proper subset of the set in the words variable. In the second case, the improper subset comparison was `True`, because the two sets are actually equal.

We also have method functions that match the various comparison operators. We can use `isdisjoint()`, `issubset()`, and `issuperset()` in addition to the `!=`, `<`, and `>` operators.

There's little practical difference between `item in set` and `{item} <= set`. It's also true that `set-{item} != set` would be true when the given `item` is in the `set`. These mathematical equivalences are interesting, but often involve extra computation.

Mappings

Python has a number of mapping collections. A mapping is an association between a key and a value. The built-in mapping collection is the `dict` class. The other mappings are defined in the `collections` library, and must be imported.

Items that are keys within a mapping must be immutable; they must provide a proper hash value as well as a matching equality test. The values within a mapping have no restrictions; they can be mutable or immutable. The order of the keys is not maintained by the `dict` class.

We can create a simple `dict` display using `{}`; each key and value are separated by the `:` character.

Here's an example of a simple mapping:

```
sieve = {2: True, 3: True, 4: False, 5: True, 6: None, 7: None}
```

We've created a simple mapping with keys that are all integers, and values which are a mixture of Boolean and None values.

We can also create a dictionary using the dict() function. This function can build a dictionary from a variety of sources. We can provide an existing dictionary as an argument; the dict() function will make a shallow copy of that source dictionary. We can provide a sequence of (key, value) two-tuples. It would look like this:

```
>>> sieve = dict(
... [(2, True), (3, True), (4, False), (5, True), (6, None), (7,
None)]
... )
```

This example created a dictionary from a list of (key, value) two-tuples. The resulting dictionary object that's created will match the literal display shown in the preceding example.

We can also create dictionaries with string keys using the dict() function. When we provide keyword arguments, they become the keys.

```
>>> cadaeic= dict( poe=3, e=1, near=4, a=1, raven=5, midnights= 9 )
>>> cadaeic
{'raven': 5, 'e': 1, 'near': 4, 'midnights': 9, 'poe': 3, 'a': 1}
```

It's important to repeat the observation that the order of the keys in a built-in dict object is not defined.

We can also build a dictionary from a set of keys, providing a single default value. We can do this as follows:

```
>>> sieve = dict.fromkeys( range(2,10) )
>>> sieve
{2: None, 3: None, 4: None, 5: None, 6: None, 7: None, 8: None, 9:
None}
```

We've used the range() function to iterate through a series of numbers which start with two and end just before ten. These numbers are then used to create keys for a dictionary. The value associated with each key is the default of None.

Using dictionary operators

All Python mappings, including the built-in `dict`, use a key in [] to get, set, and delete items. The syntax looks like this:

```
>>> cadaeic['poe']
3
>>> cadaeic['so']= 2
>>> del cadaeic['so']
```

We've provided literal strings to show how we can get an item, set an item, and use the `del` statement to delete an item.

Note that dictionary comparisons are difficult to define in a general way. It's not perfectly clear if an ordering comparison should compare only the keys, only the values, or a combination of keys and values. Consequently, only `==` and `!=` comparisons among dictionaries are defined.

Using dictionary mutators

We can use `dict[key]` on the left side of an assignment statement to modify a dictionary. This will insert the given key and value if the key does not exist; if the key already exists, it will change the value associated with the key.

We also have a number of methods that we can use to mutate a dictionary object. These methods include `clear()`, `pop()`, `popitem()`, `setdefault()`, and `update()` to modify a dictionary object.

The `clear()` and `update()` methods don't return a useful value. The `clear()` method will empty the dictionary. The `update()` method will fold additional data into an existing dictionary. This method will accept the same variety of arguments as the `dict()` function that creates a dictionary. The first positional argument can be a dictionary object or a sequence of `(key, value)` two-tuples. Additionally, we can provide any number of keyword arguments; the keywords will become keys in the updated dictionary.

Here are two examples that show some of the different ways in which the `update()` method can be used:

```
>>> cadaeic.update( {'so':2, 'dreary':6} )
>>> cadaeic.update( [('tired',5), ('and',3)], weary=5 )
>>> cadaeic
{'a': 1, 'weary': 5, 'near': 4, 'dreary': 6, 'e': 1,
'raven': 5, 'midnights': 9, 'and': 3, 'so': 2, 'poe': 3,
'tired': 5}
```

We've updated the `cadaeic` dictionary object using another dictionary with two items. Then we applied further updates using a sequence of (`key, value`) two-tuples. The second example also included an additional keyword argument, which inserted the key `'weary'` into the dictionary.

The `setdefault()` method function is an interesting special case. This is a variation on the `get()` accessor. The `get()` method (and the `pop()` method) has a provision for a default value. The `setdefault()` method doesn't merely return the default value if the key is missing — paralleling what `get()` does. The `setdefault()` method updates the dictionary to be sure that the default value is now in the dictionary. All subsequent `setdefault()` or `get()` methods will find the key in the dictionary.

The sequence of operations might look something like this:

```
>>> counter = {}
>>> counter.setdefault('a',0)
0
>>> counter['a'] += 1
>>> counter
{'a': 1}
```

We've created an empty dictionary and assigned it to the `counter` variable. When we use `counter.setdefault('a',0)`, we'll get the value associated with a key of `'a'`, or we'll get the default value of zero. In addition to returning, the default value will also be used to update the dictionary, assuring that there is a value associated with the given key.

We can then do a simple, easy-to-understand `counter['a'] += 1` knowing that the key, `'a'`, has a value in the dictionary. Either the key already existed, and the `setdefault()` function did nothing or the key did not exist, and the `setdefault()` function provided that default value.

Since `setdefault()` returns a value, we can optimize this into something like this:

```
>>> counter['b'] = counter.setdefault('b',0) + 1
```

This `setdefault()` process is so common that there are two closely-related classes in `collections`. The `defaultdict` class simply treats all `get()` operations like `setdefault()`. The `Counter` class will implicitly do the `count[key] +=1` process for any iterable, building on the `defaultdict` class.

There are two variations on the `pop()` method. The typical implementation of `pop()` will remove a given key and return the value associated with that key. Beyond this, the `popitem()` method will remove and return one (`key, value`) pair from a dictionary. The pair will be chosen arbitrarily. In both cases, the dictionary is updated to remove the value.

Using methods for accessing items in a mapping

We have a number of methods to access items in a mapping. First and foremost, we have the `dict[key]` construct which locates the value associated with the given key. If the key does not exist, the `KeyError` exception is raised.

The `get()` method will also return the value associated with a key in the dictionary. The `get()` method can also provide a default value. We can use `cadaeic.get("word", 4)` to locate the key (`"word"` in this example). If the key is not found the default, `4`, is returned.

The `copy()` method returns a shallow copy of the dictionary. We can do `a=dict(d)` or `a= d.copy()` to make a new dictionary, which is a copy of an original dictionary. Both are equivalent.

There are three methods which expose important features of a mapping:

- `keys()` is the sequence of keys from the mapping. By default, this is used when converting a mapping to another collection. If we use `set(cadaeic)` or `list(cadaiec)`, we'll see just the key values in the set or list object. The value of `sorted(cadaeic)` is the same as `sorted(cadaeic.keys())`.

- `values()` is the sequence of values from the mapping.

- `items()` is the sequence of (`key, value`) pairs from the mapping. This list of two-tuples can be used to rebuild the dictionary. If we use `tuple(cadaeic.items())`, we've created a tuple of two-tuples. This tuple is immutable, and can be used as a key to another mapping or as an item in a set. This is a way of "freezing" a dictionary to create an immutable copy.

Using extensions from the collections module

The *Python Standard Library* includes the `collections` module. This module offers us a number of alternatives to the built-in collections. This module has the following additional collections:

- We can import the `namedtuple` function and use this to create variations on the basic `tuple` that includes named attributes in addition to attributes identified by their positional index.

- The `deque` class defines a double-ended queue, like a `list` collection that can perform fast `append()` and `pop()` functions on either end. A subset of the features of this class will create single-ended stack (LIFO) or queue (FIFO) structures.

- In some cases, we can use a `ChainMap` instead of merging mappings, via `update()`. The result is a view of multiple mappings rather than a single, updated mapping. This can be built very quickly; a search takes longer than a single mapping.

- An `OrderedDict` mapping is a mapping which maintains the order in which the keys were created.

- The `defaultdict` class is a subclass of the built-in `dict` that uses a factory function to provide values for missing keys.

- The `Counter` class is a `dict` subclass that counts objects to create frequency tables. It is also used as a more sophisticated data structure called a multiset or bag.

We can create letter frequencies using a `Counter` class quite simply. A `Counter` will count the occurrences of items in the sequence. Given a string, which is an iterable sequence of characters, creating a `Counter` leads directly to a frequency table. Here's an example:

```
>>> from collections import Counter
>>> text = """Poe, E.
... Near a Raven
...
... Midnights so dreary, tired and weary,
... Silently pondering volumes extolling all by-now obsolete lore.
... During my rather long nap - the weirdest tap!
... An ominous vibrating sound disturbing my chamber's antedoor.
... "This", I whispered quietly, "I ignore"."""
>>> freq= Counter(text)
>>> freq.most_common(5)
[(' ', 35), ('e', 23), ('n', 18), ('r', 17), ('i', 17)]
```

We've imported the `Counter` class from the `collections` module. We've also set a variable, `text`, to a piece of a poem by Mike Keith. For more of this poem, see `http://www.cadaeic.net/naraven.htm`.

We created a `Counter` object using the string of characters as the source. A `Counter` object will iterate through each item in the sequence, counting the number of occurrences of that item. When we use the `most_common()` method, we'll see the five most common items in the collection. If we were to simply print the value of the `freq` variable, we'd see all of the character frequencies.

Each of these collections offers unique features. If the built-in `dict`, `list`, or `tuple` doesn't meet our needs, one of these additional collections may be more suitable for the problem we're tying to solve.

Processing collections with the for statement

The `for` statement is an extremely versatile way to process every item in a collection. We do this by defining a target variable, a source of items, and a suite of statements. The `for` statement will iterate through the source of items, assigning each item to the target variable, and also execute the suite of statements. All of the collections in Python provide the necessary methods, which means that we can use *anything* as the source of items in a `for` statement.

Here's some sample data that we'll work with. This is part of Mike Keith's poem, *Near a Raven*. We'll remove the punctuation to make the text easier to work with:

```
>>> text = '''Poe, E.
...      Near a Raven
...
... Midnights so dreary, tired and weary.'''
>>> text = text.replace(",","").replace(".","").lower()
```

This will put the original text, with uppercase and lowercase and punctuation into the `text` variable. We used some method functions from *Chapter 2, Simple Data Types*, to remove the common punctuation marks and return a version of the entire string entirely composed of lowercase letters.

When we use `text.split()`, we get a sequence of individual words. The `for` loop can iterate through this sequence of words so that we can process each one. The syntax looks like this:

```
>>> cadaeic= {}
>>> for word in text.split():
...      cadaeic[word]= len(word)
```

We've created an empty dictionary, and assigned it to the `cadaeic` variable. The expression in the `for` loop, `text.split()`, will create a sequence of substrings. Each of these substrings will be assigned to the `word` variable. The `for` loop body—a single assignment statement—will be executed once for each value assigned to `word`.

The resulting dictionary might look like this (irrespective of ordering):

```
{'raven': 5, 'midnights': 9, 'dreary': 6, 'e': 1,
'weary': 5, 'near': 4, 'a': 1, 'poe': 3, 'and': 3,
'so': 2, 'tired': 5}
```

There's no guaranteed order for mappings or sets. Your results may differ slightly.

In addition to iterating over a sequence, we can also iterate over the keys in a dictionary.

```
>>> for word in sorted(cadaeic):
...     print(word, cadaeic[word])
```

When we use `sorted()` on a `tuple` or a `list`, an interim list is created with sorted items. When we apply `sorted()` to a mapping, the sorting applies to the keys of the mapping, creating a sequence of sorted keys. This loop will print a list in alphabetical order of the various *pilish* words used in this poem.

 Pilish is a subset of English where the word lengths are important: they're used as mnemonic aids.

A `for` statement corresponds to the "for all" logical quantifier, ∀. At the end of a simple `for` loop we can assert that all items in the source collection have been processed. In order to build the "there exists" quantifier, ∃, we can either use the `while` statement, or the `break` statement inside the body of a `for` statement.

Using literal lists in a for statement

We can apply the `for` statement to a sequence of literal values. One of the most common ways to present literals is as a `tuple`. It might look like this:

```
for scheme in 'http', 'https', 'ftp':
    do_something(scheme)
```

This will assign three different values to the `scheme` variable. For each of those values, it will evaluate the `do_something()` function.

From this, we can see that, strictly-speaking, the `()` are not required to delimit a `tuple` object. If the sequence of values grows, however, and we need to span more than one physical line, we'll want to add `()`, making the `tuple` literal more explicit.

Using the range() and enumerate() functions

The `range()` object will provide a sequence of numbers, often used in a `for` loop. The `range()` object is iterable, it's not itself a sequence object. It's a generator, which will produce items when required. If we use `range()` outside a `for` statement, we need to use a function like `list(range(x))` or `tuple(range(a,b))` to consume all of the generated values and create a new sequence object.

The `range()` object has three commonly-used forms:

- `range(n)` produces ascending numbers including 0 but not including n itself. This is a half-open interval. We could say that `range(n)` produces numbers, *x*, such that $0 \leq x < n$. The expression `list(range(5))` returns `[0, 1, 2, 3, 4]`. This produces *n* values including 0 and *n* - 1.

- `range(a,b)` produces ascending numbers starting from a but not including b. The expression `tuple(range(-1,3))` will return `(-1, 0, 1, 2)`. This produces *b* - *a* values including *a* and *b* - 1.

- `range(x,y,z)` produces ascending numbers in the sequence $(x, x+z, x+2z, ..., x+k \times z < y)$. This produces $(y-x)//z$ values.

We can use the `range()` object like this:

```
for n in range(1, 21):
    status= str(n)
    if n % 5 == 0: status += " fizz"
    if n % 7 == 0: status += " buzz"
    print(status)
```

In this example, we've used a `range()` object to produce values, *n*, such that $1 \leq n < 21$.

We use the `range()` object to generate the index values for all items in a list:

```
for n in range(len(some_list)):
    print(n, some_list[n])
```

We've used the `range()` function to generate values between 0 and the length of the sequence object named `some_list`.

The `for` statement allows multiple target variables. The rules for multiple target variables are the same as for a multiple variable assignment statement: a sequence object will be decomposed and items assigned to each variable. Because of that, we can leverage the `enumerate()` function to iterate through a sequence and assign the index values at the same time. It looks like this:

```
for n, v in enumerate(some_list):
    print(n, v)
```

The `enumerate()` function is a generator function which iterates through the items in source sequence and yields a sequence of two-tuple pairs with the index and the item. Since we've provided two variables, the two-tuple is decomposed and assigned to each variable.

There are numerous use cases for this multiple-assignment `for` loop. We often have list-of-tuples data structures that can be handled very neatly with this multiple-assignment feature. In *Chapter 8, More Advanced Functions*, we'll look at a number of these design patterns.

Iterating with the while statement

The `while` statement is a more general iteration than the `for` statement. We'll use a `while` loop in two situations. We'll use this in cases where we don't have a finite collection to impose an upper bound on the loop's iteration; we may suggest an upper bound in the `while` clause itself. We'll also use this when writing a "search" or "there exists" kind of loop; we aren't processing all items in a collection.

A desktop application that accepts input from a user, for example, will often have a `while` loop. The application runs until the user decides to quit; there's no upper bound on the number of user interactions. For this, we generally use a `while True:` loop. Infinite iteration is recommended.

If we want to write a character-mode user interface, we could do it like this:

```
quit_received= False
while not quit_received:
    command= input("prompt> ")
    quit_received= process(command)
```

This will iterate until the `quit_received` variable is set to `True`. This will process indefinitely; there's no upper boundary on the number of iterations.

This `process()` function might use some kind of command processing. This should include a statement like this:

```
if command.lower().startswith("quit"): return True
```

When the user enters `"quit"`, the `process()` function will return `True`. This will be assigned to the `quit_received` variable. The `while` expression, `not quit_received`, will become `False`, and the loop ends.

A "there exists" loop will iterate through a collection, stopping at the first item that meets certain criteria. This can look complex because we're forced to make two details of loop processing explicit.

Here's an example of searching for the first value that meets a condition. This example assumes that we have a function, `condition()`, which will eventually be `True` for some number. Here's how we can use a `while` statement to locate the minimum for which this function is `True`:

```
>>> n = 1
>>> while n != 101 and not condition(n):
...     n += 1
>>> assert n == 101 or condition(n)
```

The `while` statement will terminate when `n == 101` or the `condition(n)` is `True`. If this expression is `False`, we can advance the `n` variable to the next value in the sequence of values. Since we're iterating through the values in order from the smallest to the largest, we know that `n` will be the smallest value for which the `condition()` function is true.

At the end of the `while` statement we have included a formal assertion that either `n` is 101 or the `condition()` function is `True` for the given value of `n`. Writing an assertion like this can help in design as well as debugging because it will often summarize the loop invariant condition.

We can also write this kind of loop using the `break` statement in a `for` loop, something we'll look at in the next section.

The continue and break statements

The `continue` statement is helpful for skipping items without writing deeply-nested `if` statements. The effect of executing a `continue` statement is to skip the rest of the loop's suite. In a `for` loop, this means that the next item will be taken from the source iterable. In a `while` loop, this must be used carefully to avoid an otherwise infinite iteration.

We might see file processing that looks like this:

```
for line in some_file:
    clean = line.strip()
    if len(clean) == 0:
        continue
    data, _, _ = clean.partition("#")
    data = data.rstrip()
    if len(data) == 0:
        continue
    process(data)
```

In this loop, we're relying on the way files act like sequences of individual lines. For each line in the file, we've stripped whitespace from the input line, and assigned the resulting string to the `clean` variable. If the length of this string is zero, the line was entirely whitespace, and we'll continue the loop with the next line. The `continue` statement skips the remaining statements in the body of the loop.

We'll partition the line into three pieces: a portion in front of any "#", the "#" (if present), and the portion after any "#". We've assigned the "#" character and any text after the "#" character to the same easily-ignored variable, _, because we don't have any use for these two results of the partition() method. We can then strip any trailing whitespace from the string assigned to the data variable. If the resulting string has a length of zero, then the line is entirely filled with "#" and any trailing comment text. Since there's no useful data, we can continue the loop, ignoring this line of input.

If the line passes the two if conditions, we can process the resulting data. By using the continue statement, we have avoided complex-looking, deeply-nested if statements. We'll examine files in detail in *Chapter 10*, *Files, Databases, Networks, and Contexts*.

It's important to note that a continue statement must always be part of the suite inside an if statement, inside a for or while loop. The condition on that if statement becomes a filter condition that applies to the collection of data being processed. continue always applies to the innermost loop.

Breaking early from a loop

The break statement is a profound change in the semantics of the loop. An ordinary for statement can be summarized by "for all." We can comfortably say that "for all items in a collection, the suite of statements was processed."

When we use a break statement, a loop is no longer summarized by "for all." We need to change our perspective to "there exists". A break statement asserts that at least one item in the collection matches the condition that leads to the execution of the break statement.

Here's a simple example of a break statement:

```
for n in range(1, 100):
    factors = []
    for x in range(1,n):
        if n % x == 0: factors.append(x)
    if sum(factors) == n:
        break
```

We've written a loop that is bound by $1 \leq n < 100$. This loop includes a break statement, so it will not process all values of n. Instead, it will determine the smallest value of n, for which n is equal to the sum of its factors. Since the loop doesn't examine all values, it shows that at least one such number exists within the given range.

We've used a nested loop to determine the factors of the number n. This nested loop creates a sequence, factors, for all values of x in the range $1 \le x < n$, such that x, is a factor of the number n. This inner loop doesn't have a break statement, so we are sure it examines all values in the given range.

The least value for which this is true is the number six.

It's important to note that a break statement must always be part of the suite inside an if statement inside a for or while loop. If the break isn't in an if suite, the loop will always terminate while processing the first item. The condition on that if statement becomes the "where exists" condition that summarizes the loop as a whole. Clearly, multiple if statements with multiple break statements mean that the overall loop can have a potentially confusing and difficult-to-summarize post-condition.

Using the else clause on a loop

Python's else clause can be used on a for or while statement as well as on an if statement. The else clause executes after the loop body if there was no break statement executed. To see this, here's a contrived example:

```
>>> for item in 1,2,3:
...     print(item)
...     if item == 2:
...         print("Found",item)
...         break
... else:
...     print("Found Nothing")
```

The for statement here will iterate over a short list of literal values. When a specific target value has been found, a message is printed. Then, the break statement will end the loop, avoiding the else clause.

When we run this, we'll see three lines of output, like this:

```
1
2
Found 2
```

The value of three isn't shown, nor is the "Found Nothing" message in the else clause.

If we change the target value in the if statement from two to a value that won't be seen (for example, zero or four), then the output will change. If the break statement is not executed, then the else clause will be executed.

The idea here is to allow us to write contrasting `break` and non-`break` suites of statements. An `if` statement suite that includes a `break` statement can do some processing in the suite before the `break` statement ends the loop. An `else` clause allows some processing at the end of the loop when none of the `break`-related suites statements were executed.

Summary

We've looked at three mutable collections: lists, sets and dictionaries. The built-in dictionary class is only one of many mappings available in Python, the others are defined in the collections module of the standard library. The list allows us to collect items which are identified by their positions in the list. The set allows us to collect a set of unique items, in which each item is simply identified by itself. A mapping allows us to identify items by a key.

For sets, each item must be immutable. For mappings, the object used as a key must be immutable. This means that numbers, strings, and tuples are often used as mapping keys.

We've looked at the `for` statement, which is the primary way we'll process the individual items in a collection. A simple `for` statement assures us that our processing has been done for all items in the collection. We've also looked at the general purpose `while` loop.

In *Chapter 7, Basic Function Definitions*, we'll look at how we can define our own functions. We'll also look at the wide variety of ways we can evaluate a function in Python.

7

Basic Function Definitions

Mathematically, a function is a mapping of values in a domain to values in a range. Functions like sine or cosine map values from a domain of angles to a range of real values between -1 and +1. The details of the mapping are summarized in the name, domain, and range. We'll use this function concept as a way to package our Python programming into something that allows us to summarize the implementation details using a name.

We'll look at how to define and evaluate Python functions. In this chapter, we'll focus on Python functions that simply return Python objects as the range of values. In *Chapter 8, More Advanced Functions*, we'll look at generator functions; these are iterators, which are used with a `for` loop to produce sequences of values.

Python functions offer optional parameters as well as a mixture of positional and keyword parameters. This allows us to define a single function which has a number of variant signatures, allowing considerable flexibility in how the function is used.

Looking at the five kinds of callables

Python offers five variations on the theme of a function. Each of these is a kind of callable object: we can call the object with argument values and it returns a result. Here's how we'll organize our exploration:

- Basic functions created with the `def` statement are the subject of this chapter.
- Lambda forms are a function definition reduced to parameters and an expression; this is also a topic within this chapter.
- Generator functions and the yield statement are something we'll look at in *Chapter 8, More Advanced Functions*. These functions are iterators which can provide multiple results.

- Function wrappers for class methods are something we'll look at in *Chapter 11, Class Definitions*. These are built-in functions which leverage features of a class. A function like `len()` is implemented by the `__len__()` method of a collection.

- Callable objects are also part of *Chapter 11, Class Definitions*. These are classes which include the `__call__()` method so that an instance of the class behaves like a basic function created with the `def` statement.

All of these are variations on a common theme. They are ways to package some functionality so that it has a name, input parameters, and a result. This allows us to decompose large, complex programs into smaller, easier-to-understand functions.

Defining functions with positional parameters

The essential Python function definition is built with the `def` statement. We provide a name, the names of the parameters, and an indented suite of statements that is the body of the function. The `return` statement provides the range of values.

The syntax looks like this:

```
def prod(sequence):
    p= 1
    for item in sequence:
        p *= item
    return p
```

We've defined a name, `prod`, and provided a list of only one parameter, `sequence`. The body of the function includes three statements: assignment, `for`, and `return`. The expression in the `return` statement provides the resulting value.

This fits the mathematical idea of a function reasonably well. The domain of values is any numeric sequence, the range will be a value of the a type which reflects the data types in the sequence.

We evaluate a function by simply using the name and a specific value for the argument in an expression:

```
>>> prod([1,2,3,4])
24
>>> prod(range(1,6))
120
```

In the first example, we provided a simple list display, [1, 2, 3, 4], as an argument. This was assigned to the parameter of the function, `sequence`. The evaluation of the function returned the product of that sequential collection of items.

In the second example, we provided a `range()` object as the argument to the `prod()` function. This argument value is assigned to the parameter of the function. When used with a `for` loop, the range object behaves like a sequence collection, and a product is computed and returned.

Defining multiple parameters

Python offers us a variety of ways to assign values to parameters. In the simplest case, the argument values are assigned to the parameters based on position. Here's a function with two positional parameters:

```
def main_sail_area(boom, mast):
    return (boom*mast)/1.8
```

We've defined a function that requires the length of the sail's boom, usually called the "E" dimension, and the height of the mast along which the sail is rigged, usually called the "P" dimension. Given these two numbers, and an assumption about the curvature of the sail, we return the approximate sail area.

We can evaluate this function providing the two positional parameters for boom length and mast height.

```
>>> main_sail_area(15, 45)
375.0
```

We can define a function with any number of parameters. A function with a large number of parameters will tend to push the edge of the envelope on comprehensibility. A good function should have a tidy summary that makes it possible to understand the function's purpose without having to struggle with too many details.

Using the return statement

The `return` statement has two purposes: it ends the function's execution, and it can optionally provide the result value for the function. The `return` statement is optional. This leads to three use cases:

- No `return` statement: The function finishes at the end of the suite of statements. The return value is `None`.

- A `return` statement with no expression: The function finishes when the `return` statement is executed, the result is `None`.

- A `return` statement with an expression: The function finishes when the `return` statement is executed, the value of the expression is the result. A `return` statement with a list of expressions creates a `tuple`, suitable for multiple assignment.

Here's a function with no `return` statement:

```
def boat_summary(name, rig, sails):
    print( "Boat {0}, {1} rig, {2:.0f} sq. ft.".format(
        name, rig, sum(sails))
    )
```

This function consists of a single expression statement that uses the `print()` function. There's no explicit `return` so the default return value will be `None`.

It's common to use a `return` statement to finish early when an exception condition has been met, otherwise you execute the rest of the suite of statements in the function definition. It looks like this:

```
def mean_diff(data_sequence):
    s0, s1 = 0, 0
    for item in data_sequence:
        s0 += 1
        s1 += item
    if s0 < 2:
        return
    m= s1/s0
    for item in data_sequence:
        print(item, abs(item-m))
```

This function expects a collection of data. It will compute two values from that collection: `s0` and `s1`. The `s0` value will be a count of items, the `s1` value will be the sum of the items. If the count is too small, the function simply returns. If the count is large enough, then additional processing is done: the values are printed along with the absolute difference between the value and the average.

There's no `return` statement at the end of the suite of statements, since this is not required. Using a `return` statement in the middle of a function allows us to avoid deeply-nested `if` statements.

Note that the variables `s0`, `s1`, and `m`, are created in a local namespace that only exists while the function is being evaluated. Once the function is finished, the local namespace is removed, the reference counts are decremented and the interim objects are cleaned up. We'll look at additional details in the *Working with namespaces* section later in this chapter.

The built-in function `divmod()` returns two results. We often use multiple assignments like this: `q, r = divmod(n, 16);` it will assign the two results to two variables, `q` and `r`. We can write a function that returns multiple values by including multiple expressions on the `return` statement.

In the *Mutable and immutable argument values* section, we'll show a function that has multiple return values.

Evaluating a function with positional or keyword arguments

Python allows us to provide argument values with explicit parameter names. When we provide a name, it's called a keyword argument. For example, the `boat_summary()` function in the previous section can be used in a number of different ways.

We can provide the argument values positionally, like this:

```
>>> sails =  [358.3, 192.5, 379.75, 200.0]
>>> boat_summary("Red Ranger", "ketch", sails)
```

The arguments are assigned to the parameter variables of `name`, `rig`, and `sails` based on their position.

We can, as an alternative, do something like this:

```
>>> boat_summary(sails=sails, rig="ketch", name="Red Ranger" )
```

This example provides all three arguments with keywords. Note that the position doesn't matter when providing keyword arguments. The keyword arguments must be provided *after* any positional arguments, but the order among the keyword arguments doesn't matter, since they are assigned to parameters by name.

We can use a mixture of positional and keyword arguments. For this to work, Python uses two rules to map argument values to a function's parameters:

1. Match all positional arguments to parameters from left-to-right.
2. Match all keyword parameters by name.

There are several additional rules to handle duplicates and default values — which include optional parameters — described later, in the section called *Defining optional parameters via default values*.

In order for these rules to work properly, we must provide all positional parameters first, and then we can provide any keyword parameters after the positional parameters. We can't provide two values for the same parameter via position as well as keyword. Nor, for that matter, can we provide a keyword twice.

Here's a good example and a bad example:

```
>>> boat_summary("Red Ranger", sails=sails, rig="ketch")
>>> boat_summary("Red Ranger", sails=sails, rig="ketch", name="Red
Ranger")
```

In the first example, the `name` parameter is matched positionally. The `sails` and `rig` parameters were matched by keyword.

In the second example, there are both positional and keyword values for the `name` variable. This will raise a `TypeError` exception.

Because of this, it's very important to choose parameter variable names wisely. A good choice of parameter name can make keyword argument function evaluation very clear.

Writing a function's docstring

In order to save space, we haven't provided many examples of functions with docstrings. We'll address docstrings in detail in *Chapter 14, Fit and Finish – Unit Testing, Packaging, and Documentation*. For now, we need to be aware that every function should, at the very least, have a summary. The summary is included as a triple-quoted string that must be the very first expression in the suite of statements of the function.

A function with a docstring looks like this:

```
def jib(foot, height):
    """
    jib(foot,height) -> area of given jib sail.

    >>> jib(12,40)
    240.0
    """
    return (foot*height)/2
```

This particular triple-quoted string serves two purposes. First, it summarizes what the function does. We can read this when we look at the source file. We can also see this when we use `help(jib)`.

The second purpose for this docstring is a way to provide a concrete example of how the function is used. The examples always look like they are simply copied from a REPL session and pasted into the docstring comment.

These REPL-formatted examples are located by using the `doctest` tool. After locating the examples, this tool can run the code to confirm that it works as advertised. All of the examples in this book were tested using `doctest`. While the details of testing are part of *Chapter 14, Fit and Finish – Unit Testing, Packaging, and Documentation*, it's important to consider writing docstrings in every function.

Mutable and immutable argument values

In some programming languages, there are multiple function evaluation strategies, including call-by-value and call-by-reference. In call-by-value semantics, copies of argument values are assigned to the parameter variables in a function. In call-by-reference semantics, a reference to a variable is used in the function. This means that an assignment statement inside a function could replace the value of a variable outside the function. Neither of these types of semantics apply to Python.

Python uses a mechanism named "call-by-sharing" or "call-by-object". A function is given a reference to the original object. If that object is mutable, the function can mutate the object. The function cannot, however, assign to variables outside the function via the parameter variables. The function shares the objects, not the variables to which the objects are assigned.

One of the most important consequences is that the body of a function can assign new values to parameter variables without having any impact on the original arguments which are passed to a function. The parameter variables are strictly local to the function.

Here's a function that assigns new values to the parameter variable:

```
def get_data(input_string):
    input_string= input_string.strip()
    input_string, _, _ = input_string.partition("#")
    input_string= input_string.rstrip()
    name, _, value = input_string.partition('=')
    return name, value
```

This function evaluates the `strip()` method of the `input_string` variable and assigns the resulting string to the parameter variable. It applies the `partition()` method to the new value of the `input_string` variable and assigns one of the three resulting strings to the parameter variable. It then returns this string object, assigning it to the parameter variable yet again.

None of the assignment statements to the `input_string` parameter variable have any effect on any variables outside the function. When a function is evaluated, a separate namespace is used for the parameters and other local variables.

Another consequence of the way Python works is that when we provide mutable objects as arguments, these objects can be updated by methods evaluated inside a function. The function's parameter variables will be references to the original mutable objects, and we can evaluate methods like the `remove()` or `pop()` functions that change the referenced object.

Here's a function which updates a `list` argument by removing selected values:

```
def remove_mod(some_list, modulus):
    for item in some_list[:]:
        if item % modulus == 0:
            some_list.remove(item)
```

This function expects a mutable object like a list, named `some_list`, and a value, named `modulus`. The function makes a temporary copy of the argument value using `some_list[:]`. For each value in this copy that is a multiple of the `modulus` value, we'll remove that copy from the original `some_list` object. This will mutate the original object.

When we evaluate this function, it looks like this:

```
>>> data= list(range(10))
>>> remove_mod(data, 5)
>>> remove_mod(data, 7)
>>> data
[1, 2, 3, 4, 6, 8, 9]
```

We've created a simple list and assigned it to the `data` variable. This object referred to by the `data` variable was mutated by the `remove_mod()` function. All multiples of five and seven were discarded from the sequence.

In this function, we need to create a temporary copy of the input `list` object before we can start removing values. If we try to iterate through a `list` while simultaneously removing items from that `list`, we'll get results that don't appear correct. It helps to have the original values separate from the mutating `list`.

A function can create variables in the global namespace, and other non-local namespaces, by making special arrangements. This is done with the `global` and `nonlocal` statements shown in the *Working with namespaces* section.

Defining optional parameters via default values

Python lets us provide a default value for a parameter. Parameters with default values are optional. The standard library is full of functions with optional parameters. One example is the `int()` function. We can use `int("48897")` to convert a string to an integer, assuming that the string represents a number in base 10. We can use `int("48897", 16)` to explicitly state that the string should be treated as a hexadecimal value. The default value for the `base` parameter is 10.

Remember that we can use keyword arguments for a function. This means that we might want to write something like this: `int("48897", base=16)`, to make it abundantly clear what the second argument to the `int()` function is being used for.

Earlier, we listed two rules for matching argument values to parameters. When we introduce default values, we add two more rules.

1. Match all positional arguments to parameters from left-to-right.
2. Match all keyword parameters. In case of already-assigned positional parameters, raise a `TypeError` exception.
3. Set default values for any missing parameters.
4. In case there are parameters with no values, raise a `TypeError` exception.

 Note: This is not the final set of rules; there are a few more features to cover.

One important consequence of these rules is that the required parameters—those without default values—must be defined first. Parameters with default values must be defined last. The "required parameters first, optional parameters last" rule assures us that the positional matching process works.

We provide the default value in the function definition. Here's an example:

```
import random
def dice(n=2, sides=6):
    return [random.randint(1,sides) for i in range(n)]
```

We've imported the `random` module so that we can use the `random.randint()` function. Our `dice()` function has two parameters, both of which have default values. The n parameter, if not provided, will have a value of 2. The `sides` parameter, if omitted, will have a value of 6.

The body of this function is a list comprehension: it uses a generator expression to build a list of individual values. We'll look at generator expressions in detail in *Chapter 8, More Advanced Functions*. For now, we can observe that it uses the `random.randint(1,sides)` function to generate numbers between 1 and the value of the `sides` parameter. The comprehension includes a `for` clause that iterates through n values.

We can use this function in a number of different ways. Here are some examples:

```
>>> dice()
[6, 6]
>>> dice(6)
[3, 6, 2, 2, 1, 5]
>>> dice(4, sides=4)
[3, 3, 4, 3]
```

The first example relies on default values to emulate the pair of dice commonly used in casino games like Craps. The second example uses six dice, typical for games like 10,000 (sometimes called Zilch or Crap Out.). The third example uses four four-sided dice, typical of games that use a variety of polyhedral dice.

[A note on testing: in order to provide repeatable unit tests for functions that involve the `random` module, we've set a specific seed value using `random.seed("test")`.]

A warning about mutable default values

Here's a pathological example. This shows a very bad programming practice; it's a mistake that many Python programmers make when they first start working with default values.

This is a very bad idea:

```
def more_dice(n, collection=[]):
    for i in range(n):
        collection.append(random.randint(1,6))
    return collection
```

We've defined a simple function with only two parameter variables, n and collection. The collection has a default value of an empty list. (Spoiler alert: this will turn out to be a mistake.) The function will append a number of simulated six-sided dice to the given collection.

The function returns a value as well as mutating an argument. This means that we'll see the return value printed when we use this function in the REPL.

We can use this for games like Yacht, also called Generala or Poker Dice. A player has a "hand" of dice from which we'll remove dice and append new dice rolls.

One use case is to create a list object and use this as an argument to the more_dice() function. This list object would get updated nicely. Here's how that would work:

```
>>> hand1= []
>>> more_dice(5, hand1)
[6, 6, 3, 6, 2]
>>> hand1
[6, 6, 3, 6, 2]
```

We've created an empty list and assigned it to the hand variable. We provided this sequence object to the more_dice() function to have five values appended to the hand object. This gave us an initial roll of three sixes, a three, and a two. We can remove the two and three from the hand1 object; we can reuse it with more_dice(2, hand1) to put two more dice into the hand.

We can use another empty sequence as an argument to deal a second hand. Except for the results, it's otherwise identical to the first example:

```
>>> hand2= []
>>> more_dice(5, hand2)
[5, 4, 2, 2, 5]
>>> hand2
[5, 4, 2, 2, 5]
```

Everything seems to work properly. This is because we're providing an explicit argument for the collection parameter. Each of the hand objects is a distinct, empty list. Let's try to use the default value for the collection parameter.

In this third example, we won't provide an argument, but rely on the default sequence returned by the more_dice() function:

```
>>> hand1= more_dice(5)
>>> hand1
[6, 6, 3, 6, 2]
>>> hand2= more_dice(5)
>>> hand2
[6, 6, 6, 2, 1, 5, 4, 2, 2, 5]
```

Wait. What just happened? How is this possible?

As a hint, we'll need to search through the code for an object with a hidden, shared state. Earlier, we noted that a default list object would be a problem. This hidden list object is getting reused.

What happens is this:

1. When the def statement is executed, the expressions that define the parameter defaults are evaluated. This means that a single mutable list object is created as the default object for the collection parameter.

2. When the more_dice() function is evaluated without an argument for the collection parameter, the one-and-only mutable list object is used as the default object. What's important is that a single mutable object is being reused. If, at any point, we update this object, that mutation applies to all shared uses of the object. Since it's returned by the function, this single list could be assigned to several variables.

3. When the more_dice() function is evaluated a second time without an argument for the collection parameter, the mutated list object is re-used as the default.

From this, we can see that a mutable object is a terrible choice of a default value.

Generally, we have to do something like this:

```
def more_dice_good(n, collection=None):
    if collection is None:
        collection = []
    for i in range(n):
        collection.append(random.randint(1,6))
    return collection
```

This function uses an immutable and easily-recognized default value of None. If no argument value is provided for the collection variable, it will be set to None. We can replace the None value with a brand new list object created when the function is evaluated. We can then update this new list object, confident that we're not corrupting any mutable default object which is being reused.

> Don't use a mutable object as a default value for a parameter.
>
> Avoid list, dict, set, and any other mutable type, as default parameter values. Use None as a default; replace the None with a new, empty mutable object.
>
> You've been warned.

This can lead to mistakes. It's a consequence of the way that function definition works and call-by-sharing semantics.

It's possible to exploit this intentionally: we can use a mutable default value as a cache to retain values, creating functions which have hysteresis. A callable object may be a better way to implement functions with an internal cache or buffer. See *Chapter 11*, *Class Definitions*, for more information.

Using the "everything else" notations of * and **

Python offers even more flexibility in how we can define positional and keyword parameters for a function. The examples we've seen are all limited to a fixed and finite collection of argument values. Python allows us to write functions that have an essentially unlimited number of positional as well as keyword argument values.

Python will create a `tuple` of all unmatched positional parameters. It will also create a dictionary of all unmatched keyword parameters. This allows us to write functions that can be used like this:

```
>>> prod2(1, 2, 3, 4)
24
```

This function accepts an arbitrary number of positional arguments. Compare this with the `prod()` function shown previously. Our previous example required a single sequence object, and we had to use that function as follows:

```
>>> prod([1, 2, 3, 4])
24
```

The `prod2()` function will create a product of all argument values. Since the `prod2()` function can work with an unlimited collection of positional arguments, this leads to slightly simpler syntax for this function.

In order to write a function with an unlimited number of positional arguments, we must provide one parameter which has a `*` prefix. It looks like this:

```
def prod2(*args):
    p= 1
    for item in args:
        p *= item
    return p
```

The definition of `prod2()` has all positional arguments assigned to the `*` prefix parameter, `*args`. The value of the `args` parameter is a tuple of the argument values.

Here's a function which uses a mixture of positional and keyword parameters:

```
def boat_summary2(name, rig, **sails):
    print("Boat {0}, {1} rig, {2:.0f} sq. ft.".format(
name, rig, sum(sails.values())))
```

This function will accept two arguments, `name` and `rig`. These can be supplied by position or by keyword. Any additional keyword parameters—other than `name` and `rig`—are collected into a dictionary and assigned to the `sails` parameter. The `sails.values()` expression extracts just the values from the `sails` dictionary; these are added together to write the final summary line.

Here's one of many ways that we can use this function:

```
>>> boat_summary2("Red Ranger", rig="ketch",
...     main=358.3, mizzen=192.5, yankee=379.75, staysl=200 )
```

We've provided the first argument value by position; this will be assigned to the first positional parameter, `name`. We've provided one of the defined parameters using a keyword argument, `rig`. The remaining keyword arguments are collected into a dictionary and assigned to the parameter named `sails`.

The `sails` dictionary will be assigned a value similar to this:

```
{'main': 358.3, 'mizzen': 192.5, 'yankee': 379.75, 'staysl': 200}
```

We can use any dictionary processing on this mapping since it's a proper `dict` object.

Earlier, we provided four rules for matching argument values with parameters. Here is a more complete set of rules for matching argument values with function parameters:

1. Match all positional arguments to parameters from left-to-right.
2. If there are more positional arguments than parameter names:
    1. If there's a parameter name with a `*` prefix, assign a `tuple` of remaining values to the prefixed parameter.
    2. If there's no parameter with the `*` prefix, raise a `TypeError` exception.
3. Match all keyword parameters. In case of already-assigned positional parameters, raise a `TypeError` exception.
4. If there are more keyword arguments than parameter names:
    1. If there's a parameter name with a `**` prefix, assign `dict` of remaining keywords and values to the prefixed parameter.
    2. If there's no parameter with the `**` prefix, raise a `TypeError` exception.
5. Apply default values to missing parameters.
6. In case of parameters which still have no values, raise a `TypeError` exception.

A consequence of these rules is that, at most, only one parameter can have a `*` prefix; similarly, at most, only one parameter can have a `**` prefix. These special cases must be given after all of the other parameters. The `*` prefix variable will be assigned an empty tuple if there are no surplus positional parameters. The `**` prefix variable will be assigned an empty dictionary if there no surplus keyword parameters.

When invoking a function, we must provide positional argument values first. We can provide keyword argument values in any order.

Using sequences and dictionaries to fill in *args and *kw

The `prod2()` function, shown earlier, expects individual values which are collected into a single `*args` tuple. If we invoke the function with `prod2 (1, 2, 3, 4, 5)`, then a tuple built from the five positional parameters is assigned to the `args` parameter.

What if we want to provide a list to the `prod2()` function? How can we, in effect, write `prod2 (some_list [0], some_list [1], some_list [2], … )`?

When we call a function using `prod2 (*some_sequence)`, then the values of the given argument sequence are matched to positional parameters. Item zero from the argument sequence becomes the first positional parameter. Item one from the sequence becomes the second parameter, and so on. Each item is assigned until they're all used up. If there are extra argument values, and the function was defined with a parameter using a `*` prefix, the extra argument values are assigned to the `*` prefix parameter.

Because of this, we can use `prod2 (*range (1, 10))` easily. This is effectively `prod2 (1, 2, 3, 4, 5, …, 9)`. Since all of the positional argument values are assigned to the `*`-prefix `args` variable, we can use this function with individual values, like this: `prod2 (1, 2, 3, 4)`. We can provide a sequence of values, like this: `prod2 (*sequence)`.

We have a similar technique for providing a dictionary of keyword arguments to a function. We can do this:

```
>>> rr_args = dict(
...     name="Red Ranger", rig="ketch",
...     main=358.3, mizzen=192.5, yankee=379.75, staysl=200
... )
>>> boat_summary2 (**rr_args)
Boat Red Ranger, ketch rig, 1131 sq. ft.
```

We've created a dictionary with all of the arguments defined via their keywords. This uses a handy feature of the `dict()` function where all of the keyword arguments are used to build a dictionary object. We assigned that dictionary to the `rr_args` variable. When we invoked the `boat_summary2()` function, we used the `**rr_args` parameter to force each key and value in the `rr_args` dictionary to be matched against parameters to the function. This means that the values associated with the `name` and `rig` keys in the dictionary will be matched with the `name` and `rig` parameters. All other keys in the dictionary will be assigned the `sails` parameter.

These techniques allow us to build function arguments dynamically. This gives us tremendous flexibility in how we define and use Python functions.

Nested function definitions

We can include anything inside a function definition, even another function definition. When we look at decorators in *Chapter 13*, *Metaprogramming and Decorators*, we'll see cases of a function which includes a nested function definition.

We can include `import` statements within a function definition. An `import` statement is only really executed once. There's a global collection of imported modules. The name, however, would be localized to the function doing the import.

The general advice is given in the *Zen of Python* poem by Tim Peters:

> *Flat is better than nested.*

We'll generally strive to have functions defined in a relatively simple, flat sequence. We'll avoid nesting unless it's truly required, as it is when creating decorators.

Working with namespaces

When a function is evaluated, Python creates a local namespace. The parameter variables are created in this local namespace when the argument values (or default values) are assigned. Any variables that are created in the suite of statements in the function's body are also created in this local namespace.

As we noted in *Chapter 4*, *Variables, Assignment and Scoping Rules*, each object has a reference counter. An object provided as an argument to a function will have the reference count incremented during the execution of the function's suite of statements.

When the function finishes—either because of an explicit `return` statement or the implicit return at the end of the suite—the namespace is removed. This will decrement the number of references to the argument objects.

When we evaluate an expression like `more_dice_good(2, hand)`, the literal integer 2 will be assigned to the `n` parameter variable. Its reference count will be one during the execution of the function. The object assigned to the `hand` variable will be assigned to the `collection` parameter. This object will have a reference count of two during the execution of the function.

When the function exits, the namespace is removed, which removes the two parameter variables. The literal 2 object, assigned to the n variable, will wind up with a reference count of zero, and that `int` object can be removed from memory. The object assigned to the `collection` variable will have its reference count decreased from two to one; it will not be removed from memory. This object will still be assigned to the `hand` variable, and can continue to be used elsewhere.

This use of a local namespace allows us to freely assign objects to parameters without having the objects overwritten or removed from memory. It also allows us to freely create intermediate variables within the body of a function, secure in the knowledge that the variable will not overwrite some other variable used elsewhere in the script.

When we reference a variable, Python looks in two places for the variable. It looks first in the local namespace. If the variable isn't found, Python then searches the global namespace.

When we import a module, like `random`, we generally write `import` at the beginning of our script so that the module is imported into the global namespace. This means that a function which uses `random.randint()` will first check the local namespace for `random`; failing to find that, it will check the global namespace and find the imported module.

This fallback to the global namespace allows us to reuse imported modules, function definitions, and class definitions freely within a script file. We can also—to an extent—share global variables. The default behavior is that we can read the values of global variables, but we can't easily update them.

If we write `global_variable = global_variable + 1` in a function, we can fetch the value of a global variable named `global_variable`. The assignment, however, will create a new variable in the local namespace with the name `global_variable`. The actual global variable will remain untouched.

Assigning a global variable

What if we want to assign values to a variable which has not been provided as an argument? We can write a function which will update global variables. This can lead to confusing programs because several functions may share common states via the global variable.

To create names in the global namespace instead of a local namespace, we use the global statement. This identifies the variables which must be found in the global namespace instead of the local namespace. Here's a function which updates a global variable:

```
import random
def roll_dice_count_7():
    global sevens
    d= random.randint(1,6), random.randint(1,6)
    if d[0] + d[1] == 7:
        sevens += 1
    return d
```

We've defined a function and used the global statement to state that the variable named sevens will be found in the global namespace. We've created two random numbers, and assigned the pair to a local variable, d. This variable will be created in the local namespace, and won't conflict with any other variables defined in other namespaces.

Each time the pair of dice total seven, the global variable is updated. This is a side effect that can be confusing. It must be documented explicitly, and it requires some careful unit testing.

The two built-in functions, globals() and locals(), can help clarify the variables available when this function is being evaluated. If we add a print() function right before the return statement, we'll see results (with some details elided) like this:

```
globals={'__cached__': None,
'__loader__': <_frozen_importlib.SourceFileLoader object at
0x100623750>,
'sevens': 20,
'__name__': '__main__',
'__file__': '…',
… etc.
    'roll_dice_count_7': <function roll_dice_count_7 at 0x10216e710>,
    'random': <module 'random' from '...'>}
locals={'d': (2, 1)}
```

The globals function includes variables like sevens, it includes the random module, and the roll_dice_count_7 function. It includes some system variables: like __cached__, __loader__, __name__, and __file__.

The locals function includes the local variable d and nothing more.

Assigning a non-local variable

When one function is defined inside another function, the outer function can contain variables which are neither local to the inner function nor global. We call these non-local variables. There are situations where we might want to set a variable which is part of an enclosing function.

Nested function definitions are most commonly used when defining decorators. We'll look at this in *Chapter 13, Metaprogramming and Decorators*.

Here's a contrived example of nested functions and a non-local shared variable:

```
def roll_nl(n=2, d=6):
    def dice():
        nonlocal total
        points= tuple(random.randint(1,d) for _ in range(n))
        total = sum(points)
        return points
    total= 0
    dice()
    return total
```

We've defined a function, `roll_nl()`, which will simulate rolls of dice. The function's body includes a nested function definition, `dice()`. The rest of the body creates the variable `total`, evaluates the internal `dice()` function, and returns the value of the `total` variable.

How did the `total` variable get set to anything other than zero? It isn't updated in the body of the `roll_nl()` function.

Within the nested `dice()` function, there's a nonlocal reference to a variable named `total`. This variable must exist in an outer namespace, but not necessarily the global namespace. The `dice()` function creates a `tuple` object with the values of n dice. This expression builds a tuple from the result of a generator function. It updates the nonlocal `total` variable the sum of the `points` tuple. The `nonlocal` statement assures us that the `total` variable is part of the container for the `dice()` function. The return value of the `dice()` function is the tuple of dice, a value this isn't really used.

Defining lambdas

A lambda form is a degenerate kind of function. A lambda doesn't even have a name: it has only parameters and a single expression. We create a lambda by providing the parameter names and the expression. It looks like this:

```
lambda x: x[0]+x[1]
```

This kind of thing is helpful in the context of Python's higher-order functions. We often use lambdas with `max()`, `min()`, `sorted()`, `map()`, `filter()`, or `list.sort()`. Here's a simple example:

```
>>> colors = [
... (255,160,137),
... (143, 80,157),
... (255,255,255),
... (162,173,208),
... (255, 67,164),
... ]
>>> sorted(colors)
[(143, 80, 157), (162, 173, 208), (255, 67, 164),
  (255, 160, 137), (255, 255, 255)]
>>> sorted(colors,
...      key= lambda rgb: (rgb[0]+rgb[1]+rgb[2])/3)
[(143, 80, 157), (255, 67, 164), (162, 173, 208),
  (255, 160, 137), (255, 255, 255)]
```

We've created a simple list object which has four RGB color values. If we use the `sorted()` function on this list, the colors are sorted into order by the red component value. If the red components are equal, then the green component is used. In the rare case that the red and green components are equal the blue component is used.

If we want colors sorted by brightness, we can't simply sort by red, green, and blue. The perception of brightness is subtle and a number of formulae approximate the phenomena. We've picked just one, which is to average the RGB values. This formula doesn't take into account the fact that our eyes are more sensitive to green.

The `sorted()` function accepts a second parameter, `key`, which we've provided as a keyword argument in the second example. Rather than write a complete function definition that would only really embody a single expression, we've packaged the expression, `(rgb[0]+rgb[1]+rgb[2])/3`, as a lambda.

The syntax `lambda rgb: (rgb[0]+rgb[1]+rgb[2])/3` is equivalent to the following function definition.

```
def brightness(rgb):
    return (rgb[0]+rgb[1]+rgb[2])/3
```

The lambda is more compact. If we only need this expression in one place, a reusable function may not be appropriate. A lambda is an easy way to provide a simple expression with minimal overhead. If we think we need to write complex lambdas — more than a simple expression — or we need to reuse a lambda, then we should consider using a proper function.

Writing additional function annotations

The **Python Enhancement Proposal (PEP)** number 3107 specifies additional annotations which can be applied to a function definition. Additionally, PEPs 482, 483, and 484 cover some related ideas.

This is important only because Python has some optional syntax that we may see. In Python 3.5, there may be additional tools for the type of information provided in this optional syntax. The annotated code can look like this:

```
def roller( n: int, d: int = 6 ) -> tuple:
    return tuple(random.randint(1,d) for _ in range(n))
```

This function includes additional : `expression` annotations after each parameter. It also includes a `->` `expression` annotation to show the return type of the function. All of the annotation expressions in this example are the names of built-in types.

In order to describe more complex structures, an additional typing module can offer the tools for defining a more exact `Tuple[int, ...]` as the return type for this function. This is an exciting development that may avoid certain kinds of bugs.

These annotations are legal Python3 syntax. They have no formally-defined semantics, which means that they are optional. There are some enhancement projects that are working on leveraging these optional annotations and creating tools that can use the information provided there. It's rarely used, but perfectly legal.

Summary

We've looked at a number of Python features for function definition. We've looked at how we define the name, and the parameters to a function, providing default values to make parameters optional. We've also looked at how we can provide arguments to a function: we can provide arguments by position, or by using the parameter variable name as a keyword. We can evaluate `function(*args)` to map a sequence of values to parameters by position. We can also evaluate `function(**kw)` to map a dictionary of values to parameters by name. And, of course, we can combine these two techniques.

We've looked at how functions return values via the `return` statement. We've also looked at functions which don't return a value. Technically, they return a value of `None`, which the rest of the Python programming ignores.

We've looked at the all-important issue of attempting to use a mutable object as a default value in a function definition. Most of the time, a mutable object as a default is going to create problems.

In addition to the basics of function definition, we looked at how local variables are assigned to temporary namespaces. We also looked at how we can use the `global` statement to create variables in the global namespace. We also looked at how a nested function definition can manipulate variables that are nonlocal to the nested function, but not properly global to the container function.

In *Chapter 8*, *More Advanced Functions*, we'll look at generator expressions and functions. These are functions which are iterable, and work cooperatively with the `for` loop to handle collections and sequences of data.

8
More Advanced Functions

In *Chapter 7, Basic Function Definitions*, we looked at the core features of defining a function which returns a single result. Even functions with an implicit `return` statement at the end of the suite of statements, or a function with a `return` statement that has no expression, return a result: the `None` object is the default return value. In this chapter, we'll look at functions which generate multiple results. A generator function defines an iterable: it can be used with a `for` statement. This means that the generator doesn't produce a single object with all of the items in the result; instead it produces each item of the result separately.

Python offers generator expressions and comprehensions which complement the idea of generator functions. We can write simple expressions that represent a sequence of values which is generated one item at a time. We can use generator expressions to create `list`, `set`, or `dict` objects via a comprehension.

We'll review the `for` statement and its relationship with iterable data. This will help us understand how generator functions work. We'll also look at some functions which work as well with collection objects as with generator functions. This includes built-in reduction functions such as `max()`, `min()`, and `sum()`. It also includes higher-order functions such as `map()`, `filter()`, `functools.reduce()`, and the functions of the `itertools` module.

This chapter will skim over some concepts of functional programming. An entire book could be written about functional programming in Python. See `https://www.packtpub.com/application-development/functional-python-programming` for more information. We'll focus on the essentials.

Using the for statement with iterable collections

Python allows us to use the `for` statement with any kind of collection. We can write a statement like `for x in coll` to process `list`, `set`, or the keys of a `dict`. This works because all of the Python collections have common abstract base classes, defined in the `collections.abc` module.

This works via a common feature of the base classes, `Sequence`, `Set`, and `Mapping`. The `Iterable` mix in the class is part of each class definition. The implementation of this abstraction is our guarantee that all of the built-in collections will cooperate with the `for` statement.

Let's open up the internals to see how it works. We'll use this compound `for` statement as a concrete example:

```
for x in coll:
    print(x)
```

Conceptually, this compound statement starts with something very much like this assignment: `coll_i=iter(coll)`. This will get an iterator object for the `coll` collection. This `iter()` function will leverage the special method `__iter__()` to produce the iterator object. We can summarize how this works with a simple rule: if the variable `coll` doesn't reference a proper collection, a `TypeError` exception will be raised.

Given the resulting iterator object, `coll_i`, the `for` statement can then evaluate `x=next(coll_i)` to get each item from the iterator. This will leverage the special method `coll_i.__next__()` to produce an item from the original collection.

If the evaluation of `next(coll_i)` returns an item, this is assigned to x and the suite of statements is executed with this value bound to the x variable. We'll see the value of x printed.

If `next(coll_i)` raises a `StopIteration` exception, the underlying collection is out of items, and the loop will finish normally. In the case of any another exception being raised, this simply propagates according to the standard exception rules. (We'll look at exceptions in *Chapter 9, Exceptions*.)

Iterators and iterable collections

A collection is iterable when it implements the __iter__() special method. Almost universally, this means that it will be a subclass of the Iterable class defined in the collections.abc module. The presence of this special method means that evaluating iter() on a collection object will return an iterator object.

The iterator for a collection must implement the __next__() and __iter__() special methods. Generally, an iterator object implements the __iter__() method by returning itself as the result. Having this tautological redundancy available means that we can not only create an explicit iterator but also provide the iterator to a for statement without causing an exception; the for statement's processing can evaluate iter(object) without the overheads of checking to see if the object is already an iterator.

What if we have a sequence of items which has a header that we'd like to ignore? This often happens when a source data file includes a heading line that must be processed separately. We can leverage an explicit iterator object to discard items from a sequential collection.

We might write something like this:

```
source_iter= iter(source)
heading= next(source_iter)
for data in source_iter:
    print(data)
```

In this example, we've created an iterator, source_iter, based on a source collection or generator, unimaginatively named source. When we evaluated next(source_iter), we consumed the first item from the collection, which we then assigned to the heading variable. We can then use the iterator object in the for statement to consume the rest of the items in that iterator.

In effect, the preceding example is nearly identical to this:

```
heading, *rest = source
for data in rest:
    print(data)
```

This second example actually makes a shallow copy of the source collection and assigns this copy to the rest variable. We've nearly doubled the amount of memory used. For a small list, this doesn't matter. For a larger collection, this can become a problem.

If the source is an open file or a generator based on an open file, materializing the data in the `rest` collection could be impossible. Files too big to fit into memory are part of their own unique problem, sometimes called "big data". Using the `iter()` function explicitly allows us to avoid the risky attempt to create a large collection that may not fit in memory.

Consequences and next steps

There are three important consequences to the way a `for` statement uses `coll_i= iter(x)` and `x=next(coll_i)`:

- We can write generator expressions which implicitly have the required interface to work as an `Iterable` class
- Python gives us a way to write generator functions which will work as an `Iterable` class
- We can create our own classes which implement the special method names required to implement the `Iterable` abstract base class

We'll start by writing generator expressions. We can use these to create `list`, `set`, and mapping "comprehensions." A **comprehension** is an expression that defines the contents of a collection.

We'll look at writing generator functions. The `yield` statement changes the semantics of a function from being "simple" (or "ordinary") to being a generator.

While class definitions are the subject of *Chapter 11, Class Definitions*, we won't dig deeply into how we can create our own unique collections. Python already offers so many collections that defining our own is not really necessary.

Using generator expressions and comprehensions

We can think of simple generator expressions as an operator with three operands. The syntax for these three operands parallels the `for` statement:

```
(expression for target in source)
```

We specify an *expression* which is evaluated for each value assigned to a *target* variable from a *source*. There are more complex generators, which we'll look at later.

Generator expressions can be used freely in Python. They can be used anywhere in a sequence or a collection that is meaningful.

It's important to note that a generator expression is lazy, or "non-strict." It doesn't actually calculate anything until some consuming operation demands values from it. To see this, we can try to evaluate a generator expression at the REPL:

```
>>> (2*x+1 for x in range(5))
<generator object <genexpr> at 0x1023981e0>
```

Python tells us only that we've created a generator object. Since we didn't write an expression to consume the values, all we saw was the object, passively waiting to be evaluated.

The best way to explore a generator expression is to apply a function, such as `list()` or `tuple()`, that will consume the generator's values and build a collection object from them. Here's an example:

```
>>> tuple(2*x+1 for x in range(5))
(1, 3, 5, 7, 9)
```

In this example, the `tuple()` function consumed values from the generator object and created a `tuple` object from those values. Rather than display the generator object, the REPL shows us the `tuple` which was created from the generated values.

We can use generator expressions for a wide variety of processing. There are several patterns in the `itertools` module.

Limitations of generator expressions

Generator expressions have a few limitations. The most obvious limitation is that some language features are only available as Python statements. If we need to perform exception handling, context management, or exiting a loop early via a `break` statement, we can't write a generator expression. We have to resort to writing a complete generator function.

A less obvious limitation is that a generator expression behaves very much like a sequence. But it can only do that trick once. After the generator terminates the first time, it behaves like an empty sequence every time it's referenced after that. Here's a concrete example:

```
>>> x= (2*x+1 for x in range(20))
>>> sum(x)
400
>>> sum(x)
0
```

In this example, we assigned a generator expression to a variable, x. When we compute sum(x), the sum() function consumes all of the values produced by the generator expression: the sum is 400 in this example. Once we've used the generator, it is still valid, but it no longer generates values. All subsequent evaluations of sum(x) will produce 0.

There's no special exception to warn us that we're reusing an iterator that has already been exhausted. In some cases, a program may appear broken because we're using a generator expression instead of a list or tuple sequence. The fix is almost always to convert the generator into a tuple object so that it can be used twice. We can change to x= tuple(2*x+1 for x in range(20)) to see the difference.

When working with a generator function or expression, iter(some_function) will return the generator object because it is an iterator. In the case of a collection object, iter(some_collection) will create an iterator object that has a reference to the collection. The result will be a distinct object. A function can use iter(param) is iter(param) to detect the difference between a generator function and a concrete collection.

In some cases, we might include the statement assert iter(param) is not iter(param), "Collection object required" to raise an exception if a generator function is provided as an argument to a function which traverses a collection more than once.

Using multiple loops and conditions

The body of a generator can include multiple for clauses. This allows us to iterate over multiple dimensions. We can write expressions like this:

```
>>> deck= list((r,s) for s in '♣♦♥♠' for r in range(1,14))
>>> deck # doctest: +ELLIPSIS
[(1, '♣'), (2, '♣'), (3, '♣'), ... (11, '♠'), (12, '♠'), (13, '♠')]
>>> len(deck)
52
```

The generator expression has two for clauses: for s in '♣♦♥♠' and for r in range(1,14). It's clear from the results that the for clause on the right executes most frequently. This follows the nesting rules we'd see if we rewrote this as nested for statements. The for clause on the right is like an innermost for statement.

Additionally, the body of a generator can include `if` clauses. These can be used to filter values created by the `for` clauses. Here's an example of conditional processing in a generator expression:

```
>>> list(x for x in range(36) if x%5 == 0 or x%7 == 0)
[0, 5, 7, 10, 14, 15, 20, 21, 25, 28, 30, 35]
```

In this example, the expression is just the target variable, x. The source is `range(36)`, numbers that include zero and 35. We've included an `if` clause that will pass only those values which are multiples of five or seven. All other values will be rejected. In order to see a result, we collected the values from the generator into a `list` object.

Writing comprehensions

We can leverage a variation of the generator expression to create `list`, `set`, or `dict` objects. These are called comprehensions, and represent tangible objects, built from lazy generators.

Here are some simple examples:

```
[2*x+1 for x in range(5)]
{x for x in range(36) if x%5 == 0 or x%7 == 0}
{n: 2*n**2-3*n-14 for n in range(-5,6)}
```

The first example uses the `[]` to create a `list` comprehension. This will create a list of odd values from one to nine. The second example uses `{}` to create a `set` comprehension. This will be a set based on multiples of five or seven.

The third example creates a `dict` comprehension. The `{}` are used to bracket the expression. The use of the `:` character to separate key and value distinguishes a `dict` comprehension from a `set` comprehension. This dictionary provides a mapping from values of *n*.

This last example could be used as an optimization for a deeply-nested expression. Looking up a value in a mapping is faster than repeatedly recalculating. Using the `@ lru_cache` decorator gives similar performance benefits.

Defining generator functions with the yield statement

A generator function has properties similar to a generator expression. Rather than a single expression, a generator function is a full Python function. It has all of the features of the functions described in *Chapter 7, Basic Function Definitions*. It has the additional characteristic of being an iterator, capable of generating a sequence of items.

When we use a `yield` statement, the semantics of the function are changed. Without a `yield`, a function will return a single value. With a `yield` statement, a function will behave like an iterator, providing multiple values to a consumer.

Here's an example of a generator function that applies a range of values to a model to compute a domain of results. We'll apply the model to a sequence of input values to compute the results for each input:

```python
def model_iter(until):
    for n in range(0, until):
        yield n*(n+1)//2
```

This `model_iter()` function accepts a single argument, `until`, which is the number of values generated by this function. The body of the function includes a `for` statement which will set the `n` variable to values defined by the `range()` object.

The essential feature of this function is the `yield` statement. Each value created by the `yield` statement will be part of the sequence of items emitted by this statement.

Here's one way to use this function:

```python
>>> list(model_iter(6))
[0, 1, 3, 6, 10, 15]
```

In this example, we've collected the results into a single `list` object. Creating a `list` object is just one of the many things we can do. We could just as easily sum the results of the model to compute the mean value for the given range.

```python
>>> mean = sum(model_iter(6))/6
>>> round(mean, 4)
5.8333
```

In this example, we provided the results of the `model_iter()` generator to the `sum()` function. This avoids building a large collection of results. The `sum()` function will consume all of the values yielded by the generator function. We can process thousands or millions of values with this kind of construct because a large `list` or `set` is not materialized in memory. Only the individual items are processed.

Using the higher-order functions

A function which accepts a function as an argument, or returns a function as a result, is called a **higher-order function**. Python has a number of higher-order functions. The most commonly-used of these functions are `map()`, `filter()`, and `sorted()`. The `itertools` module contains numerous additional higher-order functions.

The `map()` and `filter()` functions are generators; their results must be consumed. Both of them apply a function to a collection of values. In the case of `map()`, the results of the function are yielded. In the case of `filter()`, if the result of the function is true, the original value is yielded.

Here's how we can apply a very simple function—so simple we coded it as a lambda—to a sequence of values:

```
>>> mapping= map( lambda x: 2*x**2-2, range(5) )
>>> list(mapping)
[-2, 0, 6, 16, 30]
```

The function is just an expression, `2*x**2-2`. We've applied this function to values given by the `range()` object. The result is a generator, and we need to consume the values. We've used `list()` to create a collection that we can print. The values are the result of applying the given function to each value in the source collection.

Here's how we can apply a simple logical test to a sequence of values using `filter()`:

```
>>> fb= filter( lambda n: n%5==0 or n%7==0, range(16) )
>>> [n for n in fb]
[0, 5, 7, 10, 14, 15]
```

We've defined a simple function as a lambda; the function, `n%5==0 or n%7==0`, is true for multiples of five or seven. We've applied that filter to values produced by a `range()` object. The result includes only the values for which the given function is `True`. All other values are rejected.

We used a `list` comprehension to gather the values into a `list` object. This `list` comprehension did no calculation and no filtering, so it's equivalent to `list(fb)`.

We can implement the simple versions of `map()` and `filter()` using generator expressions:

- `map(function, iterable)` is the same as `(function(x) for x in iterable)`
- `filter(function, iterable)` is the same as `(x for x in iterable if function(x))`

The `map()` function can handle additional iterables, providing more sophistication than the generator expression.

The `sorted()` function is similar to `map()` and `filter()`. The `sorted()` function follows a different design pattern for its parameters. The `map()` and `filter()` functions accept a function first, followed by an item to process. The `sorted()` function accepts an item to sort first, and an optional function which defines the keys on which to sort, as well as an optional reverse Boolean value used to reverse the sense of the key comparisons. We'll look at sorted in detail in the *Three ways to sort a sequence* section later.

The `itertools` module contains a large number of generator functions that can be combined to create sophisticated processing. For more information on how this module works, the book, *Functional Python Programming, Steven Lott, Packt Publishing*, devotes two chapters to the subject (`https://www.packtpub.com/application-development/functional-python-programming`).

Writing our own higher-order functions

Perhaps the simplest kind of higher-order function is based on a generator expression. Since a generator expression is lazy, its behavior is more like a function than an object which contains relevant data. A function which returns a generator relies on some other piece of programming to actually consume the data which is yielded by the generator.

A common file input requirement is to strip trailing punctuation and ignore blank lines. We'll assume a language which follows the Python rule for comments.

Here's an example of a function that returns a generator:

```
def text_cleaner( source ):
    stripped = (line.strip() for line in source)
    partitioned = (line.partition("#") for line in stripped)
    decommented = (data.rstrip() for data, sharp, comment in
partitioned)
    non_empty = (line for line in decommented if line)
    return non_empty
```

We've broken down the processing into four separate generator functions. The result of the function is the fourth of these generators, but this depends on the others to yield its results. Since generators are lazy, no processing happens until a function or statement consumes the data yielded by the generator. We must use the result of this function with a `for` statement or a `list()` or `tuple()` function to consume the data.

When a consuming process iterates over the result of this function, it will receive individual lines of text from the `non_empty` generator expression. The `non_empty` generator filters the lines created by the `decommented` generator expression. The `decommented` generator in turn relies on the `partitioned` and `stripped` generator expressions to remove comments and whitespace.

What's important here is that the pipeline of processing is the return value from the `text_cleaner()` function. This function does not process any data. This function returns a generator expression that will process some data.

Each of these generators can be also rewritten to use `map()` or `filter()`. We'll leave that as an exercise for the reader.

We can use the `text_cleaner()` function like this:

```
>>> text = '''
... # options
... db=name # database
...  task=delete # task
... '''.splitlines()
>>> for line in text_cleaner(text):
...     print(line)
db=name
task=delete
```

We've created some text with comments and data. The format of the data appears to be `name=value` settings. The `text_cleaner()` function isn't sensitive to the format of the data, only to the presence of comments and whitespace. We applied the `splitlines()` function to make the block of text behave like a file.

The result of `text_cleaner()` is a function which strips away comments, leading and trailing spaces, and leaves us with just the meaningful content of the file. In this example, we used a `for` statement to consume the data yielded by the generator function.

This can be part of a more complex process that uses these `name=value` lines as configuration parameters.

What's important about generator functions is that they are completely lazy. They don't create giant data structures in memory. They process the minimum amount of data to satisfy the consumer's requests. This reduces overheads. Additionally, each generator can be kept relatively simple, allowing an expressive composition to be built from simple pieces.

Using the built-in reductions – max, min, and reduce

We have two other built-in higher-order functions that can accept functions as arguments. These can be characterized as reductions: they reduce a collection of values to a single value. There's a third built-in reduction, sum, but it's not a proper higher-order function: we can't tailor its operation by plugging in a function.

The `max()` and `min()` reductions follow the design pattern for the `sorted()` function: they accept an iterable object first, and they can be customized with an optional key function. We'll show the default behavior first, then we'll show how to customize this with the key function:

```
>>> data = ["21", "3", "35", "4"]
>>> min(data)
'21'
>>> min(data, key=int)
'3'
```

In the first example, the string objects were compared using string comparison. This leads to the anomaly of seeing `"21"` appear to be less than `"3"`. In fact, a string beginning with `"2"` is sorted before a string beginning with `"3"`, but this may not be what the program needs to show as output.

In the second example, we provided the `int()` function for min to use when comparing items. This means that the strings are compared as integers, not as strings. This selects `"3"` as the string with the minimal integer value.

Note that we did not write `min(data, key=int())`. We're not evaluating the `int` function. We're providing the `int` function as an object which the `min()` function will use.

Additionally, there's a generic `functools.reduce()` function which can be used to build new kinds of reductions. This function accepts a two-valued function, an iterable and an initial value. It can compute a wide variety of reductions.

Three ways to sort a sequence

Python offers us three common approaches to the general problem of sorting a `list` of complex items.

- We can sort with the `sorted()` generator function. This will duplicate an object as part of sorting.

- We can sort a list with its `sort()` method and a key function. This will mutate the `list` into the requested order.

- We can create an intermediate sequence of objects which can be sorted easily. This is sometimes called the **wrap-sort-unwrap** design pattern.

In order to look at each of these in some detail, we need a collection of complex objects which we can sort. We'll use a simple dataset based on a case study in the *NIST Engineering Statistics Handbook*, section 7.1.6. See `http://www.itl.nist.gov/div898/handbook` for more information.

We've got metrics data that—after a little re-organization and cleanup—looks like this:

```
>>> data
[['2013-09-10', '289'], ['2013-09-11', '616'],
. . . ,
['2013-12-07', '752'], ['2013-12-08', '739']]
```

We have a list-of-list structure with 90 pairs. Since the date strings are formatted nicely as `yyyy-mm-dd`, we can easily sort this into date order using the `sorted(data)` function, or the `data.sort()` method. Note that `sorted(data)` will create a duplicate of the `data` object. The `data.sort()` method will mutate the `data` object in place.

How can we put the data into order by count? We can apply a key function to the `sorted()` function or `sort()` method. We'll look at these first. As an alternative, we can use the wrap-sort-unwrap design pattern.

Sorting via a key function

Putting the metrics data into order by count requires us to use a function which will change the way items are compared. In this case, we need a more complex key function that does two things. It must select the second item of each two item data points, and it must convert the second item to a proper integer value.

We can sort by count using either of these examples:

```
>>> data.sort(key=lambda x: int(x[1]))
>>> by_count= sorted(data, key=lambda x: int(x[1]))
```

Both examples use a lambda that performs the integer conversion of the second item in each two-item list. The first example updates the data object. The second example creates a new object which is a clone of the data object, put into order.

Sorting via wrapping and unwrapping

The wrap-sort-unwrap design pattern can be done with a pair of generator expressions. The first will create two-tuples from each original piece of data. The first item in each new two-tuple is the proper sort key. The second generator will select the second item from each of those two-tuples to recover the original object.

The whole sequence looks like this:

```
>>> wrapped = [(int(x[1]), x) for x in data]
>>> wrapped.sort()
>>> by_count = [x[1] for x in wrapped]
```

In the first step, we turned each piece of original data into a two-tuple of (sort key, original item). We've used a `list` comprehension to create a new object that we can sort, leaving the original object undisturbed. Once we've done this, the default sort operation works correctly. Once the data is sorted, we can recover the original items easily. In this case, we created yet another list object using a `list` comprehension.

In both cases, we can tweak this slightly to the `map()` function instead of with generator expressions. For example, we can wrap items using `map(lambda item: (int(item[1]), item), data)`.

Note that the `map()` function is a generator: it's lazy. A `list` comprehension consumes data and creates a tangible object. We can't easily switch from `list` to generator with a simple copy-and-paste. We'll need to either create a `list` object from the map generator, or use `sorted()`, which creates a `list` from a generator.

The wrap-sort-unwrap is often used when the wrap function is quite complex. We might have a generator which performs database lookups, file merges, or extremely complex calculations as part of the ordering. In these cases, a simple lambda might be difficult to write.

Functional programming design patterns

The presence of higher-order functions in Python allows us to leverage a great many functional programming design patterns. To learn more about these design patterns, a good place to start is the `itertools` module. The functions in this module provide many examples of how we can write simple functions that do sophisticated processing.

Additionally, we can use some of the features in the `functools` module. This contains the general-purpose `reduce()` function. It also contains some functions that can help us write decorators. A decorator, as we'll see in *Chapter 13, Metaprogramming and Decorators*, is another kind of higher-order function: it's a function that modifies the definition of an original function. This is another aspect of functional programming.

Most importantly, we have two ways to approach algorithms:

- We can process items in large collections of data, creating additional collections that are copies, subsets, or transformations.

- We can process items by iterating through a large collection of data as if we're creating additional collections. Instead of actually creating copies, subsets, or transformations, we can use iterators, filter functions, and mapping functions.

When we have alternatives, we can choose a variation that is succinct and expressive.

Summary

In this chapter, we've seen a number of the advanced features of functions. We've looked at the essential generator expression and how this is used as part of a comprehension. A `list` comprehension assembles a `list` from the generated values. Similarly, a `set` comprehension creates a `set`. A dictionary comprehension creates a `dict` structure from the keys and values in a generator expression.

We've looked at using the `yield` statement to create a generator function. This allows us to use all of the various Python statement features when creating a generator. Since a generator is iterable, it works with a `for` loop so that we can write a simple loop to process multiple values created by an iterator.

We've also looked at higher-order functions. These are functions which take functions as arguments or produce functions as a result. With higher-order functions, we can refactor our algorithms into functions that can be combined to create the desired behavior.

In *Chapter 9*, *Exceptions*, we'll look at how Python raises exceptions, how we can capture those exceptions, and what kind of exceptional processing we need to write.

9
Exceptions

Python's general approach to unexpected situations is to raise an **exception**. The idea is that an operation should either work normally and completely, or raise an exception. In some languages, complex numeric status codes are used to indicate success. In Python, success is assumed; if there's a problem, an exception is raised to indicate that the operation did not succeed.

Exceptions can be raised by all aspects of Python programs. All of the built-in classes involve exceptions for various kinds of unexpected conditions. Many library packages define their own unique exceptions which extend the built-in hierarchy of exceptions.

We'll look at the essential concept behind exceptions first. Python has a number of statements that we'll use. The `raise` statement creates an exception object. The `try` statement allows us to deal with exceptions.

The `except` clause in a `try` statement is used to match the class of exception being raised. With some kinds of programming, we narrowly match a specific class of exceptions. In other cases, we use a less specific class of exceptions, or a list of exception classes, to treat a variety of exceptions in a uniform manner.

The core exception concept

The core concept behind exceptions can be summarized as, "when in doubt, raise an exception". In a typical situation, each Python function or method will return a value or have some documented side-effect. For everything that isn't on the "happy path" that leads to success, the Python approach is to raise an exception.

Even though most exceptions describe erroneous situations, an exception is not necessarily an error. It's merely an exceptional condition that a given function can't handle. For example, iterators raise the `StopIteration` exception when they can no longer produce a result item. This is an exceptional situation that occurs just once in the life cycle of an iterator object.

When working with numbers, as a second example, division by zero is exceptional. If we divide by any other value, the happy path leads us to a result. While it's possible to contrive a **Not a Number (NaN)** value as the result of division by zero, it's simpler — and more universal — for the division operator to raise a `ZeroDivisionError` exception. Division by zero isn't a normal or expected design. Almost universally, division by zero indicates one of these things:

- **A design problem**: Zero was a possible condition, but the design didn't deal with this situation. The `ZeroDivisionError` exception is unexpected. The root cause of a design problem may be a failure to understand the requirements: perhaps a hastily groomed story, perhaps other problems in understanding the problem domain.

- **An implementation problem**: Zero is cropping up because of a bug. A `ZeroDivisionError` exception is similarly unexpected. The root cause may include inadequate unit testing.

- **A misuse of the application**: The user provided input that led to division by zero. The overall application can offer a helpful error message and await different input. Or perhaps the overall application can use a different calculation that's more appropriate to the input values.

An exception can be profound or shallow in its meaning.

When working with strings, for example, there are a number of situations where an exception is raised. There are also some situations where a status code is returned instead of raising an exception. We can compare `str.find()` and `str.index()` for two differences in approach:

```
>>> "abc".index("x")
Traceback (most recent call last):
  File "<stdin>", line 1, in <module>
ValueError: substring not found

>>> "abc".find("x")
-1.
```

The first example shows the `index()` method, which raises an exception when a substring can't be found. The second example shows the `find()` method, which returns a peculiar number if the substring can't be found.

Exceptions are used widely. Status codes are rarely used in Python.

Examining the exception object

When an exception is raised, it involves both a processing change and some data about the condition. An exception is an instance of a more general class. We'll talk generally about an `EOFError` exception without emphasizing that the given exception is an instance of the `EOFError` exception class.

The data associated with an exception can include a root cause exception, and a collection of additional arguments. Sometimes the additional arguments are merely a string message. Some exceptions may have a more complex collection of arguments.

There is also a traceback object which contains the call stack. This identifies the function which raised the exception, the function which called that function, and so on, back to the initial function that started things off. This traceback information is in a specially named attribute called `__traceback__`.

We can create an exception in several different ways:

- We can create exception objects and later raise them to signal a problem:

  ```
  obj = Exception("some message")
  raise obj
  ```

- We can create and raise the exception in one smooth motion:

  ```
  raise Exception("Some Argument", "additional details")
  ```

- We can create an exception which wraps a root-cause exception:

  ```
  raise MyError("problem") from some_exception
  ```

In the last case, where an exception wraps a root cause, the root cause information is in an attribute named `__cause__`.

Using the try and except statements

When an exception is raised, the ordinary sequential exception of statements stops. The next sequential statement is not executed. Instead, the exception handlers are examined to find an except clause which matches the given exception's class. This search proceeds down the call stack from the current function to the function which called it. If an except clause is found which matches the exception, then ordinary sequential execution resumes in that except clause. When the except clause finishes, the try statement is also finished. From there, the normal sequential statement execution continues after the try statement.

If no except clause matches the given exception, the exception and the traceback information is printed. Processing stops, and Python exits. Generally, the exit status is non-zero to indicate that the Python program ended abnormally.

A try statement inside a function looks like this:

```
def clean_number(text):
    try:
        value= float(text)
    except ValueError:
        value= None
    return value
```

We've defined a function which will convert text to a number. We're going to silence the ValueError exception and return the None object instead of raising an exception. We might use this when cleaning a CSV file so that cells without proper numeric values are replaced with the None object.

We can see it in operation when we apply it to numbers, like this.

```
>>> row = ['heading', '23', '2.718']
>>> list(map(clean_number, row))
[None, 23.0, 2.718]
>>> clean_number("1,956")
```

In this example, we're applying the clean_number() function to a row of data from the CSV reader. The sample row of data shows both the happy path and the exception path. On the happy path, the two numbers are converted from a string to a proper float value. On the exception path, the improper text was converted into a None.

We've also included a test case that isn't handled well. This number-like string, "1,956" turns into None. We might have wanted it to be turned into a proper number, in spite of the embedded comma. We can see that a simplistic except clause isn't really doing everything we'd like it to do.

Note that some financially-oriented spreadsheet values should be converted to Decimal values instead of float values. We can make a higher-order function which will use either the float() function or the Decimal() function (or any other conversion function for that matter) to create values of a desired type.

Here's a revised version that has two try statements:

```
from decimal import Decimal, InvalidOperation
def clean_number3(text, num_type=Decimal):
    try:
        value= num_type(text)
    except (ValueError, InvalidOperation):
        text= text.replace(",","").replace("$","")
        try:
            value= num_type(text)
        except (ValueError, InvalidOperation):
            value= None
    return value
```

In this version of our number cleaning function, we have an additional parameter, num_type, with a conversion function to apply. We've provided a default value, Decimal, so that it is optional. The body of the function has the same happy path as the previous version. We've updated the first except clause to do more sophisticated fallback processing. This more sophisticated processing involves creating a new string without the "," or "$" characters that commonly pollute numeric data.

If this second string is converted, we'll return a useful numeric result. If this revised string is not a number, we're stumped, and forced to return a None object.

 As an exercise, the reader can create an algorithm to convert words to numbers as a fallback. Convert "twenty one" to 21. The complexity of languages like English makes this is an interesting challenge.

Using nested try statements

The `clean_number3()` function shows one of the two ways that we can have nested `try` statements. In this case, the `try` statements are nested inside a single function. If an exception is raised in the inner `try` statement, then the inner `try` statement's `except` clause is checked first for a matching exception. The outer `try` statement's `except` clauses are checked next. If none of these match, then the function which called this is checked.

Consider this example:

```
>>> from fractions import Fraction
>>> clean_number3(',2/0,', Fraction)
```

This produces a traceback dump that shows how nested try blocks behave:

```
Traceback (most recent call last):
  ...
ValueError: Invalid literal for Fraction: ',2/0,'

During handling of the above exception, another exception occurred:

Traceback (most recent call last):
  ...
ZeroDivisionError: Fraction(2, 0)
```

We've elided some details with line numbers to focus on the relevant portions of the message. The first exception was raised by the first attempt to apply `Fraction(',2/0,')`. This raised a `ValueError` exception, knocking us off the happy path. Python resumes sequential execution in the `except` clause. This creates a new string with the `","` characters removed. The second attempt at conversion does not raise a `ValueError` exception, it raises a `ZeroDivisionError` exception.

The inner `try` statement has no `except` clause to match this exception. Python must then search the outer `try` statement's `except` clauses for a matching exception. Since the outer `try` statement doesn't match the exception, the script as a whole ends with an unhandled exception.

The more common situation is to have `try` statements in separate functions. The nesting occurs via the function call stack, not the structure of a single suite of statements. Here's a function which calls our `clean_number3()` function to create a row of `Fraction` objects.

```
def fraction_row(row):
    try:
        return [clean_number3(item,Fraction) for item in row]
    except (TypeError, ZeroDivisionError):
        return [None for item in row]
```

This function includes another `try` statement. When this function calls `clean_number3()` the calls stack will include `fraction_row()` and `clean_number3()`. If the `clean_number3()` function raises an unhandled exception, Python moves down the call stack and searches this `try` statement for matching `except` clauses.

Matching exception classes in an except clause

In the previous examples, we've shown two kinds of `except` clauses:

* `except SomeException:`
* `except (OneException, AnotherException):`

The first example matches a single specific exception. The second example matches any of the exceptions in the list of specific exceptions.

In many cases, the details of the exception are not important. On the other hand, there are some cases where we want to do some processing on the exception object's arguments. We can have the exception object assigned to a variable using this syntax:

```
except SomeException as exc:
```

This will assign the exception instance to the `exc` variable. We can then write this to a log, or examine the arguments, or modify the traceback that gets printed.

Matching more general exceptions

The Python exceptions form a class hierarchy. Generally, we match exceptions specifically. In a few cases, we'll use exception superclasses instead of specific classes. Some of the most common superclasses are the OSError and ArithmeticError exceptions. There are a number of subclasses of OSError that provide more detailed information about the exception; in many cases, we're not too interested in the nuances of the OSError superclass. Similarly, the distinction between OverflowError and ZeroDivisionError may not be helpful.

We can use the superclass exception like this:

```
import os
def names(path="."):
    try:
        return [name
            for name in os.listdir(path)
            if not name.startswith('.')]
    except OSError as exc:
        print( exc.__class__.__name__, exc )
        raise
```

We've used the superclass OSError to match all of the various OSError subclasses. While the most likely exceptions are FileNotFoundError and NotADirectoryError, we may also get one of the other subclasses of OSError. In this case, we don't care about the specific problem, so we can use a superclass error.

This example also uses the raise statement with no argument. Within an except clause, this will reraise the exception after doing some initial handling. The exception will now propagate down the call stack as Python searches for a handler.

The empty except clause

Python allows an except clause with no exception named. This is the most general exception matcher: it matches all exception classes.

Since it matches the SystemExit and KeyboardInterrupt exceptions, using this casually can create problems. When we're handling this exception, we may find that we can no longer gracefully exit from our program and must resort to the SIGKILL signal to stop the program.

The undecorated except clause should be viewed skeptically.

Creating our own exceptions

The hierarchy of exceptions has a superclass for error-related exceptions, called
Exception. All of the exceptions which reflect essentially erroneous conditions
are subclasses of the Exception class. The base class for all exceptions is the
BaseException class; some non-error-related exceptions are direct subclasses of
the BaseException class.

We can summarize the hierarchy like this:

- BaseException

    ◦   SystemExit

    ◦   KeyboardInterrupt

    ◦   GeneratorExit

    ◦   Exception

        ◦   All other exceptions

The superclass of all error-related exceptions, Exception, is quite broad. We can use
this in a long-running server like this:

```
def server():
    try:
        while True:
            try:
                one_request()
            except Exception as e:
                print(e.__class__.__name__, e)
    except Shutdown_Request:
        print("Shutting Down")
```

This example depends on a function, one_request(), which handles a single
request. The while loop runs forever, evaluating the one_request() function.
If any of the error-related subclasses of Exception are raised, the error will be
logged, but request handling will continue.

When a Shutdown_Request exception is raised, the inner try statement won't match
this. The exception will propagate out of the loop into the outer try statement. We
can log the shutdown request, do any other cleanup that's required, and exit the
server() function.

The class hierarchy assures us that two of the non-error exceptions — `KeyboardInterrupt` and `SystemExit` — will not be erroneously handled in the inner `try` statement. These exceptions are peers of the `Exception` class, which is why they will not be matched. This means that a `SIGINT` signal (the effect of hitting *Ctrl* + *C* on the keyboard) will terminate the server cleanly. Additionally, if some part of the request handling evaluates `sys.exit()`, the server will shut down gracefully.

Using a finally clause

We can include a `finally` clause on a `try` statement. This contains a suite of statements that will always be executed at the end of the `try` statement. This means that the happy path, as well as the exception paths, will always execute the `finally` suite. Here's a summary of how this looks:

```
try:
    # Something that might fail.
except SomeException:
    # Fallback plan to handle failure.
finally:
    # Always executed.
```

We use this when we have cleanup or a concluding suite of statements that must always be executed. One of the most common use cases for this is to close a file or a network connection even if an exception was raised and handled properly.

In many cases, we can use a context manager to properly close a file or network connection. We can use `contextlib.closing()` to wrap objects which have a `close()` method but are not proper context managers. We'll look at context managers in *Chapter 10, Files, Databases, Networks, and Contexts*.

Use cases for exceptions

The use cases for exceptions are very broad. We'll identify a few significant areas where exceptions are used in Python.

Some exceptions are entirely benign. The `StopIteration` exception is raised by an iterable that has run out of values. The `for` statement consumes items from the iterable until this exception is raised to signal that there's no more data. Similarly, a `GeneratorExit` is used when a generator is closed before producing all of its data. This is not an error; it's a signal that more data will not be requested.

Conditions that are entirely outside the program may be seen as exceptions. Unexpected OS conditions or errors are signaled by exceptions which are subclasses of the OSError exception. Some OS conditions can be ignored; others may indicate a serious problem in the environment or in the application. There are over a dozen subclasses of this error to provide a more detailed description of the OS condition. Additionally, internal OS error numbers are also provided as an argument to these exceptions to help distinguish the details of the problem.

Some exceptions are the result of perfectly ordinary things inside a program. When we use the str.index() method, this may raise a ValueError exception instead of returning a numeric value. We can capture and leverage this exception information as part of a program's normal operation.

We'll often detect the misuse of a program with exceptions. Bad data may be involved, or unsupported operations may be attempted. In these cases, a program may use exceptions to signal a problem that stems from user input problems. A common design pattern is to have exception handling at a high enough level to capture, log, and display these problems in a meaningful way to the user. A long-running server may merely log and then process the next request. A web page may wrap input form validation in exception handling so that the user's response is the form page decorated with error messages.

Some exceptions reflect design or implementation problems. An unexpected occurrence of a ValueError exception may indicate a design problem or an implementation problem. It might indicate inadequate test cases. In this case, it's best for the program as a whole to crash so that the traceback information can be used to locate and correct the problem.

Unexpected exceptions generally indicate that the program is broken. The program will stop; the output from the exception can provide valuable debugging information. We can interfere with this normal behavior by writing needlessly broad exception handlers, but concealing unexpected exceptions is generally a bad idea, since valuable debugging information is lost.

In *The Zen of Python* by Tim Peters, there's some poetic advice:

> *Errors should never pass silently.*

> *Unless explicitly silenced.*

The idea here is that unexpected exceptions in Python will stop the program with a big, noisy error traceback. If we need to silence exceptions, we can use broad, general except statements to capture and silence them.

Issuing warnings instead of exceptions

The Python `warnings` module handles a special subclass of exceptions. We can use the `warnings` module to identify potential problems in our application. The warnings module is used internally to track a number of internal considerations.

The warning concept fits into the middle ground between perfectly normal operations and erroneous conditions. Our program may not be performing optimally, but it's not completely broken, either.

There are three notable warning classes that we might encounter when running unit tests. Since the unit test framework displays `all` warnings, we may see some warnings in a test context that we don't see in the normal operational use of our software.

- `DeprecationWarning`: This warning is raised by modules, functions, or classes that have been deprecated. It's a reminder that we need to fix our code to stop using this feature.

- `PendingDeprecationWarning`: A function, module or class for which deprecation has been announced may raise this warning. This is a hint that we need to stop using this feature before it becomes deprecated.

- `ImportWarning`: Since some modules are optional or platform-specific, some import statements are wrapped in a `try` block; this warning is raised instead of an exception. We can expose these warnings to be sure that imports are being processed properly.

We can leverage the `warnings` module to expose the warnings which are normally silenced. We can use `warnings.simplefilter("always")` to see all warnings.

We can raise the generic `UserWarning` like this:

```
>>> import warnings
>>> warnings.warn("oopsie")
__main__:1: UserWarning: oopsie
```

Using `warnings.warn()` allows us to include warning messages in an application with very little overhead. We can use this as a debugging aid to track rare situations that are questionable or potentially confusing.

Permission versus forgiveness – a Pythonic approach

A common piece of Pythonic wisdom is the following advice from RADM Grace Murray Hopper:

"It is Easier to Ask for Forgiveness than Permission"

In the Python community, this is sometimes summarized as EAFP programming. This is in contrast to **Look Before You Leap** (**LBYL**) programming.

Python exception handling is fast. More importantly, all of the necessary precondition checks for potential problems are already part of the language itself. We never need to bracket processing with extraneous `if` statements to see whether or not the input could possibly raise an exception.

It's generally considered a bad practice to write LBYL code that looks like this:

```
if text.isdigit():
    num= int(text)
else:
    num= None
```

The bad idea shown here is an attempt to check carefully to prevent an exception from being raised. This is ineffective for a number of reasons.

- The `isdigit()` test fails to properly handle negative numbers. For a `float()` conversion, this kind of test misses a large number of valid syntax alternatives.

- The overhead of checking the validity of characters and syntax is already part of the `int()` function. Checking validity in advance duplicates the checking already in place.

The more Pythonic approach is to handle the built-in exceptions. For example:

```
try:
    num= int(text)
except ValueError:
    num= None
```

This is the same number of lines of code. It properly converts all possible Python integer strings. It does not include any redundant validity checks.

Summary

In this chapter, we've seen how we can use Python exceptions to write programs which properly handle unexpected conditions. The various kinds of exceptions reflect external conditions as well as internal conditions that may alter how our program behaves. We can use exception clauses to implement fallback processing so that our program handles these exceptional conditions gracefully.

We've also seen some things which are discouraged. The empty except clause — which matches too many kinds of exception classes — is something which is legal but should not be used.

The idea of **Look Before You Leap (LBYL)** programming is also generally discouraged. The Pythonic approach is summarized as **Easier to Ask Forgiveness than to ask Permission (EAFP)**. The general approach is to wrap operations in a try statement and write appropriate exception handlers for the meaningful exceptions.

Some exceptions, such as RuntimeError or SyntaxError, should not be handled by ordinary application programming. These exceptions usually indicate problems so serious that the program really should crash.

Other exceptions, such as IndexError or KeyError, may be an expected part of the design. When these exceptions are unexpected, we've uncovered a design problem. This may also indicate that we have inadequate unit tests.

In *Chapter 10, Files, Databases, Networks, and Contexts,* we'll look at a number of ways in which Python can be used to work with persistent data files and network data transmission. This kind of processing will often require exception handling.

10
Files, Databases, Networks, and Contexts

Files and the filesystem are central to the way modern OSs work. Many OS resources are visible as part of the filesystem. For example, the Linux `/dev/mem` is a view into the processor's memory, implemented as a device visible in the filesystem. Python provides file objects that map to these OS features.

At a fundamental level, OS files are simply collections of bytes. In practice, we often work with files that are collections of Unicode characters. Python offers both views of files. With some file formats, we need to process the bytes. With text files, we expect Python to properly decode Unicode characters from the bytes.

A Python file object will generally be entangled with an OS resource. In order to be sure that an application doesn't leak OS resources, we often use a context manager. This allows us to be sure that OS resources are released when Python files are closed. The `with` statement provides a tidy way to work with a context manager to allocate and de-allocate resources.

In addition to ordinary files, we'll look at TCP/IP sockets. The `urllib` module allows us to open a socket to a remote host. The socket is used like a file to read the data from the remote host.

A file has a physical format; all but the simplest formats require a `library` module to read and write the content properly. Additionally, within the constraints of a physical format, there may be variations in the logical layout of the data. A **comma-separated values** (**CSV**) file, for example, may use field names in the first line of the file to describe the logical layout of the columns.

A SQLite database or a `shelve` database relies on one (or more) file to make the data persistent. We'll look briefly at higher-level constructs which rely on files.

The essential file concept

Modern OSs rely on files and device drivers for a variety of services and features. Bytes on a disk drive are only one type of file.

 Since many storage devices use or include **Solid State Drives** (**SSD**) the term "disk" is technically a misnomer; we'll use the outdated term.

A network adapter is another kind of file; one in which bytes are available continuously, instead of appearing at rest. In addition to disk and network files, the Linux filesystem includes the /dev directory, which describes all of the devices on a given computer. These devices include serial ports, references to memory, and even a device which accumulates an entropy pool to provide random bytes.

The Python file object wraps an OS file. The open() function binds a Python file object to an OS file. In addition to a name, the function expects a mode string for access. The mode string combines two features:

- **Characters versus bytes**: By default, a file is opened in text mode; we can make this explicit by using t. When reading, the OS bytes are decoded to create Unicode characters. When writing, the Unicode characters are encoded into bytes. To use bytes instead of text, we include b in the mode; no encoding or decoding will be done.

- **Allowed operations**: By default, a file is opened in r mode which allows reading only. We can open a file in w mode which will remove any previous content and allow writing only. We can open a file in a mode which will search to the end of the previous content so that new content can be appended. The + modifier allows both reading and writing; this means that w+ removes any previous content and allows reading and writing; r+ leaves the previous content in place and allows reading and writing.

When we open a text file, we provide explicit encoding. In some cases, explicit encoding is required because the encoding expected by the OS isn't in the file.

In some cases, we may also need to specify how newline characters should be handled. On input, we rarely need to specify line endings: Python handles them gracefully by translating Windows \r\n to \n. On output, however, we might need to explicitly provide the line ending. If we set newline="", then no translation is performed; we'll need this so that we can create CSV files with \r\n line endings. If we set newline=None when opening a file, then \n from our program's output translates the platform-specific value in the os.linesep variable. This is the default behavior. Any other values for newline replace the \n characters in our output.

We can specify buffering. We can also specify how Unicode decoding errors are handled. There are seven choices for Unicode errors, including `strict`, `ignore`, `replace`, `xmlcharrefreplace`, `backslashreplace`, and `surrogateescape`. The `strict` error handling raises an exception. The `ignore` error handling quietly drops the illegal character. The other choices offer different kinds of replacement strategies.

Opening text files

For processing text files, here's how to create the file object using the `open()` function:

```
>>> my_file = open("Chapter_10/10letterwords.txt")
>>> text= my_file.read().splitlines()
>>> text[:5]
['consultive', 'syncopated', 'forestland', 'postmarked', 'configures']
```

We've opened a file using all of the default settings. The mode will be read-only. The file must use the system's default encoding (Mac-Roman, for example). We'll rely on the default buffering and the default Unicode error handling, which is `strict`.

In this example, we read the entire file into a giant string and then split that single string into a sequence of individual lines. We assigned the list of strings to the `text` variable. We only displayed the first five items from this list. By default, the string `split()` method does not preserve the split character.

Filtering text lines

We'll look at two key concepts in the following examples. We'll start by opening a file that's encoded using `"utf-8"`:

```
>>> code_file = open("Chapter_1/ch01_ex1.py", "rt", encoding="utf-8",
errors="replace")
>>> code_lines = list(code_file)
>>> code_lines[:5]
['#!/usr/bin/env python3\n', '"""Python Essentials\n', '\n',
'Chapter 1, Example Set 1\n', '\n']
```

We've opened a file with the mode `"rt"`, which means read-only and text. This is the default, so it could have been omitted. We've explicitly provided `"utf-8"` encoding, which is not the OS default.

We used the `list()` function to convert the file object into a sequence of lines. When we use a file object as if it is an iterable, we'll see that the file iterates over lines. If we don't change the newline setting for the file, then the "universal newlines" rules are used: \n, \r, or \r\n will end a line; they're normalized to \n. When we process a file as lines, the line ending characters are preserved.

We often want to remove newline characters from the end of each line. This is a kind of mapping from raw lines to lines with trailing whitespace stripped. We can use a generator expression or the `map()` function and the `str.rstrip()` method.

In some cases, an empty line has no meaning and can be removed. This, too, can be done with a generator expression that has an `if` clause to reject empty lines. We can also do it with a `filter()` function. It's easier if we write these map and filter operations in two lines, like this:

```
>>> txt_stripped = (line.rstrip() for line in code_file)
>>> txt_non_empty= (line for line in txt_stripped if line)
>>> code_lines= list(txt_non_empty)
```

We've broken down the input cleanup into two generator expressions. The first generator expression, `txt_stripped`, maps raw lines to lines with trailing whitespace stripped. The second generator expression, `txt_non_empty`, is a filter which rejects lines that are empty. We could easily add other filter conditions to the `if` clause. Since generator expressions are lazy, nothing is really done until the final `list()` function consumes all of the lines from the generators.

In this way, we can design fairly sophisticated file parsing as a collection of generator expressions. We can apply a number of mapping and filtering operations so that the main suite of statements has only clean data.

Working with raw bytes

Here's how we open a file and see the raw bytes:

```
>>> raw_bytes = open("Chapter_10/favicon.ico", "rb" )
>>> data = raw_bytes.read()
>>> len(data)
894
>>> data[:22]
b'\x00\x00\x01\x00\x01\x00\x10\x10\x00\x00\x00\x00\x18\x00h\x03\x00\
x00\x16\x00\x00\x00'
```

We've opened this file in binary mode. The input we get will be `bytes` instead of `str`. Since a `bytes` object has many similar features to a `str` object, we can do a great deal of string-like processing on these bytes. We've dumped the first 22 bytes from the file. Bytes are shown as a mixture of hex values and ASCII characters.

We'll need to look at the description of the ICO file format to see what the bytes mean. Here's some background at `http://en.wikipedia.org/wiki/ICO_(file_format)`.

The easiest way to decode this block of bytes is by using the `struct` module. We can do the following to pick apart the header on the file and the header on the first image of the file.

```
>>> import struct
>>> struct.unpack( "<hhhbbbbhhii", data[:22] )
(0, 1, 1, 16, 16, 0, 0, 0, 24, 872, 22)
```

The `unpack()` function requires a format that specifies different kinds of conversions to perform on the stream of bytes. In this case, the format contains three codes for groups of bytes: h means two-byte half worlds, b means single bytes, and i means four-byte integers. The bytes are assembled into numeric values and the resulting structure is a tuple of proper Python `int` values. The leading < in the format specifies that the conversion to integers uses **little-endian** byte ordering.

Using file-like objects

Because of the way objects work in Python, any object that offers an interface similar to the `file` class can be used in place of a file. This leads to the term "file-like object". We can use a file object, or any other object which is designed to behave like a file. For example, the io module has the `StringIO` class, which allows us to work with a string as if it were the contents of a file.

We often use this for creating test data. Note that an `io.StringIO` object is a lot like an open file. When we think about designing for testability — the subject of *Chapter 14, Fit and Finish – Unit Testing, Packaging, and Documentation* — we need to design functions to work with file objects, not filenames.

Here's a function that applies simple pattern matching to lines of a file to yield numeric values extracted from complex lines of text. For more information on regular expressions, see *Chapter 3, Expressions and Output*.

This function uses a pattern to filter the lines of a file or file-like object:

```
import re
def tests_run(log_file):
    data_pat = re.compile(r"\s*([\w ]+):\s+(\d+\.?\d*)\s*")
    for line in log_file:
        match= data_pat.findall(line)
        if match:
            yield match
```

We've defined a generator function, which will reduce a log file to the few lines that match the given pattern. We've used the re module to define a pattern, data_pat, that looks for a string of words ([\w]+), a : character, and a number that could be an integer or floating-point (\d+\.?\d*). The data_pat.findall(line) expression will locate all of these *words: number* pairs in a given line. A resulting list of match results is produced for each matching line.

The matches are strings. We'll need to apply additional functions to the results to convert the numeric group from a string to a proper number.

It is important when defining our function to use a filename; the function doesn't open the file. A function that opens a file is slightly more difficult to test. Instead, we defined our tests_run() function to use any file-like object. This allows us to write unit tests like the following:

```
>>> import io
>>> data = io.StringIO(
... '''
... Tests run: 1, Failures: 2, Errors: 0, Skipped: 1, Time elapsed:
0.547 sec
... Other data
... Tests run: 1, Failures: 0, Errors: 0, Skipped: 0, Time elapsed:
0.018 sec
... ''')
>>> list( tests_run(data) )
[[('Tests run', '1'), ('Failures', '2'), ('Errors', '0'), ('Skipped',
'1'), ('Time elapsed', '0.547')],
[('Tests run', '1'), ('Failures', '0'), ('Errors', '0'), ('Skipped',
'0'), ('Time elapsed', '0.018')]]
```

We've imported the io module so that we can create an io.StringIO object that contains simulated input. We can provide this file-like object to the tests_run() function. Since StringIO behaves like a file, we can use it in place of an actual file to test our function to be sure that it properly locates the Tests run lines and ignores other lines. We'll look at unit testing in *Chapter 14, Fit and Finish – Unit Testing, Packaging, and Documentation*.

Using a context manager via the with statement

A Python file object is generally entangled with OS resources. When we're done using the file, we need to be sure that the file is properly closed so that the OS resources can be released. For small command-line applications, this consideration is not that important: when we exit from Python, and the reference counts for all objects are decreased to zero, the files will be closed during object delete processing.

For a large, long-running server, however, files that are not properly closed will accumulate OS resources. Since pools of OS resources are finite, a file handle leak will, eventually, cause problems.

As a general practice, we can use a context manager to be sure that files are closed when we're done using them. The idea is to constrain an open file to the suite of statements within the context manager. Once that suite of statements is finished, the context manager will ensure that the file is closed.

We specify the context using the `with` statement. A file object is a context manager; the `with` statement uses the file as a manager. At the end of the `with` statement, the context manager will exit and the file will be closed. Some more complex file structures are also context managers. For example, a `ZipFile` object, defined in the `zipfile` module, is a proper context manager; when used in a `with` statement, the file will be neatly closed.

It should be considered a best practice to wrap all file input-output processing in a `with` statement to be absolutely sure that the file is properly closed. Here's an example of how we can use the `tests_run()` function (shown earlier) using a context manager:

```
file_in= "Chapter_10/log_example.txt"
file_out= "Chapter_10/summary.txt"
with open(file_in) as source, open(file_out, "w") as target:
    for stats in tests_run(source):
        print(stats, file=target)
```

We've opened two files to serve as context managers. The file which is opened for reading, `"Chapter_10/log_example.txt"`, is assigned to the `source` variable. The file opened for writing, `"Chapter_10/summary.txt"`, is assigned to the `target` variable. We can then process these files knowing that they will close properly.

If an exception is raised, the files will be closed. This is very important. Each of these context managers is notified if an exception occurs in the suite of statements inside the `with` statement. In this case, both of the managers are file objects. Each will see the exception and close the file—releasing all OS resources—and allow the exception handling to continue. Our application will crash with an exception, but the files will also close properly.

 Always wrap file processing in a `with` statement.

Closing file-like objects with contextlib

In some cases, we want to be sure that our application closes a file-like object that does not implement the context manager methods. Modules such as `http.client` will create an `HTTPConnection` object that may be entangled with network resources. We'd like to ensure that any network resources are released when we're done using the connection object. However, since this object is not a proper context manager, it won't be closed automatically when used in a `with` statement.

Indeed, trying to use an `HTTPConnection` object as context manager in a `with` statement will raise an `AttributeError` exception. This error will show that the `HTTPConnection` object does not implement the correct methods to behave as a context manager.

We can leverage a generic context manager in the `contextlib` module. The `contextlib.closing()` function will wrap any object that has a `close()` method with the required special methods to make the wrapped object into a context manager.

A RESTful web services request might look like this:

```
import contextlib
import http.client
with contextlib.closing(
    http.client.HTTPConnection("www.example.com")) as host:
        host.request("GET", "/path/to/resources/12345/")
        response= host.getresponse()
        print(response.read())
```

We're interested in making a GET request to a web service. The `http.client.`
`HTTPConnection` object isn't a context manager; there's no guarantee that it will
be closed if an exception occurs. By wrapping it with the `contextlib.closing()`
function, we've made it into a proper context manager. We can make requests and
process responses, in the knowledge that the `HTTPConnection` object will have its
`close()` method called properly.

Using the shelve module as a database

Files offer us persistent storage. The simple use of files is limited by the fact that the
data must be accessed sequentially. How can we access items in an arbitrary order?

We'll use the term "database" for a file (a set of files) on which we're going to perform
Create, Retrieve, Update, and Delete (CRUD) operations on data elements in an
arbitrary order. If we create objects of a consistent size, we can open an ordinary text
file in `r+` mode and use the `seek()` method to position at the start of any particular
record. This is rather complex, however, and we can do better.

The core database concept of readable and writable storage can be extended with a
seemingly endless list of ancillary features. We'll ignore locking, logging, auditing,
journaling, distributed transaction management, and many other features, for now to
focus on the core feature of persistence.

The `shelve` module provides us with a very flexible database. A shelf object
behaves like an ordinary Python mapping with the bonus feature that the content is
persistent. One additional constraint is that keys used for a shelf must be strings.

Generally, we use multi-part strings as shelf keys so that we can include some class
information along with a unique identifier for the instance of the class. We can use
a simple `class:id` format to include both the class name and an object's identifier
value as the composite key for the shelf.

Here's an example of creating a shelf that maps a key to a list of values. In this
example, the input file has a sequence of words, plus some blank lines and a trailer
line that we want to ignore. The shelf has keys which are the initial letters of words.
The value associated with each key is a list of words that share that common
first letter.

Here's the entire function:

```
import contextlib
import shelve
def populate():
    with contextlib.closing(
      shelve.open("Chapter_10/shelf","n")) as shelf:
        with open("Chapter_10/10letterwords.txt") as source:
            txt_stripped= (l.strip() for l in source)
            txt_non_empty= (l for l in txt_stripped
                            if l and not l.startswith("Tool") )
            for word in txt_non_empty:
                key = "word_list:{0}".format(word[0])
                try:
                    word_list= shelf[key]
                except KeyError:
                    word_list= []
                word_list.append(word)
                shelf[key]= word_list
```

We've opened the shelf object using `shelve.open()`. The `"n"` mode creates a new, empty shelf file each time the application runs. Since a shelf is not a proper context manager, we need to wrap it with the `contextlib.closing()` function.

The `shelve` module relies on a platform-specific database module. This may necessitate one or more underlying files to support the shelf. We've provided a base filename of `"Chapter_10/shelf"`. We may see a `.dat` or `.db` file get created, depending on the OS we're using.

The `for` loop traverses the input sequence of words generated by the `txt_non_empty` expression. The suite starts by building a two-part key. The first part is the string `word_list`; this is clearly not the Python data class, but it serves as a summary of what the data means. After the colon, we've put the first character of the word.

We fetch the current list of words associated with this key. If there is no such key in the shelf, we handle the `KeyError` exception by creating a fresh, empty list. Once we have a list—either new or fetched from the shelf—we can update the list by appending our new word. We then save the word list in the shelf.

To query words with a certain first letter, we can use `shelf["word_list:"+letter]`. We need to create a complete key string that includes a classifier so that we have a shelf with multiple collections.

To retrieve and summarize the data, we use a simple loop based on this generator expression:

```
sorted(k for k in shelf.keys() if k.startswith("word_list:"))
```

This will select only the keys from our `word_list` collection in the shelf database. In a more sophisticated database, there may be other collections with other key prefixes.

Using the sqlite database

The `sqlite` module provides us with a SQL-based database. An application that leverages SQL is—in principle—portable. We should be able to use MySQL or PostgreSQL as our database instead of SQLite without making dramatic changes to our Python application.

While there are several applicable standards for SQL, each implementation seems to suffer from its own particular problems. SQL-based applications are therefore rarely perfectly portable between database platforms.

SQL databases require a formal schema definition. This means that SQL applications must always include some provision for creating or confirming the schema. As in the previous example, we'll work with a database that has a single table with two columns: a non-unique key which is the initial letter of a word, and the word which has that initial letter.

Here's the table definition in SQL:

```
CREATE TABLE IF NOT EXISTS word(
    letter VARCHAR(1),
    word VARCHAR(10),
    PRIMARY KEY (letter))
```

This defines a table that has two columns, `letter` and `word`. To find all of the words which have a common first letter, we'll need to retrieve multiple rows from this table. This is a common type of SQL design. It doesn't fit neatly with Python's object-oriented design, a common limitation when using SQL.

We need to execute the SQL `CREATE TABLE` statement to create (or confirm the existence of) the table in a SQLite database. Here's a function that will establish (or confirm) the schema:

```
def schema():
    with SQL.connect("Chapter_10/sqlite.sdb") as db:
```

```
db.execute( """CREATE TABLE IF NOT EXISTS word(
        letter VARCHAR(1),
        word VARCHAR(10),
        PRIMARY KEY (letter))
        """)
```

The essential statement is the `execute()` method of the SQLite connection object. We've provided the SQL with a triple-quoted string. If there's a problem, an exception will be raised.

Here's a function that will load this table with data from a text file:

```
def populate():
    with SQL.connect("Chapter_10/sqlite.sdb") as db:
        db.execute( """DELETE FROM word""" )
        with open("Chapter_10/10letterwords.txt") as source:
            txt_stripped= (l.strip() for l in source)
            txt_non_empty= (l for l in txt_stripped
                            if l and not l.startswith("Tool") )
            for word in txt_non_empty:
                db.execute( """INSERT INTO WORD(letter, word)
                        VALUES (:1, :2)""", (word[0], word) )
```

Note that we begin by deleting all the rows from the `word` table. This parallels the way that our previous example worked by creating a fresh, empty `shelve` database. There may be high overheads in creating an empty SQL database; this example expects an established database with a table already defined, and deletes rows from the defined table.

As with the previous example, we've used two generator expressions to filter out these lines of junk from the input file. The loop traverses the words generated by the `no_summary` expression. The suite executes a SQL `INSERT` statement binding two values for the `letter` and `word` columns of the table. This statement creates a new row in the word table in our database.

To see counts of words which begin with a given letter, we can use SQL aggregation. We would execute the following `SELECT` statement.

```
SELECT letter, COUNT(*) FROM word GROUP BY letter
```

When we execute this, we get a SQL iterator (called a "cursor") that yields a sequence of two-tuples based on the `SELECT` clause. Each tuple will have the letter and the number of words that share that letter. We can use this to display a summary of counts of words with a given initial letter.

Using object-relational mapping

Many popular SQL databases offer Python drivers. Some have better levels of support than others. When working with SQL databases, it's sometimes difficult to locate SQL syntax that is effective and portable. A feature on one database may be a problem on another.

More importantly, however, there's a mismatch between the completely flat column-and-row structure of a SQL table and the requirements of more complex class definitions in an object-oriented language like Python. This impedance mismatch is often addressed with an **object-relational mapping (ORM)** package. Two popular packages are SQLAlchemy or SQLObject.

These packages help with the mapping of complex objects to simple SQL tables. It also helps by divorcing the application programming for the details of a particular SQL database.

Databases which don't use SQL, such as `shelve`, MongoDB, CouchDB, and other NoSQL databases, don't have the same object-relational impedance mismatch problem that SQL databases have. We have many choices for persistence technology; Python can be used with a wide variety of databases.

Web services and Internet protocols

As we noted earlier, many TCP/IP protocols, like HTTP, depend on the socket abstraction. Sockets are designed to be file-like: we can use ordinary file operations to read or write a socket. At a very low level, we can use the Python `socket` module. We can create, read, and write sockets to connect client and server programs.

Rather than work directly with sockets, however, we'll make use of higher-level modules, such as `urllib` and `http.client`. These give us the client-side operations of the HTTP protocol, allowing us to connect to a web server, make requests, and get replies. We looked briefly at the `http.client` module in the previous *Closing file-like objects with contextlib* section.

To implement a server, we can use `http.server`. In practice, though, we'll often leverage a frontend application, such as Apache HTTPD or NGINX, to provide the static content of a website. For the dynamic content, we'll often use a WSGI gateway to pass web requests from the frontend to a Python framework. There are several Python web server frameworks, each with a variety of features, strengths, and weaknesses.

Physical format considerations

The Python library offers us a number of modules to help process common physical file formats. *Chapter 13, File Formats*, of the *Python Standard Library* describes file compression and archiving; this includes modules to handle files compressed using zip or BZip2. *Chapter 14, Cryptographic Services* describes modules which handle file formats such as CSV, configuration files, and PLIST files. *Chapter 19, Structured Markup Processing Tools* describes Internet data handling, which includes the JSON file format. *Chapter 20, Internet Protocols and Support* describes modules to handle markup languages such as HTML and XML. For modules that are not part of the standard library, the **Python Package Index** (**PyPI**) may have a package that handles the file format. See `http://pypi.python.org`.

We'll look quickly at the CSV module because it is often used when working on "big data" problems. For example, the Apache Hadoop software library — a framework that allows for the distributed processing of large datasets — leverages simple programming models. We can use Python with Hadoop streaming.

A Hadoop file is often a CSV-formatted file. In some instances, it will have "|" instead of a comma, and quoting or escapes won't be used. In other cases, an `\x01` (ASCII SOH) character could be used as a separator. This is relatively simple to handle with the Python CSV module.

When we create a CSV file from a spreadsheet, the first row may have header information. This can be very helpful. The `csv.DictReader()` class uses the first line of a CSV file as the header. Each remaining line is transformed into a `dict`. The keys in this `dict` will be the column names from the first line.

When working with other CSV files, a header line may not be present. This means that we'll need a separate schema definition to determine the meaning of each column. In most cases, we can simply represent the schema as a list or tuple of column names.

We might have a line like this to provide the missing column names:

```
TEST_LOG_SUMMARY = (
    "module", "datetime", "tests_run", "failures",
    "errors", "skipped", "time_elapsed",
)
```

This gives us pleasant Python-friendly column names in a simple tuple. We've included a gratuitous comma at the end of the items in the tuple to make it easier to add new columns without getting a syntax error. In general, we can simply put this into a file and import this schema definition.

Let's assume that we have a function named `log_parser()` that can parse a complex log file to extract the fields shown earlier. This function will use regular expressions to locate lines with the test results, the module name, and the time stamp in the log. The data from a log will be used to build a simple dictionary with the keys defined by the `TEST_LOG_SUMMARY` global variable. The parser will return a sequence of `dict` objects which looks like this:

```
{'module': 'com.mycompany.app.AppTest', 'errors': '0', 'time_elapsed':
'0', 'failures': '0', 'datetime': 'Thu Oct 06 08:12:17 MDT 2005',
'tests_run': '1'}
```

We can use this `log_parser()` function to write a CSV summary file from a log. We'll call this function `mapper()` because it maps a sequence of filenames to file to a sequence of data rows, preserving the relevant details:

```
def mapper(name_iter, result):
    writer= csv.DictWriter(result, fieldnames=TEST_LOG_SUMMARY,
delimiter='|')
    for name in name_iter:
        with open(name) as source:
            writer.writerow( log_parser(source) )
```

This function expects two parameters: an iterator which yields log file names, and an open file into which the results are written. This function will create a CSV `DictWriter` object using the output file, the set of field names that will be part of each dictionary to be written, and finally, a delimiter.

For each name, the log is opened and parsed. The results of the parse, `dict`, are written to the CSV file to summarize the processing. We might use this function in a script that looks like this:

```
mapper(glob.glob("Chapter_10/log_*.txt"), sys.stdout)
```

We've written the output to the OS standard out. This allows us to pipe these results into a separate program which computes statistics on the log summaries. We might call the statistical summary a reducer, since it reduces a large number of values to single results. The reducer would share the `TEST_LOG_SUMMARY` variable to assure that both programs agree on the content of the file that passes between them.

Summary

In this chapter, we've seen how we can use Python exceptions to write programs which work with files of various kinds. We've focused on text files, since they are easy to work with. We've also looked at parsing binary files, which often require support from the `struct` module.

A file is also a context manager. The best practice is to use files in a `with` statement so that the file is closed properly and all OS resources are released. In a command-line program, this may not be that important; in long-running servers, it's absolutely essential to be sure that resources don't leak from improperly closed files.

We've also looked at more complex persistence mechanisms, including the `shelve` module and the SQLite database. These provide us with ways to perform CRUD operations on data objects in a file. The SQLite database requires us to use the SQL language to describe data access: this can make our programs more portable to other databases. It can also be confusing to leverage SQL in addition to Python. We can overcome that small problem by using a library such as SQLAlchemy so that we can work entirely in Python, and leave it to SQLAlchemy to create the SQL appropriate for our database.

The standard library has numerous packages to handle different physical file formats. One of these can help to create and retrieve data in the CSV format. The role of the comma delimiter can be any sequence of characters, extending the concept so that many kinds of delimited files can be read or written by this module.

In *Chapter 11, Class Definitions*, we'll look at how we can define our own customized classes in Python. Class definitions are the heart of object-oriented programming. We'll touch on several of the class design patterns that are common in Python programming.

11
Class Definitions

A Python object is an instance of a class. A **class** defines the behavior of an object via the method functions. In this chapter, we'll look at creating our own classes and our own objects. We'll start by looking at the basics of creating classes and objects. Once we've seen the essential tools, we can summarize some of the ways that we can class definitions to create objects, and how objects should interact to create the behavior we intend.

We'll look at some elements of more sophisticated class definition. Advanced topics will include the concepts of class methods and static methods. An entire book can be written on advanced object-oriented programming in Python, so we'll take a broad, but shallow, approach to looking at class definitions.

We'll also look at the built-in abstract base classes. We can use these to simplify our own class definitions. In many cases, we have container-like classes that can leverage a base class, saving us some programming and assuring a seamless fit with other Python features.

Creating a class

The core of the object-oriented program is the class definition. The class statement creates an object that is used to create instances of the class. When we create a new class, `SomeClass`, we can then use that `SomeClass()` function to create objects that share the common definitions of the class. This is the way the built-in classes all work; for example, the `int()` function creates an instance of the `int` class.

In Python, a `class` statement includes the method functions that describe the behavior of each instance. In addition to ordinary methods, there are several varieties of "special" methods which are intimately bound to the way Python operates.

We aren't obligated — in any formal way — to provide specific attributes (also called instance variables) for a class. The instance variables of an object are flexible, and are not defined in advance.

The initial clause of a `class` statement provides the class name. It can also name any superclasses, from which features are inherited. The bulk of the class body contains method definitions, created with the indented `def` statements.

In some cases, we don't need to provide a suite of statements. We often create customized exception classes like this

```
class MyAppError(Exception):
    pass
```

In this example, we've provided a new class name, `MyAppError`, and specified that it inherits the features of the `Exception` class. We don't need to make any changes to that base definition; since we must provide an indented suite of statements, we use the pass statement to complete the syntax of the `class` statement.

Since this class works like any other exception, we can use statements like `raise MyAppError("Some Message")` to raise an instance of this new class of exceptions.

Writing the suite of statements in a class

The suite of statements inside a `class` statement is generally a collection of method definitions. Each method is a function that's bound to the class. The suite of statements can also include assignment statements; these will create variables that are part of the class definition as a whole.

Here's a simple class for an (x, y) coordinate pair:

```
class Point:
    """
    Point on a plane.
    """
    def __init__(self, x, y):
        self.x= x
        self.y= y
    def __repr__(self):
        return "{cls}({x:.0f}, {y:.0f})".format(
            cls=self.__class__.__name__, x=self.x, y=self.y)
```

We've provided a class name, `Point`. We haven't explicitly provided a superclass; by default our new class will be a subclass of `object`. By convention, the names of most built-in classes, like `object`, begin with lowercase letters. All of the other classes that we will define should begin with uppercase letters; hence, our name of `Point`. We've also provided a minimal docstring for this class. In *Chapter 14, Fit and Finish – Unit Testing, Packaging, and Documentation*, we'll look at expanding this docstring.

We've defined two methods in the class. The first has a special name of `__init__()`. The first parameter to any method defined within a class must include the instance variable. This variable, usually `self`, will be the reference to the relevant object. When we assign a value to the variable `self.x`, this will set the x attribute of a specific instance of the `Point` class. The instance variable is provided implicitly when the method is called.

Instead of any formal definition of the allowed instance variables, Python relies on the `__init__()` special method to initialize appropriate instance variables. By default, an object can have additional attributes added at any time.

The second method has a special name of `__repr__()`. To be a proper method, the first parameter must be the instance variable, `self`. This method must return a string that represents our coordinate pair. If we don't override this special method, we'll get a default string representation that looks like this: `<__main__.Point object at 0x100623e10>`. Our implementation uses `self.__class__.__name__` to leverage the class of an object so that any subclass will have the proper class name inserted into the resulting output.

Special method names are ubiquitous in Python. Using them allows a seamless integration between our classes and built-in Python features. There are a large number of special method names—too many to review in this book. All such names begin and end with `__` (two underscores). It's easy to avoid conflicts with this naming convention. There is no good reason to use `__` names that are part of our application programming; any name in this form that we choose may turn out to be a hidden feature of Python.

Note that we did not include placeholder docstrings on the two method functions. We've omitted them to keep the example short, and focused on class definitions. In general, every method of a class will have a docstring to provide a pithy, helpful summary of that method.

In *Chapter 4, Variables, Assignment and Scoping Rules*, we introduced the concept of a namespace as a container for variables. The `self` variable is the object, which is a namespace into which we can insert attribute variables.

We can create an instance of a class like this:

```
>>> p_1 = Point(22, 7)
>>> p_1.x
22
>>> p_1.y
7
```

We've used the class name, `Point`, like a function. An empty object is created first. Then the argument values are provided to the __init__() special method to initialize that empty object. Note that we did not explicitly provide a value for the instance variable, `self`.

To execute the __repr__() special method, we can do this:

```
>>> p_1
Point(22, 7)
```

When an object is printed, the built-in `repr()` function is applied to get a string representation of the object. This built-in function relies on the __repr__() special method of an object to provide a string representation for the object. The object, p_1, was implicitly assigned to the instance variable, `self`, when evaluating the __repr__() method.

Our implementation of the __repr__() special method produced a string with the *x* and *y* coordinate values. We used `.0f` as the format specification, providing zero places to the right of the decimal point for the `x` and `y` attributes of the self instance variable.

Using instance variables and methods

The `Point` class definition in the previous section included only two special methods. We'll now add a third method that's not special. Here's the third method for this class:

```
def dist(self, point):
    return math.hypot(self.x-point.x, self.y-point.y)
```

This method function accepts a single parameter, named `point`. The body of this method function uses `math.hypot()` to compute the direct distance between two points on the same plane.

Here's how we can use this function:

```
>>> p_1 = Point(22, 7)
>>> p_2 = Point(20, 5)
>>> round(p_1.dist(p_2),4)
2.8284
```

We've created two `Point` objects. When the `p_1.dist(p_2)` expression is evaluated, the object that was assigned to the `p_1` variable will be assigned to the `self` variable. This is the instance of `Point` that's doing the relevant processing. The argument to the `dist()` method, assigned to the `p_2` variable, will be assigned to the `point` parameter variable.

 When we evaluate `obj.method()`, the `obj` object will be the `self` instance variable.

By default, the objects we create are mutable. Here's another method of the `Point` object — this changes the internal state:

```
def offset(self, d_x, d_y):
    self.x += d_x
    self.y += d_y
```

This method requires two values which are used to offset the coordinates of the `Point` object. The method assigns new values to the `x` and `y` attributes of the object.

Here's what happens when we use this method:

```
>>> p_1.offset(-3, 3)
>>> p_1.x
19
>>> p_1.y
10
```

We've evaluated the offset method associated with object `p_1`. As noted earlier, the `self` instance variable will be the same object referred to by `p_1`. When we assign a value to `self.x`, that will mutate the object referred to by `p_1`, setting `p_1.x`.

Pythonic object-oriented programming

We've seen a few important features of Python's approach to object-orientation. Perhaps the most important is that Python lacks a static binding between variable name and type; any type of object can be assigned to any variable. Names are not resolved statically by a compiler. Python's dynamic name resolution means that we can think of our programs as being entirely generic with respect to class.

When we evaluate `obj.attribute` or `obj.method()`, there are two steps. First the name, `attribute` or `method`, must be resolved. Second the referenced attribute or method is evaluated.

For the name resolution step, there are several namespaces that are searched to determine what the name means.

- The local namespace of the `obj` instance is searched to resolve the name. The object's namespace is available as `obj.__dict__`. Attribute names (and values) are generally found in the object's own namespace. Methods, on the other hand, are not generally part of an object instance.

- If the name isn't local to the object, the local namespace of the object's class is searched. The class namespace is available as `obj.__class__.__dict__`. Method names are generally found in the class's namespace. An attribute of the class may also be found here.

- If the name isn't in the class, the superclasses are searched for the name. The entire lattice of superclasses is assembled into the `obj.__class__.__mro__` value. This defines the **Method Resolution Order** (**MRO**); each of the classes in this sequence is searched for the name.

Once the name has been found, Python must determine the value. For names that do not refer to callable methods, that is, attributes — the object referred to by the name is the value of the attribute. A name that refers to a callable method will have argument values bound and it will be evaluated as a function. The result of that function is the value.

The "search" described previously relies on the built-in `dict` class. This uses hashing to make an extremely fast determination of the presence or absence of a name. There's remarkably little performance cost from the sophisticated and flexible class behavior available in Python.

If an object of an inappropriate type is provided at run-time, a method name or attribute name won't be found in the object, and an `AttributeError` exception is raised. In our preceding example, we can try to evaluate `p_1.copy()`. The `copy` name is not defined in our class nor any of the superclasses, so an `AttributeError` exception is raised.

Trying to do type casting

While Python variables are merely names attached to objects, the underlying objects are very strongly typed. There's no way to assign a new value to the `__class__` name that defines the class of an object.

Type casts are required by some statically-compiled languages to make it possible to create generic data structures. In those languages, we can cast a reference from one type to another type. Because of the dynamic nature of method resolution, there's no need for this kind of type casting in Python.

All Python collections can contain objects of mixed types. We can easily evaluate this:

```
>>> map(lambda x:x+1, [1, 2.3, (4+5j)])
```

The lambda expression, `x+1`, can be applied to an `int`, a `float`, or a `complex` type without resorting to any kind of type cast operation. This works because each class provides appropriate special method functions to implement the addition of an integer.

Designing for encapsulation and privacy

A common question about Python class definitions is how we can achieve **encapsulation** if all attribute and member names are public. Some programmers worry about this:

```
>>> p_2 = Point(20, 5)
>>> p_2.y = 6
>>> p_2
(20, 6)
```

We've created an object, `p_2`. Then we modified an attribute value of the object without using any of the object's method functions. This is not a failure to use the encapsulation design principle: the class has a properly encapsulated design. The class doesn't have an implementation that can be checked statically by a compiler.

The Pythonic principle is summarized with the following observation:

We're all adults here.

There's no compelling reason to create the complexity of private, public, and protected methods and attributes of an object, because Python code is distributed as source and anyone can inspect the source to see what the consequences of bending or breaking encapsulation might be. The preferred approach is to write clear docstrings for classes and methods, and to provide unit tests to demonstrate that attributes and methods are being used properly.

We can prefix a name with a single _ to indicate that the method or attribute is not part of the public interface to a class. Python documentation tools will politely ignore these names so that these implementation details can be changed freely. Names that begin with _ are considered to be subject to change without notice; depending on these names may lead to a program breaking in unexpected ways.

In some languages, "getter and setter" methods are required to expose the attributes of a class. In Python, we can use the object's __dict__ directly, simplifying introspection. We can also use the built-in functions getattr(), setattr(), and delattr() to work with attribute names as strings. For example:

```
>>> p_2.__dict__.keys()
dict_keys(['y', 'x'])
>>> getattr(p_2, "x")
20
```

This shows how we can get an attribute's names and values dynamically. In the first example, we looked at the object's internal namespace, __dict__, to get the attributes. In the second example, we used the built-in getattr() function to get the value of an attribute.

Using properties

Python allows us to create methods that can be used as if they were attributes. This gives us very pleasant syntax for getting a derived value from an object. A method that appears to be an attribute is called a **property**. We'll extend our Point class with two more methods:

```
@property
def r(self):
    return math.sqrt(self.x**2 + self.y**2)
@property
def θ(self):
    return math.atan2(self.y, self.x)
```

We've defined two functions using the @property decorator. This decorator can be used with a function that has only the instance variable, self, as a parameter.

Here's how we can use these properties:

```
>>> p = Point(12, 5)
>>> round(p.r, 1)
```

```
13.0
>>> round(math.degrees(p.θ), 1)
22.6
```

We've accessed these methods as if they were simple attributes of the object, p. Using p.r and p.θ can be more pleasant than having to write p.r() and p.θ() in a complex formula. The preceding properties are explicitly *read-only*. We get an exception if we try to assign a value to p.r or p.θ.

We'll return to the topic of the @property decorator in *Chapter 13, Metaprogramming and Decorators.*

Using inheritance to simplify class definitions

We can use **inheritance** — reuse of code from a superclass in subclasses — which can simplify a subclass definition. In an earlier example, we created the MyAppError class as a subclass of Exception. This means that all of the features of Exception will be available to MyAppError. This works because of the three-step search for a name: if a method name is not found in an object's class, then the superclasses are all searched for the name.

Here's an example of a subclass which overrides just one method of the parent class:

```
class Manhattan_Point(Point):
    def dist(self, point):
        return abs(self.x-point.x)+abs(self.y-point.y)
```

We've defined a subclass of Point named Manhattan_Point. This class has all of the features of a Point. It makes a single change to the parent class. It provides a definition for the dist() method that will override the definition in the Point superclass.

Here's an example that shows how method resolution works:

```
>>> p_1 = Point(22, 7)
>>> p_2 = Manhattan_Point(20, 5)
>>> round(p_1.dist(p_2),4)
2.8284
>>> round(p_2.dist(p_1),4)
4
```

We've created two objects: p_1 is an instance of Point, and p_2 is an instance of Manhattan_Point. We didn't write the __init__() method of Manhattan_Point; it was inherited from Point. When we evaluate p_1.dist(), we're using the dist() method that's part of p_1's class, Point. When we evaluate p_2.dist(), on the other hand, we're using the dist() method that's part of p_2, which is the method of Manhattan_Point.

Reuse through inheritance is a way to guarantee that several classes have identical behavior. This is an import object-oriented design principle, sometimes called the **Liskov Substitution Principle (LSP)**. An instance of Manhattan_Point can be used anywhere an instance of Point is used.

Using multiple inheritance and the mixin design pattern

Inheritance is sometimes visualized as a simple hierarchy of related classes. If each subclass has at most one parent class, there's a chain of relationships between any given subclass and the object superclass. This single inheritance model isn't always appropriate. In some cases, a class will include a number of disparate features that don't fit the linear ancestry idea.

The collections abstract base class module, collections.abc, contains a number of examples of multiple inheritance. The overall design pattern here is to have a central class hierarchy that defines the essential features of the List, Set, or Mapping collections. Other features are included via reusable **mixin** classes.

For example, the Set class is a subclass of Container. Mixed into this definition are features from the Sized and Iterable class definitions. The Sized mixin incorporates the __len__() special method. The Iterable mixin incorporates the __iter__() special method.

This leads to the final class being an assembly of reusable superclasses. We can leverage this to create our own classes which contain different mixtures of features.

Python manages multiple inheritance by relying on the order in which classes are named in the class statement. This builds the __mro__ value used to search for names in the inheritance lattice. Here's an example:

```
>>> from collections.abc import Mapping
>>> Mapping.__mro__
(<class 'collections.abc.Mapping'>, <class
'collections.abc.Sized'>,
```

```
<class 'collections.abc.Iterable'>, <class
'collections.abc.Container'>,
<class 'object'>)
```

We've imported one of the abstract base classes. When we look at the MRO, we see that Python will search for a name in `Mapping`, `Sized`, `Iterable`, `Container`, and `object`, in that order.

When designing with mixin classes like this, we generally divide responsibility among the various classes so that we avoid any name collisions between the various superclasses that are used to assemble the final class definition.

Using class methods and attributes

Generally, we expect objects to be stateful and classes to be stateless. While typical, a stateless class is not a requirement. We can create class objects which have attributes as well as methods. A class can also have mutable attributes, in the rare cases that this is necessary.

One use for class variables is to create parameters that apply to all instances of the class. When a name is not resolved by the object instance, the class is searched next. Here is a small hierarchy of classes that rely on a class-level attribute:

```
class Units(float):
    units= None
    def __repr__(self):
        text = super().__repr__()
        return "{0} {1}".format(text, self.units)

class Height(Units):
    units= "inches"
```

The `Units` class definition extends the `float` class. It introduces a class-level attribute named `units`. It overrides the `__repr__()` special method of `float`. This method uses the superclass `__repr__()` method to get the essential text representation of a value. It then includes the value of the `units` attribute.

When we evaluate `self.units`, there will be a three-step search for this name. An instance of `Height` will not provide the `units` attribute. The `Height` class, however, will provide the `units` attribute; the value will be `inches`.

When we create an instance of a `Height` object, we'll see the units:

```
>>> Height(61.5)
61.5 inches
```

When we print an instance of `Height`, the `print()` function will use the built-in `repr()` function to get a string representation. The `repr()` function uses the `__repr__()` special method of an object. We've overridden the `__repr__()` special method to include the text from the `units` attribute.

Since all attributes are publicly available, we can write something like `Height.units= "furlongs"`, which will cause all further uses of objects of the `Height` class to display different units. Changing the class level attributes is generally a bad idea, but it is not prohibited in any formal way.

Recall the policy: *We're all adults here.*

Using mutable class variables

Some applications may call for a properly mutable variable that's part of an overall class. A class-level attribute name is found during the three-step search for a name: first the object, then the class, then the superclasses. This means that we can successfully evaluate `self.class_level_name`, even if the name is not in the object instance, but is defined in the class or one of the parent superclasses.

If we try to assign a class-level variable, however, using a name like `self.class_level_name`, we'll be creating a new attribute in the instance. The class-level name will no longer be visible because the instance name will now be found first.

If we want to update a class-level variable, we must explicitly use the class name, avoiding the self instance variable. Here's a class which assigns a sequence number to each instance that is created:

```
class Sample:
    counter= 0
    def __init__(self, measure):
        Sample.counter += 1
        self.sequence = Sample.counter
        self.measure = measure
```

We have created a class-level variable, `counter`, which is initialized to zero when the class is created. The `__init__()` method will increment the class-level `counter` attribute. In order to avoid creating a variable in the instance, the class name, `Sample`, is used instead of `self`. In addition to updating `Sample.counter`, this method also sets two attributes of the instance: the current value of `Sample.counter` is assigned to the sequence attribute, and the given value for the measure is also saved.

It's essential to note that, inside a method function, we can use `self.counter` and `Sample.counter` to access the same object. This will be true when there's no instance variable named `counter`. In order to assign a variable in the class, however, we can only use `Sample.counter`.

Writing static methods

In some cases, we'll include a method in a class that does not actually depend on any instance variables. In many languages, this kind of method is called **static**. Using the word *static* to refer to class-level features comes from C++ and Java; it has also been adopted for Python.

We don't have any syntax complications for class-level attributes. As we've seen in previous examples, any attribute that's not part of the instance will be searched for in the class; the distinction between instance variables and class variables doesn't require any additional syntax.

A class-level method, however, cannot have an instance variable as the first defined parameter. This is an important syntactic change. We use the `@staticmethod` decorator to annotate methods that do not have an instance variable.

We'll expand the `Sample` class shown earlier to include a validity check. Checking for validity isn't a proper instance method: we should not create an instance with invalid values. We'll add this method to the class:

```
@staticmethod
def validate(measure):
    m= float(measure)
    if 0 <= m < 12:
        pass
    else:
        raise ValueError("Out of range")
```

We've marked this method with the `@staticmethod` decorator. The method does not have a `self` variable, since it doesn't apply to an instance of the class. This method can only be invoked via `Sample.validate(some_value)`. The method will confirm that the value of the `measure` parameter is valid, or it will raise an exception which details the reason why the value is invalid.

We might use this method to create and use an instance of the `Sample` object:

```
try:
    Sample.validate(some_data)
    s= Sample(some_data)
    ... etc. ...
except Exception as ex:
    print(ex)
```

We'll start the `try` statement by simply evaluating the `Sample.validate()` method. If this method does not raise an exception, the given value is valid. If this method does raise an exception, we'll write an error message and continue processing. Often, we'll have this kind of processing in a file input loop: we'll process good data and write messages about bad data to the log.

Python also offers a `@classmethod` decorator. This is a more specialized tool. It provides the class as an argument instead of the instance. It allows us to write a method that can work with a variety of classes. This might be used in a metaclass.

We'll return to the topic of decorators in *Chapter 13, Metaprogramming and Decorators*.

Using __slots__ to save storage

The default behavior of the `object` superclass is to create a `dict` for an object's attributes. This provides fast resolution of names. It means that an object can have attributes added and changed very freely. Because a hash is used to locate the attribute by name, the internal `dict` object can consume quite a bit of memory.

We can modify the behavior of the `object` superclass by providing a list of specific attribute names when we create a class. When we assign these names to the specially named __slots__ variable, these will be the only available attributes. A `dict` is not created, and memory use is reduced considerably.

If we're working with very large datasets, we might need to use a class that looks like this:

```
class SmallSample:
    counter= 0
    __slots__ = ["sequence", "measure"]
    def __init__(self, measure):
        SmallSample.counter += 1
        self.sequence = SmallSample.counter
        self.measure = measure
```

This class uses the __slots__ attribute to define the only two attributes that can be used for an instance. This avoids using a dict to represent the attributes of instances of this class.

The ABCs of abstract base classes

In *Chapter 6, More Complex Data Types*, we looked at the collections module, which offers a number of variations on the mapping theme. These different kinds of collections are built on a foundation of abstract base classes, defined in the collections.abc module. Looking at this module exposes the common features, and the differences, among the collections.

We can see how Sequence is the basis for the built-in tuple class, and MutableSequence is the basis for the built-in list. The Set abstract base class is the basis for the frozenset built-in class, and MutableSet is the basis for the set class. There's no concrete implementation of the Mapping class, but the dict class is the built-in implementation of the MutableMapping class.

If we need to implement a unique kind of collection, one not already provided by the collection module, we're encouraged to use the collections.abc module as a starting point. If we leverage these common base classes, we're assured that our new collection will fit seamlessly with other Python features.

Writing a callable class

The abstract base class Callable is defined in the collections.abc module. This class doesn't seem to have much to do with collections. It's a useful abstraction, nonetheless.

A class that derives from Callable must define the __call__() special method. The objects created from this class are callable, and can be used as if they were functions. This allows us to create fairly complex functions based on a class definition.

Here's a function to compute the *n*th Fibonacci number. There are three relevant rules for computing this value:

$$F_0 = 0$$
$$F_1 = 1$$
$$F_n = F_{n-1} + F_{n-2}$$

The first two Fibonacci numbers are defined as zero and one. Other Fibonacci numbers are the sum of the two preceding numbers. If we use a naïve algorithm, it's quite expensive to compute a large Fibonacci number. We can, however, define a `Callable` that uses an internal cache to reduce the workload to a manageable level. This technique is called **memoization**.

The class definition for a `Callable` looks like this:

```
from collections.abc import Callable
class Fibonacci(Callable):
    def __init__(self):
        self.cache= {0: 0, 1: 1}
    def __call__(self, n):
        if n not in self.cache:
            self.cache[n]= self.__call__(n-1) + self.__call__(n-2)
        return self.cache[n]
```

We've defined a class, `Fibonacci`, which extends the `Callable` abstract base class. The `__init__()` method initializes a cache with two defined values for Fibonacci numbers. The `__call__()` method only computes a Fibonacci number, n, if the number is not already in the cache. It does this by recursive calls to compute Fibonacci numbers n-1 and n-2. Once the result is in the cache, it can be returned.

When we create an instance of this class, we have created a callable function. Given that function, we can compute Fibonacci numbers. Here's an example:

```
>>> fib= Fibonacci()
>>> fib(7)
13
```

We've created an instance of the `Fibonacci` class, and assigned this to the variable `fib`. The `fib` object is callable; when we evaluate it with an argument value of six, we get the seventh Fibonacci number.

Summary

In this chapter, we've seen the basics of defining a class and using objects of that class. We've looked at how we create the methods that define the behavior of a class. The internal state of the class is the result of the various methods: in Python we don't formally declare instance variables. We generally rely in the __init__() method to provide the initial or default values for the object's state.

We've looked at the way Python resolves attribute and method names by searching the object, the class, and then the superclasses. The method resolution order is based on the order the classes are presented in the initial class statement.

The @properties decorator can be used to create methods that have the same syntax as an attribute. This can help clarify otherwise complex algorithms. We've also looked at the @staticmethod decorator, which is used to create methods that belong to the class as a whole and are independent of any specific instance of the class.

In order to save some memory, we can use the __slots__ variable. This will construct an object that isn't based on a dict for storing attributes. The object is quite a bit smaller, but also suffers from some limitations.

We also looked at how we can create a callable object. This is an object that can be used like a function, but has all of the powerful features of an object.

In *Chapter 12, Scripts, Modules, Packages, Libraries, and Applications*, we'll look at how we can package our functions and classes into modules. We'll see how modules are grouped into packages. The *Python Standard Library* is a collection of packages that we install with Python. We'll look at the tiny distinctions between modules and script files, and how we can create more complete Python applications.

12
Scripts, Modules, Packages, Libraries, and Applications

While it's easy to work with Python at the **Read-Evaluate-Print Loop (REPL)** >>> prompt, our real goal is to create Python application files. A Python file may be a script, which means it should be able to do some useful work when it's executed by the Python program. A file may be a module, which means that it is designed to be imported to provide useful definitions. A directory of Python modules is a **package**. These are formal definitions, implemented by the language.

More generic terms like **library**, **application**, or **framework** aren't formalized by the language. We have ways to implement these common concepts in Python. We can think of a collection of modules or packages as a library. The *Python Standard Library*, for example, is a large collection of modules and packages. An "application" will be at least a script. A more complex application may involve a script plus several additional modules and packages. A framework will be a Python application into which we'll inject our customized modules or packages. Many frameworks will also include non-Python files: a web framework may include a great deal of HTML and CSS; a GUI framework may include image files and fonts.

We'll look at creating and running script files. We'll also look at creating modules and packages of modules. Finally, we'll look at a very clever Python feature that allows us to write a script that can also be used as a module. This design pattern allows us to build composite applications that are based on other applications.

Script file rules

A Python script file must adhere to only one simple rule: *it must be pure text*. In some cases, a poorly-chosen filename can lead to problems, so we'll add two recommendations that are often helpful:

- The content must be pure text; ideally encoded in UTF-8, although ASCII is also popular.
- The filename should follow the Python identifier rules. It should start with a letter and use only letters, digits, and the _ character. Filenames that begin and end with __ (two underscores) are reserved and have special meanings for Python.
- The extension should be .py.

The two additional recommendations are essential for writing modules and packages, but are not required to write a simple script.

A script is simply a sequence of statements; it's identical to what we might do at the REPL prompt with only one difference: a script has no implicit printed output. We must use the print() function in a script to see any results. In larger applications, we often use the logging module to produce more sophisticated output. In some cases, we'll carefully replace all the print() functions we put into an early technology spike with logging.debug() functions as our application matures.

To run a script, we need to provide it as input to the Python program. We'll look at three common ways to do this.

Running a script by the filename

The most common way to run a script is to provide the filename to the Python command. Let's assume we have a file with the unpleasant name of ch12_script1. py in a directory named Chapter_12.

In Linux and Mac OS X, the full name will be Chapter_12/ch12_script1.py. In Windows, the full filename will be Chapter_12\ch12_script1.py. We'll stick with the Linux standard filenames for the remaining examples.

Here's how we can run a script by giving the filename:

```
MacBookPro-SLott:Code slott$ python3 Chapter_12/ch12_script1.py
Temperature °C: 8
C=8°, F=46°
```

This output shows the OS prompt. The `python3` command that we entered is highlighted. The prompts and the outputs from the script are also shown. This example is typical for an OS that uses Python 2 internally; we have to distinguish our new Python 3 from the OS's internal `python` command.

The application prompted us, and we entered a temperature of 8. The output shows that 8°C is about 46°F. We'll need to wear a coat.

The script file, `ch12_script1.py`, looks like this:

```
c= float(input("Temperature °C: "))
f = 32+9*c/5
print("C={c:.0f}°,  F={f:.0f}°".format(c=c,f=f))
```

The script uses the `input()` function to prompt an interactive user at the console. The output is displayed with the simple `print()` function.

We've kept the script small to emphasize ways that scripts can be run. There are numerous **user experience (UX)** issues with this, but that is not the focus of this section.

Running a script by its module name

In most cases, our scripts can either be installed in the `site-packages` directory inside the Python library, or we can extend the Python path using the `PYTHONPATH` environment variable to include the location of our scripts. Either of these approaches makes a script file visible on Python's search path.

To install a script in `site-packages`, we can rely on Python's `distutils` package. We'll create a `setup.py` file, which describes the module we'd like to install. We can then run `python3 setup.py install` to have our module placed into the `site-packages` directory. Installers like `pip` and `easy-install` require use of `distutils` following this standard pattern.

We can also locate the `site-packages` directory and manually copy our module into that directory. This location varies from OS to OS. This directory is the last item in the `sys.path` variable.

Setting the `PYTHONPATH` environment variable is another alternative. We can use the Linux `export` command to make a change to environment variables. We often put this in our `~/.bash_profile` file. For Windows, we have to make a change to the advanced system settings where the environment variables are set. We can easily create private libraries with many modules, made visible via the `PYTHONPATH` variable.

Once our module is visible on Python's search path, we can execute the module like this:

```
MacBookPro-SLott:Code slott$ python3 -m Chapter_12.ch12_script1
Temperature °C: 8
C=8°, F=46°
```

When we provide the -m option, we're naming a module to be executed. In this example, we've used a qualified name: Chapter_12 is a package and ch12_script1 is the module within that package. We'll look at packages in the later sections; packages are essentially the directories in which module files can be found.

Running a script using OS shell rules

The third way that we can run a script is by making the script file executable and including an OS association between the script file and the Python3 program.

In Linux and Mac OS X, the file association is set by the first line of the file. We'll often use something like this as the first line in a file, to associate a given .py file and the Python3 program:

```
#!/usr/bin/env python3
```

This will use the OS env program to locate and start the python3 environment. The shell will provide the entire file as input to the program named on a #! line. This means that the env program will be started with the script file as input. The env program will prepare the environment and then hand the file to the Python3 program.

To mark a file as executable in Linux and Mac OS X, we use the chmod +x command. We can do this to mark our script as executable:

```
MacBookPro-SLott:Code slott$ chmod +x Chapter_12/ch12_script1.py
```

This command will add the execute, x, option to the file's mode. When we do an ls -l, we'll see this as part of the file's details.

In Windows, all files are considered executable. The association between file extension and program is done through the Windows Control Panel. The setting was put in place when you installed Python.

Once the file is marked as executable, we can run it simply by providing the name:

```
MacBookPro-SLott:Code slott$ Chapter_12/ch12_script1.py
```

Under Windows, the file extension of `.py` is bound to the Python program, and Windows will launch Python providing this filename as input. The binding of filename to script is outside the application.

Under Linux and Mac OS X, the processing is based on the magical first line of the file. The Linux shell checks the file's mode to see that it's executable. It then reads the first few bytes of the file. In this case, the first few bytes are `#!`, which marks the file as a script. The first full line of a script includes the command that must be used to process this script. In this case, the command is `/usr/bin/env python3`. The shell launches this program with the given file as input.

Choosing good script names

Script names should be kept short and meaningful. As with filenames, it's generally best practice to avoid complex prefixes and suffixes. The Linux or Windows DOS commands provide some guidance on what makes a good (and bad) name for a script. One of the best examples is the `git` command, which has numerous subcommands. Rather than invent dozens of complex-looking names, **git** uses a simple command name as a prefix.

The `argparse` module, used for parsing command-line arguments, supports this nicely. We can define a few common arguments that apply to all subcommands. We can also define arguments that are unique to each subcommand.

In order to keep the code for this book organized by the publishing pipeline, the script names are long. The redundancy in these names (`Chapter_12/ch12_...`) is not the best practice, and should be avoided where possible. As with variable names and function names, script names should be kept reasonably short and meaningful.

Creating a reusable module

In Python, the module is the unit of software reuse. When we have a feature that must appear in more than one script, we'll put this feature into a module and import that module into each script that shares the feature.

It's important to note two slightly different senses of the word "reuse" as follows:

- We can define a class hierarchy to achieve localized reuse within an application. Inheritance is an elegant way to share code among related objects. Often we'll define all of these related classes in a single module file.
- We can define a module to achieve a less local reuse across applications.

To create a module that can be imported, we merely have to be sure that a Python file is visible in a directory that's part of the Python search path. Since the local directory is always visible, we can create a module simply by creating a file in the current working directory.

A module designed for import should consist mostly of `import`, `class`, and `def` statements. We can also use assignment statements to create module global variables, but we need to be cautious of how much processing is done. Any name that's created (via assignment, `class`, `def`, or `import`) will be in that module's namespace.

A module is only imported once. The `import` implementation checks a global cache of loaded modules, visible as `sys.modules`, to see if the module is known. Because of this, a module that actually does some kind of processing will only do it once. After that, the import is ignored. This behavior makes it easy to create a global **Singleton** object inside an imported module.

Examples of modules that do significant processing on `import` are `this` and `antigravity`. When we execute `import this` or `import antigravity`, these modules will immediately do some interesting processing. After having been imported once, they won't do this again. While handy in some specialized situations, it's not a general pattern to follow.

> We generally expect an `import` statement to provide definitions of classes, functions, and module global variables.
>
> We don't generally expect an `import` statement to do useful processing.

A module may define a unique exception. We might want to create a generic exception class named `Error` in a module. It would look like this:

```
class Error(Exception): pass
```

Because this name will be qualified by the module name when the module is imported, we are able to reference this exception via `some_module.Error`. It might look like this:

```
import some_module
try:
    some_module.some_function()
except some_module.Error as e:
    logger.exception("some_function broke: {0}".format(e))
```

The module name, `some_module`, acts as a nice qualifier to show the origin of the `Error` class definition. We don't need to give the `Error` class a more complex, globally unique name.

Creating a hybrid library/application module

A script may import modules, perhaps define some functions or classes, but it will always do the relevant processing. Our first example script had just three lines of relevant processing: two assignment statements, and a function statement that printed a result. This shows the Pythonic ideal of having programs without any boilerplate; we try to avoid syntax that's just overhead.

A possible downside of a perfectly clean approach to scripting is that it's difficult to create unit tests. Each unit test would have to invoke the script as a subprocess; something that can involve quite a bit of OS overhead. The goal of unit testing is to isolate each unit—each function, class, module, package, or script—so that it can be tested separately. Having the OS launch the script file doesn't seem to be properly isolated.

Also, as an application matures, a good script may become a component in a larger, and more comprehensive, application. It can become difficult to create a composite application from a script file. It's far easier to create composite processes from functions or classes.

This leads to the following suggested structure for a script:

```
def c_to_f():
    c= float(input("Temperature °C: "))
    f = 32+9*c/5
    print("C={c:.0f}°,  F={f:.0f}°".format(c=c,f=f))

if __name__ == "__main__":
    c_to_f()
```

We've taken our script and wrapped it with a `def` statement to make a function. We've then written an `if` statement that distinguishes between a main script and an imported module by examining the __name__ variable. The `if` statement makes the following conditions:

- When a module is imported, Python sets the global variable __name__ to the actual module name

- When run as a main script, Python sets the global variable __name__ to __main__

This pattern can be used to write library modules which run their own unit tests. We can include the following in a library module that is never used as a main script:

```
if __name__ == "__main__":
    import doctest
    doctest.testmod( verbose=1 )
```

This will run all of the unit tests that are embedded in docstrings. We'll look more closely at testing in *Chapter 14, Fit and Finish – Unit Testing, Packaging, and Documentation*.

Creating a package

A package is a directory that contains module files plus one additional file. Each package must have an __init__.py file. This file must be present and is often empty.

The poem, *Zen of Python*, by Tim Peters, offers the following advice:

> *Flat is better than nested.*

The idea is to organize Python applications into a flat collection of modules to the greatest extent possible. A deeply-nested, complex hierarchy of packages isn't considered helpful.

We can use a package in two ways. We can import a module that's part of a package. The standard library, for example, has an XML package with several XML parser modules. We can use import `xml.etree` to import the `etree` module from the XML package. In this case, the __init__.py file has a comment and a list of sub-packages.

In other cases, we can import the package, as a whole, as if the package were a module. When we write import collections, for example, we're really importing the module `collections/__init__.py`.

The `__init__.py` file is a top-level module for the package as a whole. It can be empty, in which case we can only pick specific modules from within the package. Or the `__init__.py` file may have content, allowing us to import the package as a single complex structure.

Designing alternative implementations

We can easily offer alternative implementations of a given feature. If we want more speed, more accuracy, or less memory use, we should be able to import an alternative definition of a given library.

We can compare the `math` and `cmath` modules for a concrete example of this principle. Here's an example of how they differ:

```
>>> import math
>>> import cmath
>>> math.sqrt(-1)
Traceback (most recent call last):
  File "<stdin>", line 1, in <module>
ValueError: math domain error
>>> cmath.sqrt(-1)
1j
```

The `math` module includes a square root function, which we used as `math.sqrt()`. This produces only real-valued results, and must raise an exception when confronted with an expression that's not real-valued.

The `cmath` module also includes a square root function. The `cmath.sqrt()` function can return complex values instead of raising an exception. Since the packages are so similar, we can substitute one for the other in a variety of ways.

Both of these modules offer a similar set of function definitions. The components within the module have the same names. The modules, which are namespaces, have different names to distinguish the origin of a definition.

This technique is often used to support different platforms. We can create a package with platform-specific modules within the package. The package's top-level `__init__.py` can choose which module to import and provide the platform-specific definitions. We can also use this to write enterprise software that must run in different environments: development, quality assurance, and final production. A single package can include different configuration modules. The standard library `os` package demonstrates this concept.

Seeing the package search path

The Python search path can be seen by importing the `sys` package to see `sys.path`:

```
>>> import sys
>>> sys.path
['', '/Library/Frameworks/Python.framework/Versions/3.3/lib/python3.3/
site-packages/setuptools-2.0.2-py3.3.egg',
..., etc.
'/Library/Frameworks/Python.framework/Versions/3.3/lib/python33.zip',
'/Library/Frameworks/Python.framework/Versions/3.3/lib/python3.3',
'/Library/Frameworks/Python.framework/Versions/3.3/lib/python3.3/plat-
darwin',
'/Library/Frameworks/Python.framework/Versions/3.3/lib/python3.3/lib-
dynload',
'/Library/Frameworks/Python.framework/Versions/3.3/lib/python3.3/site-
packages']
```

We've elided a number of lines from this output to show the essentials of how the standard library fits into the way we develop Python code. This list of places to search for modules is built by the `sites` package when Python starts running.

The zero-length directory name, `''`, is first. This means that the current working directory is the preferred place to locate modules. This allows us to import our own modules from the local directory. After our local directory, a number of locations are searched, ending with the `.../site-packages` directory.

The next group of names, starting with `setuptools-2.0.2-py3.3.egg`, is a list of all external packages added to this installation in the form of downloaded `.egg` files. The exact list will vary from installation to installation. These names are created by the `pip` and `easy_install` programs.

When we set the `PYTHONPATH` environment variable, those names are spliced into the path *after* the various installed packages. The final group of names, starting with `python33.zip`, is a common list of modules that come with Python. The last entry lists the generic site-packages portion of the library. If you download a package and run the package's `setup.py` script, it is copied into this directory where it will be found by Python.

The `sys.path` object is a proper mutable list. We can dynamically change the path in our script files. This can make it difficult to determine all the modules that a script depends on. It's almost always clearer to explicitly depend on the modules being properly installed or the `PYTHONPATH` environment variable being set.

Summary

In this chapter, we've looked at the higher-level ways to organize software. A function contains many statements, a class contains many method functions, and a module can contain many classes and functions. A package can contain many modules.

We've looked at a number of ways of executing a Python script. We have a great deal of flexibility because there are many contexts in which we need to execute software. Generally, we'll focus on executing Python programs by module name rather than by filename. The distinction is tiny. Since a module must be on the search path, we can create a directory that contains the script and any supporting modules and libraries, and ensure that this directory is named on the PYTHONPATH.

We've looked at how we can create library modules that contain definitions and will be imported into other scripts. This is our primary method of reuse. We've also looked at how we can create a script, that is reusable as a library module. This supports unit testing as well as maturation of our software.

In *Chapter 13, Metaprogramming and Decorators*, we'll look at some more advanced programming techniques. These will allow us to create more sophisticated class and function definitions. We can use these design patterns to write more flexible and more reusable software.

13
Metaprogramming and Decorators

The bulk of what we've covered has been programming — writing Python statements to process data. We can also use Python to process Python instead of processing data. We'll call this metaprogramming. We'll look at two aspects: decorators and metaclasses.

A decorator is a function that accepts a function as an argument and returns a function. We can use this to add features to a function without repeating the feature in several different function definitions. A decorator prevents copy-and-paste programming. We often use this for logging, audit, or security purposes; these are things that will cut across a number of class or function definitions.

A metaclass definition will extend the essential object creation that happens when we make an instance of a class. Implicitly, the special method name of __new__() is used to create a bare object that is subsequently initialized by the __init__() method of the class. A metaclass allows us to change some of the fundamental features of object creation.

Simple metaprogramming with decorators

Python has a few built-in decorators that will modify a function or a method of a class. For example, in *Chapter 11*, *Class Definitions*, we saw @staticmethod and @property, which are used to alter the behavior of a method in a class. The @staticmethod decorator changes a function to work on the class instead of an instance of the class. The @property decorator makes evaluating a no-argument method available via the same syntax as an attribute.

A function decorator that's available in the `functools` module is `@lru_cache`. This modifies a function to add memoization. Having cached results can be a significant speed-up. It looks like this:

```
from functools import lru_cache
from glob import glob
import os

@lru_cache(100)
def find_source(directory):
    return glob(os.path.join(directory, "*.py"))
```

In this example, we've imported the `@lru_cache` decorator. We've also imported the `glob.glob()` function and the `os` module so that we can use `os.path.join()` to create filenames irrespective of OS-specific punctuation.

We've provided a size parameter to the `@lru_cache()` decorator. The parameterized decorator modifies the `find_source()` function by adding a cache that will hold 100 previous results. This can speed up a program that does a lot of work with the local file system. The **last recently used (LRU)** algorithm assures that recent requests are preserved and older requests are quietly forgotten to limit the cache to the requested size.

The `@lru_cache` decorator embodies a reusable optimization that can be applied to a variety of functions. We have separated the memoization aspect from other aspects of a function's implementation.

The *Python Standard Library* defines a few decorators. For more examples of decorator metaprogramming, see the Python Decorator Library page, `https://wiki.python.org/moin/PythonDecoratorLibrary`.

Defining our own decorator

In some cases, we can extract a common aspect from a number of functions. Concerns like security, audit, or logging are common examples of something we might want to implement consistently across many functions or classes.

Let's look at a way to support enhanced debugging. Our goal is to have a simple annotation that we can use to provide consistent, detailed output from several unrelated functions. We'd like to create a module with definitions like this:

```
@debug_log
def some_function(ksloc):
    return 2.4*ksloc**1.05
@debug_log
```

```
def another_function(ksloc, a=3.6, b=1.20):
    return a*ksloc**b
```

We've defined two simple functions that will be wrapped by a decorator to provide consistent debugging output.

A decorator is a function that accepts a function as an argument and returns a function as a result. What we've shown in the preceding piece of code is evaluated as follows:

```
>>> def some_function(ksloc):
...     return 2.4*ksloc**1.05
>>>  some_function = debug_log(debug_log)
```

When we apply a decorator to a function, we're implicitly evaluating the decorator function with an original function as the argument. This will create the decorated function as a result. Using a decorator creates a result with the same name as the original function—the decorated version replaces the original.

For this to work, we'll need to write a decorator that creates the debugging log entries. This must be generic so that it will work for any function. As we noted in *Chapter 7*, *Basic Function Definitions*, we can use the * and ** modifiers to collect "all other" positional arguments and all other keyword arguments into a single sequence or a single dictionary. This allows us to write completely generic decorators.

Here's the @debug_log decorator function:

```
import logging
from functools import wraps
def debug_log(func):
    log= logging.getLogger(func.__name__)
    @wraps(func)
    def decorated(*args, **kw):
        log.debug(">>> call(*{0}, **{1})".format(args, kw))
        try:
            result= func(*args, **kw)
            log.debug("<<< return {}".format(result))
            return result
        except Exception as ex:
            log.exception( "*** {}".format(ex) )
            raise
    return decorated
```

The body of the decorator definition does three things. First, it creates a logger based on the original function's name, func.__name__. Second, it defines an entirely new function, named decorated(), which is based on the original function. Finally, it returns that new function.

Note that we used a decorator from the functools library, @wraps, to show that the new decorator function wraps the original function. This will assure that the name and docstring are properly copied from the original function to the decorated function. The decorated version will be indistinguishable from the original.

We can use these functions normally:

```
>>> round(some_function(25),3)
70.477
```

The decoration has no impact on the value of the function. It has a small performance impact.

If we have logging enabled, and we set the logging level to DEBUG, we'll see additional output in the log. The preceding example would lead to the following in the logger's output:

```
DEBUG:some_function:>>> call(*(25,), **{})
DEBUG:some_function:<<< return 70.47713658528114
```

This shows the debugging detail produced by this decorator. The log shows the argument values and the result value. If there's an exception, we'll see the argument values as well as the exception message, which can be more useful than the default behavior of just showing the exception message.

An easy way to enable the logger is to include the following in the application:

```
import sys
logging.basicConfig(stream=sys.stderr, level=logging.DEBUG)
```

This will direct the log output to the standard error stream. It will also include all messages that have a severity level above the debug level. We can change this level setting to a value like logging.INFO to silence the debugging messages, leaving informational messages intact.

A decorator that also accepts parameters values — in a manner similar to the @lru_cache decorator — is more complex. The argument values are first applied to create a decorator. The decorator that results from this initial binding is then used to build the decorated function from the original function.

More complex metaprogramming with metaclasses

In some cases, the default features built into a class aren't appropriate for our particular application. We can see a few common situations where we might want to extend the default behavior of object construction.

- We can use a metaclass to preserve some of the original source code that defined a class. By default, each class object uses dict to store the various methods and class-level attributes. We might want to use an ordered dictionary to retain the original source code ordering for class-level attributes. An example of this is shown in the *Python Standard Library*, section 3.3.3.5.

- The **abstract base classes** (**ABC**) rely on a metaclass __new__() method to confirm that the concrete subclass is complete when we attempt to create an instance of the class. If we fail to provide all of the required methods in a subclass of an ABC, we can't create an instance of that subclass.

- Metaclasses can be used to simplify object serialization. A metaclass can incorporate information required for XML or JSON representation of an instance.

- We can use a metaclass to inject additional attributes into an object. Because a metaclass provides the implementation of the __new__() method used to create an empty object, it is able to inject attributes before the __init__() method is evaluated. For some immutable classes, such as tuples, there is no __init__() method, and a subclass of the tuple must use the __new__() method to set the value.

The default metaclass is type. This is used by application classes to create the new, bare object prior to the __init__() method being invoked. The built-in type.__new__() method requires four argument values — the metaclass, the application class name, the base classes for the application class, and a namespace of system-defined initial values.

When we create a metaclass, we'll override the __new__() method. We'll still use the type.__new__() method to create the bare object. We can then extend or modify this bare object before returning the object.

Here's a metaclass that inserts a logger prior to __init__():

```
import logging
class Logged(type):
    def __new__(cls, name, bases, namespace, **kwds):
```

```
result = type.__new__(cls, name, bases, dict(namespace))
result.logger= logging.getLogger(name)
return result
```

We've defined a class that extends the built-in `type` class. We've defined an overriding special method, `__new__()`. The special method uses the superclass `type.__new__()` method to create the bare object, which is assigned to the `result` variable.

Once we have the bare object, we can create a logger and inject this logger into the bare object. This `self.logger` attribute will be available from the very first line of the `__init__()` method in each class that's created using this metaclass.

We can create application classes that leverage this metaclass, like this:

```
class Machine(metaclass=Logged):
    def __init__(self, machine_id, base, cost_each):
        self.logger.info("creating {0} at {1}+{2}".format(
            machine_id, base, cost_each))
        self.machine_id= machine_id
        self.base= base
        self.cost_each= cost_each
    def application(self, units):
        total= self.base + self.cost_each*units
        self.logger.debug("Applied {units} ==> {total}".format(
            total=total, units=units, **self.__dict__))
        return total
```

We've defined a class that explicitly depends on the `Logged` metaclass. If we don't include the `metaclass` keyword parameter, the default metaclass of `type` will be used. In this class, the `logger` attribute was created before the `__init__()` method was invoked. This allows us to use the logger in the `__init__()` method without any further overhead.

Summary

In this chapter, we've looked at two common metaprogramming techniques. The first is writing decorator functions—these can be used to transform an original function to add new features. The second is using a metaclass to extend the default behavior of class definitions.

We can use these techniques to develop application features that cut across many functions and classes. Writing a feature once and applying it to a number of classes assures us of consistency and can help during debugging, as well as upgrades or refactoring.

In *Chapter 14, Fit and Finish – Unit Testing, Packaging, and Documentation*, we'll look at a number of features that characterize a complete Python project. Rather than address technical language features, we'll look at ways we can use Python features to create polished, complete solutions.

14
Fit and Finish – Unit Testing, Packaging, and Documentation

Beyond the Python language and its libraries, there are several other aspects to Python programming. We'll start by looking closely at the docstrings, which should be viewed as an essential ingredient in every package, module, class, and function definition. These have several purposes, one of which is to clarify what the object does.

In this chapter, we'll also look at the different approaches to unit testing. The `doctest` and `unittest` modules provide a comprehensive suite of tools. External tools like Nose are also widely used.

We'll also look at how we can leverage the `logging` module as part of a complete application. The Python logger is quite sophisticated as well, so we'll focus on a few of the essential features.

We'll examine some tools that are used to build Python documentation from the embedded docstring comments. Using tools to extract documentation allows us to focus on writing proper code and deriving the reference documents from the code. In order to create complete documentation—more than just an API reference—many developers use the Sphinx tool.

We'll also address the organization of files in a large Python project. Because Python is used in so many different contexts and has so many different frameworks, the layout for a web application built with Flask will look nothing like a web application built with Django. However, there are a few essential principles that we can follow for keeping Python programs neat and well organized.

Writing docstrings

In *Chapter 7, Basic Function Definitions*, we noted that all functions should have a docstring that describes the function. In *Chapter 11, Class Definitions*, and *Chapter 12, Scripts, Modules, Packages, Libraries, and Applications*, we offered similar advice, without providing many details.

The `def` statement and the `class` statement should, universally, be followed by a triple-quoted string that describes the function, method, or class. It's not required by the language—it's required by all of the people who will try to read, understand, extend, improve, or repair our code.

We'll revisit an example from *Chapter 11, Class Definitions*, to show the kinds of docstrings that were omitted. Here's how we might create a more complete class definition:

```
class Point:
    """
    Point on a plane.

    Distances are calculated using hypotenuse.
    This is the "as a crow flies" straight line distance.

    Point on a plane.

    Distances are calculated using hypotenuse.
    This is the "as a crow flies" straight line distance.

    >>> p_1 = Point(22, 7)
    >>> p_1.x
    22
    >>> p_1.y
    7
    >>> p_1
    Point(22, 7)
    """
    def __init__(self, x, y):
        """Create a new point

        :param x: X coördinate
        :param y: Y coördinate
        """
        self.x= x
        self.y= y
    def __repr__(self):
        """Returns string representation of this Point."""
```

```
                    return "{cls}({x:.0f}, {y:.0f})".format(
                        cls=self.__class__.__name__, x=self.x, y=self.y)
            def dist(self, point):
                """Distance to another point measured on a plane.

                >>> p_1 = Point(22, 7)
                >>> p_2 = Point(20, 5)
                >>> round(p_1.dist(p_2),4)
                2.8284

                :param point: Another instance of Point.
                :returns: float distance.
                """
                return math.hypot(self.x-point.x, self.y-point.y)
```

In this class definition, we've provided four separate docstrings. For the class as a whole, we provided an overview of what the class does, plus an example of how the class behaves. This is shown as a copy and paste from the Python REPL, showing the input prefixed with >>> prompts.

For each method function, we've provided a docstring that shows what the method function does. In the case of the dist() method, we've included another example interaction in the docstring to show an example of the expected behavior of the method.

The documentation of parameters and return values uses the **ReStructuredText (RST)** markup language. This is widely used because of tools like docutils and Sphinx, which can format RST into nice-looking HTML or LaTeX. We'll look at RST in the section *Writing documentation with RST markup* later in this chapter.

For now, we can focus on :param name: and :returns: as markup syntax that helps tools understand the semantics of these constructs. The tool can then give them special formatting to reflect their meaning.

Writing unit tests with doctest

It is a widely adopted practice to provide concrete examples of classes and functions in docstrings. As shown in the preceding example, we can provide the following kind of example text in a docstring:

```
>>> p_1 = Point(22, 7)
>>> p_2 = Point(20, 5)
>>> round(p_1.dist(p_2),4)
2.8284
```

A concrete example has many benefits. The goal of Python code is to be beautiful and readable. If the code sample is obscure or confusing, this is a design problem that really should be resolved. Writing more words in comments to try to explain bad code is a symptom of a deeper problem. A concrete example should be as clear and expressive as the code itself.

An additional benefit of concrete examples is that they are test cases. The doctest module can scan each docstring to locate these examples, build, and execute test cases. This will confirm that the output in the example matches the actual output.

One common approach to using doctest is to include the following in a library module:

```
if __name__ == "__main__":
    import doctest
    doctest.testmod(verbose=1)
```

If the module is executed as the main script instead of being imported, then it will import doctest, scan the module for docstrings, and execute all the tests in those docstrings. We've set the verbose level to one, which produces output that shows the tests in some detail. If we leave the verbose level to it's default value of zero, success is silent; not even an Ok is displayed.

We can also run doctest as a command-line application. Here's an example:

```
MacBookPro-SLott:Code slott$ python3 -m doctest Chapter_1/ch01_ex1.py -v
Trying:
    355/113
Expecting:
    3.1415929203539825
ok
...
1 items had no tests:
    ch01_ex1
9 items passed all tests:
    2 tests in __main__.__test__.assignment
    4 tests in __main__.__test__.cmath
    2 tests in __main__.__test__.division
    1 tests in __main__.__test__.expression
    3 tests in __main__.__test__.import 1
```

```
1 tests in __main__.__test__.import 2
2 tests in __main__.__test__.import 3
2 tests in __main__.__test__.mixed_math
2 tests in __main__.__test__.print
19 tests in 10 items.
19 passed and 0 failed.
Test passed.
```

We've run the doctest module as an application, providing it with the name of a file that should be examined to locate test examples inside docstrings. The output starts with the first example found. The example is this:

```
>>> 355/113
3.1415929203539825
```

The verbose output shows the expression and the expected results. The output of ok indicates that the test was passed.

What about the one item that had no tests? That's the docstring for the module itself. This shows us that our test case coverage is incomplete. We should consider adding a test in the module docstring.

The summary showed that 9 items had 19 tests. The items are identified with strings such as ch01_ex1.__test__.assignment. The special name __test__ is neither a function nor a class; it's a global variable. If there's a variable named __test__, it must be a dictionary. The keys in the __test__ dictionary are documentation, and the values are strings that must include doctest examples.

The __test__ variable might look like this:

```
__test__ = {
    'expression': """
        >>> 355/113
        3.1415929203539825
    """,
etc.
}
```

Each key identifies the test. Each value is a triple-quoted string that includes a snippet of REPL interaction showing the expected results.

As a practical matter, this particular test suffers from one of the potential limitations of doctest examples.

As we noted in *Chapter 5, Logic, Comparisons, and Conditions*, we should not use exact equality tests between floating point values. The proper way to write a test like this is to use `round(355/113, 6)` to truncate the trailing digits; the final digits might differ slightly depending on the hardware or underlying floating point libraries. It's better to write tests that are independent of implementation nuances.

There are a number of potential limitations with `doctest` examples. Dictionary keys have no defined order. Therefore, a `doctest` can fail when the keys are displayed in an order that differs from the expected output in the test. Similarly, set items have no defined order. Additionally, an error traceback message may not match precisely because it will have a line like `File "<stdin>", line 1, in <module>` that may vary depending on the context in which the test runs.

For some of these potential limitations, `doctest` offers directives that can be used to annotate the tests. The directives appear as special comments like this: `# doctest: +ELLIPSIS`. This will enable flexible pattern matching to cope with the variations in displayed output. For other limitations, we need to construct our test cases properly. We can use `sorted(some_dict.values())` to transform a dictionary result into a sorted list of tuples where the order is guaranteed.

Docstrings are an essential feature of good Python programming. Examples are an essential feature of well-written documentation. Given a tool that can verify the correctness of the examples, this kind of testing should be considered mandatory.

Using the unittest library for testing

For more complex testing, the `doctest` examples may not provide enough depth or flexibility. A docstring with a large number of cases would become too long to be effective as documentation. A docstring with complex test setup, teardown, or mock objects may not be useful as documentation either.

For these cases, we'll use the `unittest` module to define test cases and test suites. When using `unittest`, we'll generally create separate modules. These test modules will contain `TestCase` classes that contain test methods.

Here's a quick overview of a typical test case class definition:

```python
import unittest

from Chapter_7.ch07_ex1 import FtoC

class Test_FtoC(unittest.TestCase):
    def setUp(self):
```

```
            self.temps= [50, 60, 72]
        def test_single(self):
            self.assertAlmostEqual(0.0, FtoC(32))
            self.assertAlmostEqual(100.0, FtoC(212))
        def test_map(self):
            temps_c = list(map(FtoC, self.temps))
            self.assertEqual(3, len(temps_c))
            rounded = [round(t,3) for t in temps_c]
            self.assertEqual([10.0, 15.556, 22.222], rounded)
```

We've shown a `setUp()` method and two test methods. The default `runTest()` method will search for all methods with a name that begins with `test`; it will then run the `setUp()` method that is executed prior to each individual `test...` method.

We can use the Python `assert` statement to compare actual and expected results. Because there are so many common comparisons, the `TestCase` class offers handy methods for comparing different kinds of expected results with actual results. We've shown `assertEqual()` and `assertAlmostEqual()`. Each of these methods parallels the `assert` statement — they succeed silently. If there's a problem, they raise an `AssertionError` exception.

Using the `unittest` module allows us to write voluminous test cases. A `doctest` string is most useful when it expresses a few helpful concrete examples. A unit test is a better way to include many edge and corner cases.

The `unittest` module is also handy for test examples that involve interaction with the filesystem. We might have a `.csv` format file that has a number of examples. We can write a `runTest()` method that reads this file and treats each row as a test case.

When pursuing **acceptance test-driven development (ATDD)**, the test cases themselves can become quite complex. The test case setup may involve seeding a database with sample data prior to executing a big application feature, and then examining the resulting database contents. The essential structure of ATDD testing fits the unit testing design patterns offered by the `unittest` module. The "unit" under test is not an isolated class; instead, we're testing a complete web API or command-line application.

Combining doctest and unittest

We can incorporate `doctest` test cases into the `unittest` suite of tests. This assures us that the `doctest` examples are not overlooked when using `unittest` cases. We'll do this by using the `TestSuite` class, which can contain other `TestCase` classes as well as `TestSuite` classes.

A `doctest.DocTestSuite` object will create a proper `unittest.TestSuite` method from the `doctest` strings embedded in a given module. We can use a function like the following to locate all test cases in a large collection of packages and modules:

```
def doctest_suite():
    files = glob.glob("Chapter*/ch*_ex*.py")
    by_chxx= lambda name: name.partition(".")[2].partition("_")[0]
    modules = sorted(
        (".".join(f.replace(".py","").split(os.sep)) for f in files),
        key=by_chxx)
    suites= [doctest.DocTestSuite(m) for m in modules]
    return unittest.TestSuite(suites)
```

This function will return a `TestSuite` object built from other `TestSuite` objects. This function has five steps:

1. It uses `glob.glob()` to get a list of all matching module names in the packages. This particular pattern will locate all of the example code for this book. We might have to change this to pass or reject other kinds of names that might be available.

2. It defines a lambda object that extracts the chapter number from the module, ignoring the package. The expression uses `name.partition(".")` to split the complete module name into the package, the dot character, and the module name. Item number 2 from this sequence is the module name. This is partitioned on the `"_"` into chapter prefix, underscore, and example suffix. We use item number 0, the chapter prefix, as the sort order for the modules.

3. The input to the `sorted()` function is a sequence of filenames restructured into module names. This transformation involves replacing the `".py"` filename suffix and then splitting the filename on the OS path separator (`"/"` on most OSes, but on Windows it is `"\"`) into separate substrings. When we join the substrings using `"."` we get a module name, which we can use for sorting and test case discovery.

4. We build a list comprehension of the test suites that can be built from the `doctest` examples in each module. This includes over 100 individual tests culled from the examples throughout this book.

5. We assemble a single test suite from the list of test suites. This can then be executed to confirm that all of the examples produce the expected results.

We can merge this doctest `TestSuite` object with a `TestSuite` object built from tests based on the `unittest.TestCase` definitions. This complete suite can then be executed to show that the code works as expected.

We often use something like the following:

```
if __name__ == "__main__":
    runner= unittest.TextTestRunner( verbosity=1 )
    all_tests = unittest.TestSuite( suite() )
    runner.run( all_tests )
```

This will create a test runner that produces a summary of tests and test failures. The `suite()` function—not shown—returns a `TestSuite()` method built from the `doctest_suite()` function and a function that scans files for `unittest.TestCase` classes.

The output summarizes the tests run and the failures. When we build a comprehensive test suite like this, we include both `unittest` and `doctest` cases. This allows us to freely mix complex suites with simple docstring examples.

Using other add-on test libraries

The `doctest` and `unittest` modules allow us to write a number unit tests conveniently. In many cases, we want even more sophistication. One of the more popular additional features is test discovery. The `nose` package gives us a way to painlessly examine modules and packages for tests. See `http://nose. readthedocs.org/en/latest/` for more information.

There are several benefits of using `nose` as an extension to `unittest`. The `nose` module can collect tests from `unittest.TestCase` subclasses, as well as simple test functions, and also from test classes that are not subclasses of `unittest.TestCase`. We can use `nose` for writing timing tests too—something that can be a little awkward in `unittest`.

Because `nose` is particularly good at collecting tests automatically, there's no need to manually collect test cases into test suites; we don't need some of the examples shown earlier. Furthermore, `nose` supports test fixtures at the package, module, and class level, so expensive initialization can be done as infrequently as possible. This allows us to populate a test database for multiple modules of related testing—something that `unittest` can't do as easily.

Logging events and conditions

A well-behaved application can produce a variety of processing summaries. For command-line applications, the summary might be a simple "everything went okay" message. For GUI applications, this summary is inverted—silence means things are working well, and a dialog box with an error message indicates things didn't work properly.

In some command-line processing contexts, the summary might include some additional details on the number of objects that were processed. In financial applications, some counts and the total values of various objects must balance properly to show that all objects that were received as input became proper outputs.

When we need additional details, beyond a simple "works or breaks" summary, we can leverage the print() function. The output can be redirected to the sys.stderr file to produce a handy log. While this is effective in small programs, it has a number of desirable features offered by the logging module.

The first step in using the logging module is to create logger objects and use the loggers to produce useful output. Each logger has a name that fits into a tree using names delimited with the . character. The logger names parallel the standards for module names; we can use the following:

```
import logging
logger = logging.getLogger(__name__)
```

This will create a module-wide logger object with a name that matches the module name. The root logger has the name ""; that is, an empty string.

We can also create class-wide loggers as well as object-specific loggers. We can, for example, create a logger during the __init__() method part of object creation. We might use the __qualname__ attribute of an object's class to provide a qualified class name for the logger. To create a logger for a specific instance of a class, we can suffix the class name with the . character and some unique identifier for the instance.

We use the logger to create messages with a severity level from DEBUGGING (the least severe) to FATAL or CRITICAL (synonyms for the most severe level.) We do this with a method name that reflects the severity level. Messages are created with methods like these:

```
logger.debug("Finished with {0} using {2}".format(message, details))
logger.error("Error due to {0}".format(data))
```

The logging module has a default configuration that does nothing. This means that we can include logging requests in an application without any further consideration. As long as we properly create a Logger instance and use methods of the logger instance, we don't need to do anything else.

To see output, we'll need to create a handler that will write the messages to a particular stream or file. This is usually done as part of the overall configuration of the logging system.

Configuring the logging system

We have several ways to configure the logging system. For small applications, we might provide the logging setup using the `logging.basicConfig()` function. We've shown this in *Chapter 13, Metaprogramming and Decorators*. A simple initialization will send the output to the standard error stream and explicitly set a level that filters the messages being displayed. This uses the `stream` and `level` keyword arguments.

A slightly more complex configuration might look like this:

```
logging.basicConfig(filename='app.log', filemode='a', level=logging.
INFO)
```

We've opened a named file, assigned a mode of `a` to append, and set the level to show messages with a severity that's equal to or greater than `INFO`.

Since each individual logger is named, we can adjust the level of detail for a specific logger. We can include a line like the following to enable debugging on a specific logger:

```
logging.getLogger('Demonstration').setLevel(logging.DEBUG)
```

This allows us to see details for a specific class or module. This is often a great help when debugging.

The `logging.handlers` module offers a large number of handlers for routing, printing, or saving the sequence of logging messages. The preceding example shows the file handler. The stream handler is used to write to the standard error stream. In some cases, we need to have multiple handlers. We can apply filters to each handler, so that the handlers will reflect different kinds of details.

Logging configurations often get too complex for the `basicConfig()` function. The `logging.config` module offers several functions that can be used to configure the logging for an application. One general approach is to use the `logging.config.dictConfig()` function. We can create a Python `dict` object directly in Python, or read some serialized version of the `dict` object. The standard library documentation uses examples written in the YAML markup language because it's simple and flexible.

We might do something like this to create a configuration object:

```
config = {
    'version': 1,
    'handlers': {
        'console': {
            'class' : 'logging.StreamHandler',
```

```
                    'stream': 'ext://sys.stderr',
                }
        },
        'root': {
            'level': 'DEBUG',
            'handler': ['console'],
        },
    }
```

This object has the required `version` attribute to specify the structure of the configuration. A single handler is defined; it's named `console` and uses `logging`. `StreamHandler` is used to write to the standard error stream. The root logger is configured to use the `console` handler. The severity level is defined to include any message at or above the DEBUG level.

Only in configuration files is the root logger named `'root'`. In application code, the root logger is named with an empty string.

Larger and more sophisticated applications will rely on logging configurations in external configuration files. This permits flexible and sophisticated logging configurations.

Writing documentation with RST markup

While Python code should be beautiful and informative, it doesn't easily provide background or context to show why a particular algorithm or data structure was chosen. We often need to provide these additional details to help people maintain, extend, and make effective use of our software. While we can include a lot of information in a module docstring, it seems best to keep docstrings focused on implementation details, and provide the additional material separately.

We can write additional documentation in a variety of formats. We can use a sophisticated editor with complex file formats, or we can use simple text editors and plain text format. We can even write our documentation entirely in HTML. Python also offers a hybrid approach—we can write using a text editor with simplified **ReStructuredText (RST)** markup, and use the `docutils` tools to create nice-looking HTML pages or LaTeX files suitable for publication from that markup.

The RST markup language is widely used for creating Python documentation. This markup allows us to write plain text, while adhering to a few formatting rules. In the next section, we'll look at using the `docutils` tools to parse the RST and create an output document.

The rules of RST markup are simple. There is paragraph-level markup that applies to big blocks of text. Paragraphs must be separated by blank lines. When a line is "underlined" with a sequence of characters, it is taken as a heading. When a paragraph starts with an isolated punctuation mark, it's a bullet. When a paragraph starts with a letter or digit, and a punctuation mark, this indicates numbers instead of bullets. The `docutils rst2html.py` tool transforms each paragraph of the input to the proper kind of HTML structure.

There are many paragraph-level "directives" that can be used to insert an image, a table, an equation, or a large block of code. These directives are prefixed with `..` and end with `::`. We might use the directive `.. contents::` to add the table of contents to our document.

We can write inline markup inside the body of a paragraph. Inline markup includes a few simple constructs. If we surround a word with the `*` character, like `*this*`, we'll see the word in an *italic*-style font in the final document; we can use `**bold**` for **bold** characters. If we want to write a `*` character without confusing the tool, we can escape it with the `\` character. In many cases, however, we'll need to use a more complex semantic markup that looks like this: `:code:`code sample``. This includes the text role, `:code:`, as a prefix that shows how to classify the marked characters; the content is surrounded by the `` ` `` character. The text roles of `:code:` and `:math:` are widely used.

When we write a docstring, we'll often use additional RST markup. We'll use `:param name:` when defining the parameter to a function or class method. We use `:returns:` to annotate the return values from a function. When we provide this additional markup, we're assured that various formatting tools will produce elegant documentation from our docstrings.

Here's an example of what an RST file might contain:

```
Writing RST Documentation
===========================

For more information, see http://docutils.sourceforge.net/docs/user/
rst/quickref.html

1.  Separate paragraphs with blank lines.

2.  Underline headings.

#.  Prefix with one character for an unordered list. Otherwise it may
be
```

```
        interpreted as an ordered list.

#.   Indent freely to show structure.

#.   Inline markup.

    -   Use ``*word*`` for *italics*, and ``**word**`` for **bold**.

    -   Use ``:code:\`word\``` for more complex semantic markup.
```

We've shown a heading, underlined with a sequence of = characters. We've provided a URL; in the final HTML output, this will become a proper link using the <a> tag. We've shown numbered paragraphs. When we omit the leading number and use #, the docutils tools will assign increasing numbers. We've also shown indented bullet point within the last numbered paragraph.

While this example shows numbering and simple hyphen bullets, we can use lettering or Roman numerals as well. The docutils tools are generally able to parse a wide variety of formatting conventions.

Creating HTML documentation from an RST source

To create HTML or LaTeX (or any of the other supported formats), we'll use one of the docutils frontend tools. There are many individual conversion tools that are part of the docutils package.

The docutils tools are not part of Python. See http://docutils.sourceforge.net for the download.

All of the tools have a similar command-line interface. We might use the following command to create an HTML page from some RST input:

```
MacBookPro-SLott:Chapter_14 slott$ rst2html.py ch14_doc.rst ch14_doc.rst.
html
```

We've provided the rst2html.py command. We've named the input file and the output file. This will use default values for the style sheet, and other optional features for the resulting document. We can configure the output through the command line or by providing a configuration file that assures a common look for all of our generated HTML files.

To create LaTeX, we can use the `rst2latex.py` or `rst2xetex.py` tool, and then a LaTeX formatter. TeX Live distribution works nicely for creating a PDF file from LaTeX. See `https://www.tug.org/texlive/`.

For large and complex documents, creating a single RST file isn't ideal. While we can use the `.. include::` directive to insert material from separate files, the document must be built as a whole, which requires a large amount of memory; rebuilding a document after a small change might require a disproportionate amount of processing.

For a multipage website, we have to use a tool like Make, Ant, or SCons to rebuild the relevant HTML pages when a source RST file has been updated. This is the kind of overhead that calls out for a tool to automate and simplify production of large or complex documents.

Using the Sphinx tool

The Sphinx tool allows us to easily build multipage websites or complex documents. For more information, see `http://sphinx-doc.org`. When we install Sphinx using `pip` or `easy_install`, the installer will also include `docutils` for us.

To create sophisticated documentation, we'll start with the `sphinx-quickstart` script. This application will build the template file structure, the configuration files, and a Makefile that we can use to rebuild our documents efficiently.

Sphinx adds a large number of directives and text roles to the basics of RST. These additional roles and directives make it easier to write about code with properly formatted references to modules, classes, and functions. Sphinx simplifies inter-document references — we can have multiple documents with consistent references to a target location; we can move the target and the references will all be updated.

The `sphinx-build` command is used to construct the target files from the RST source. Sphinx can build over a dozen different kinds of target documents, making it a versatile tool.

The Python documentation is built with Sphinx. This means that our projects can include documentation that looks as polished and elegant as Python's documentation.

Organizing Python code

Python programs should be beautiful. To that end, the language has few syntactic overheads; we should be able to write short scripts without unpleasant boilerplate. The principle is sometimes articulated as *Simple things should be simple*. The "Hello World" script really is a single line of code that uses the `print()` function.

A more complex file will generally have a few major sections:

- A `!#` line, often `#!/usr/bin/env python3`.

- A docstring comment explaining what the module does.

- The function or class definitions. We often group multiple functions and classes into a single module. The module is the proper unit of reuse in Python.

- If the module can be run as a main script, we'll include an `if __name__ == "__main__":` section that defines the file's behavior when run as the main script.

Many applications are too complex for a single file. When designing larger applications, the Pythonic ideal is to keep the resulting structure as flat as possible. While the language supports nested packages, deep nesting is not seen as desirable. In *Chapter 12*, *Scripts, Modules, Packages, Libraries, and Applications*, we looked at the details of defining modules and packages.

Summary

In this chapter, we've looked at several features of polished and complete Python projects. The most important feature of working code is a suite of unit tests that demonstrate that the code works. Code without test cases simply cannot be trusted. In order to make use of any software, we must have tests that show us that the software is trustworthy.

We've looked at including tests in docstrings. The `doctest` tool can locate these tests and execute them. We've looked at creating `unittest.TestCase` classes. We can combine the two into a script that will locate all `doctest` and `unittest` test cases into a single master test suite.

One other feature of good software is some explanation of how to install and use the software. This may be as short as a `README` file that provides basic information. Often, however, we need a more sophisticated document that provides a variety of additional information. We might want to provide context, design background, or examples that are too big to be packaged into module or class docstrings. We'll often write documentation using tools above and beyond the basic components that come with Python.

In *Chapter 15*, *Next Steps*, we'll look at the next steps in our exploration of Python. Once we've mastered the essentials, we need to add depth to the areas that are relevant to the problems we need to solve. We might want to study big data applications, web applications, or game development. Each of these more specialized areas will involve additional Python concepts, tools, and frameworks.

15
Next Steps

After studying the Python basics, what's next? Each developer's journey will vary, based on the general architecture of the application that they're going to build. In this chapter, we'll look at four kinds of Python applications. We'll look at **command-line interface (CLI)** applications in some depth. We'll look briefly at **graphical user interface (GUI)** applications. There are a number of graphics libraries and a number of frameworks that we might use for this; it's difficult to address all of the alternatives.

Web server applications often involve a sophisticated web framework that handles the standardized overheads. Our Python code will plug into this framework. As with GUI applications, there are several commonly used frameworks. We'll look quickly at a few common features of web frameworks. We'll also look at the big data context as epitomized by the Hadoop server's streaming interface.

This isn't intended to be complete or even representative. Python is used in many different ways.

Leveraging the standard library

When implementing Python solutions, it's helpful to scan the standard library for relevant modules. The library is large, making it somewhat intimidating at first. We can, however, focus our search.

We can break the *Python Standard Library* document into three portions. The first five chapters are general reference material that all Python programmers need to understand. The next 20 chapters, plus chapters 28 and 32, describe modules that we might incorporate into a wide variety of applications. The remaining chapters are less useful; they're more focused on Python internals and ways in which to extend the language itself.

The name and the summary of a module in the library table of contents may not provide enough information to see all of the ways in which a module might be used. The `bisect` module, for example, can be extended to create a fast dictionary that retains its keys in a defined order. This isn't obvious without careful reading of the description of the module.

Some of the library modules have relatively small, easy-to-understand implementations. For larger modules and packages, there are often pieces that can be lifted out of context and reused widely. As an example, consider an application that uses `http.client` to make REST web services requests. We often need functions from the `urllib.parse` module to encode a query string or properly quote parts of the URL. It's common to see a long list of imports at the front of Python applications.

Leveraging PyPI – the Python Package Index

After scanning the library, the next place to look for additional Python packages is the **Python Package Index (PyPI)**at `https://pypi.python.org/pypi`. There are thousands of packages listed here, with varying degrees of support and quality.

As we noted in *Chapter 1, Getting Started*, Python 3.4 also installs two scripts to help us add packages, `pip` and `easy_install`. These search PyPI for the requested package. Most packages can be found by using their name; the tools locate the appropriate release for the platform and Python version.

We've mentioned a few external libraries in other chapters:

- `nose` for writing tests, see `https://pypi.python.org/pypi/nose/1.3.6`
- `docutils` for writing documentation, see `https://pypi.python.org/pypi/docutils/0.12`
- `Sphinx` for writing complex documentation, see `https://pypi.python.org/pypi/Sphinx/1.3.1`

Additionally, there are bundles of packages available: we might install Anaconda, NumPy, or SciPy, each of which includes a number of other packages in one tidy distribution. See `http://continuum.io/downloads`, `http://www.numpy.org`, or `http://www.scipy.org`.

In some cases, we may have Python configurations that are incompatible with each other. For example, we may have to work in two environments, one using the older Beautiful Soup 3 with the other using the newer version 4. Refer to `https://pypi.python.org/pypi/beautifulsoup4/4.3.2`. To simplify this switch, we can use the `virtualenv` tool to create isolated Python environments with their own complex trees of interdependent modules. See `https://virtualenv.pypa.io/en/latest/`.

The Python ecosystem is large and sophisticated. There's no good reason to invent a solution in a vacuum. It's often best to locate the appropriate components or partial solutions, then download and extend them.

Types of applications

We'll look at four types of Python applications. These are neither the most common nor the most popular kinds of Python applications; they were selected more or less randomly based on the author's narrow experience. Python is used widely, and any attempt to summarize all of the various places where Python is used runs the risk of misleading rather than informing.

We'll look at CLI applications for two reasons. Firstly, they can be relatively simple, relying on fewer additional packages or frameworks than other kinds of applications. Secondly, more complex applications will often be launched from a CLI main script. For these reasons, the CLI features seem to be fundamental to most uses of Python.

We'll look at GUI applications because they are popular on the desktop. The difficulty here is that there are many GUI frameworks available for Python software development. Here's one list: `https://wiki.python.org/moin/GuiProgramming`. We'll focus on the `turtle` package because it's simple and built-in.

We'll look at web applications because Python is used with frameworks such as Django or Flask (among many others) to build high-volume websites. Here's a list of Python web frameworks: `https://wiki.python.org/moin/WebFrameworks`. We'll focus on Flask because it's relatively simple.

We'll also look at how Python can be used with Hadoop streaming to perform data analytics. Rather than download and install Apache Hadoop, we'll touch on how we build and test pipelined map-reduce processing on our desktop.

Building CLI applications

Our focus from the initial script example in *Chapter 1, Getting Started*, was on using CLI scripting to learn Python basics. CLI applications have a number of common features:

- They often read from the standard input file, write to a standard output file, and produce logs or errors in the standard error file. The OS assures us that these files are always available. Python provides them as `sys.stdin`, `sys.stdout`, and `sys.stderr`. Furthermore, functions such as `input()` and `print()` use these files by default.

- They often use environment variables for configuration. These values are available through `os.environ`.

- They may also rely on shell features, like expanding ~ into a user's home directory, something done by `os.path.expanduser()`.

- They often parse command-line arguments. While the variable `sys.argv` has the argument strings, these are awkward to work with directly. We'll use the `argparse` module to define the argument patterns, parse the strings, and create an object with the relevant argument values.

These basic features cover many programming alternatives. A web server, for example, can be thought of as a CLI program that runs forever, servicing requests that come from a specific port number. A GUI application might start from the command line, but then open windows to permit user interaction.

Getting command-line arguments with argparse

We'll create a parser to use the command-line arguments, using the `argparse` module. Once configured, we can use that parser to create a small namespace object which has all of the argument values that were provided on the command line, or has default values. Our application can use this object to control its behavior.

Generally, we want to isolate command-line handling from the rest of our application. Here's a function that handles parsing, and then uses the parsed options to invoke another function to do the real work:

```
logger= logging.getLogger(__name__)
def main():
    parser= argparse.ArgumentParser()
    parser.add_argument("-v", "--verbose",
```

```
            action="store_const", const=logging.DEBUG, default=logging.
    INFO)
        parser.add_argument("c", type=float)
        options= parser.parse_args()

        logging.getLogger().setLevel(options.verbose)
        logger.debug("Converting '{0!r}'".format(options.c))
        convert(options.c)
```

We've built an `ArgumentParser` method using all of the default parameters. We could have identified the program name, provided a summary of usage, or have had anything else displayed when someone uses the -h option to get help. We omitted these extra bits of documentation to keep the example small.

We've defined two arguments for this application: an optional argument and a positional argument. The optional argument, -v or --verbose, stores a constant value in the resulting collection of options. The name of this attribute is the long name of the argument, `verbose`. The constant provided is `logging.DEBUG`; the default value if the option isn't present is `logging.INFO`.

The positional argument, `c`, accepts one command-line argument after all of the options have been parsed. The value for `nargs` can be omitted; it can be `'*'` to collect all arguments. We've provided a requirement that the input value is converted by the `float()` function, which means that non-numeric values will be rejected with an error during argument parsing. This will be set as the `c` attribute of the resulting object.

When we evaluate the `parse_args()` method, the defined arguments are used to parse the command-line values in `sys.argv`. The `options` object will have the resulting values or defaults.

In the second part of `main()`, we've used the `options` object to set the logging level for the root logger using the `verbose` argument value. We've then used a global `logger` object to dump the single positional argument value that will be assigned to the `c` attribute of the `options` object.

Finally, we've evaluated our application function with the input argument value; the parser assigned this to the `options.c` variable. The function which does the real work is designed to be entirely separate from the command-line interface that is used to invoke it. The function accepts a floating-point value and prints a result to a standard output. It can leverage the module global `logger` object.

Our goal in designing a CLI application is to completely separate the useful work from all interface considerations. This allows us to import the function which does the real work, and build larger or more complex applications from individual pieces. It generally means that the command-line arguments are transformed into ordinary function arguments or class constructor arguments.

Using the cmd module for interactive applications

Some CLI applications require user interaction. The sftp command, for example, can be used from the command line to exchange files with a server. We can create similar interactive applications using Python's cmd module.

To build a more complex interactive application, we can create a class which extends the cmd.Cmd class. Each method in this class that has a name starting with do_ defines an interactive command. For example, if we define a method do_get(), this means that our application now has an interactive get command.

Any subsequent text after the user's input of get will be provided as an argument to the do_get() method. The do_get() function is then responsible for any further parsing and processing of the text after the command.

We can create an instance of this class, and call that inherited cmdloop() method to have a working interactive application. This allows us to deploy a working, interactive application very quickly and simply. While we're limited to a character-mode, command-line interface, we can easily add features without much extra work.

Building GUI applications

We can differentiate between applications which merely work with graphics and applications which are deeply interactive. In the first case, we might have a command-line application which creates or modifies image files. In the second case, we'll define an application which responds to input events. These interactive applications create an event loop which accepts mouse clicks, screen gestures, keyboard characters, and other events, and responds to those events. In some respects, the only unique feature of a GUI program is the wide variety of events it responds to.

The tkinter module is an interface between Python and the **Tk** user interface widget toolkit. This module helps us build richly interactive applications. When we use Python's built-in IDLE editor, we're using an application that was built with tkinter. The tkinter module documentation includes background information on the **Tk** widgets.

The turtle module also depends on the underlying **Tk** graphics. This module also allows us to build simple interactive applications. The turtle idea comes from the Logo programming language, in which graphic commands are used to animate a "turtle" which traverses the drawing space. The turtle model provides a very handy specification for certain types of graphics. For example, drawing a rotated rectangle can involve a rather complex calculation involving sine and cosine to determine the final locations of the four corners. Alternatively, we can direct the turtle to use commands such as forward(w), forward(l), and right(90) to draw a rectangle of the size $w \times l$ from any starting position and any initial rotation.

In order to make it easy to learn Python, the turtle module provides some essential classes that implement a Screen and a Turtle. The module also includes a rich collection of functions that implicitly work with a singleton Turtle and Screen object, eliminating any need to set up the graphics environment. For beginners, this function-only environment is a language of simple verbs that can be used to learn the foundations of programming.

Simple programs look like this:

```
from turtle import *

def on_screen():
    x, y = pos()
    w, h = screensize()
    return -w <= x < w and -h <= y < h

def spiral(angle, incr, size=10):
    while on_screen():
        right(angle)
        forward(size)
        size *= incr
```

We've used from turtle import * to introduce all of the individual functions. This is the common setup for beginners.

We've defined a function, on_screen(), which compares the turtle's position, given by the pos() function, with the overall size of the screen, given by the screensize() function. Our function uses a simple logical expression to determine if the current turtle position is still within the display boundaries.

For people learning to program, the implementation details of the pos() and screensize() functions may not be that helpful. More advanced programmers may want to know that the pos() function uses the Turtle.pos() method of a singleton, global Turtle instance. Similarly, the screensize() function uses the Screen.screensize() method of a singleton, global Screen instance.

The function `spiral()` will draw a spiral-like shape using three parameters that define the line segments that comprise the spiral. This function relies on the `right()` and `forward()` functions from the `turtle` package to set the turtle's orientation and then draw a line segment. While the calculation of the end point of the segment drawn by `forward()` may involve a bit of trigonometry, a new programmer is able to learn the basics of iteration without struggling with sine or cosine.

Here's how we can use this function:

```
if __name__ == "__main__":
    speed(10)
    spiral(size=10, incr=1.05, angle = 67)
    done()
```

As part of the initialization, we've set the turtle speed to 10, which is fast. For people struggling with loops or conditions, a slower speed can help them follow their code as they watch the turtle. We've evaluated the `spiral()` function with a set of argument values.

The `done()` function will start a GUI event processing loop that will wait for user interaction. We've started the loop *after* the interesting part of the drawing because the only expected event is the closing of the graphics window. When the window is closed by the user, the `done()` function will also finish. Our script can then end normally.

If we're going to build more complex interactive applications, there's a proper `mainloop()` function which we can use. This captures events so that our programs can respond to those events.

The Logo language—and the related `turtle` package—allow a novice programmer to learn the essentials of programming without having to master too many details at one time. The `turtle` package isn't designed to produce the same kinds of sophisticated technical graphics as a package such as **matplotlib** or **Pillow.**

Using more sophisticated packages

We can create complex image-processing applications using the Pillow library. This package allows us to create thumbnails of large images, convert image formats, and verify that a file actually contains encoded image data. We can also use this package to create simple scientific graphics showing two-dimensional plots of data points. This package isn't designed to build a complete GUI since it doesn't handle input events for us. For more information, see `https://pypi.python.org/pypi/Pillow/2.8.1`.

For mathematical, scientific, and statistical work, the matplotlib package is widely used. This includes very sophisticated tools for creating essential data plots in two and three dimensions. This package is bundled with SciPy and Anaconda. For more information, see `http://matplotlib.org`.

There are several more generalized graphical frameworks. One that's often used to learn more about Python is the **Pygame** framework. This has a large number of components which include tools for graphics as well as sound and image processing. The Pygame package includes a number of graphics drivers and is capable of smooth animation with a large number of moving objects. See `http://www.pygame.org/news.html`.

Building web applications

Web applications involve a great deal of processing, which is best described as boilerplate. The essential handling of the HTTP protocol, for example, is often standardized, with libraries that handle it gracefully. The details of parsing request headers and mapping a URL path to a specific resource don't need to be reinvented.

There is, however, a profound distinction between simply handling the HTTP protocol and mapping a URL to an application-specific resource. These two layers drive the definition of the **Web Services Gateway Interface** (**WSGI**) design and the `wsgi` module is in the standard library. For more information, see **Python Enhancement Proposal** (**PEP**) 3333, `https://www.python.org/dev/peps/pep-3333/`.

The idea behind WSGI is that all web services should adhere to a single, minimum standard for handling the details of HTTP requests and responses. This standard allows a complex web server to include a variety of Python tools and frameworks that are fitted together using WSGI to ensure that components interconnect properly. The mapping of URLs to resources must be handled in the context of this standard.

A `mod_wsgi` module can be plugged into an Apache HTTPD server. This module will pass requests and responses between the Apache frontend and backend Python instances. With a little bit of planning, we can be sure that static content—graphics, style sheets, JavaScript libraries, and so on—are handled by the frontend web server. The dynamic content—HTML pages, XML, or JSON documents—are handled by our Python application.

For more information on `mod_wsgi`, see `http://www.modwsgi.org/`.

Using a web framework

Web applications in this context are generally built using a framework that parses URLs and invokes a Python function to return the resource located by the URL. While this is clearly the minimum required to create a web server, there are often a large number of additional features that we'd like to have.

Authentication and authorization, for example, are features we often need and would prefer not to have to implement. It's much nicer to work with a framework that allows us to add OAuth client code. A website that uses cookies will also benefit from having session management features that integrate seamlessly.

Many websites offer RESTful web services. Sometimes these services are thin wrappers around database access. When the database is relational, we often want an **Object Relational Mapper (ORM)** layer that allows us to expose more complete objects through the RESTful service. This, too, is a good option for a web server framework.

There are two broad approaches to providing web services in Python: kits and parts. The kits approach is epitomized by packages such as Django which offer just about everything that could possibly be required in a unified collection of modules and packages. See `https://www.djangoproject.com`.

The parts approach can be seen in projects such as Flask. This is called a **microframework** because it does relatively little. A Flask server focuses on URL routing, making it ideal for building RESTful services. It may include session management, allowing it to be used for HTML sites. It cooperates well with other projects such as Jinja2, WTForms, SQLAlchemy, OAuth authentication modules, and many other modules. For more information, see `http://flask.pocoo.org/docs/0.10/`.

Building a RESTful web service with Flask

We'll demonstrate a very simple web service. We'll use the algorithm shown earlier in the turtle example, with some minor modifications, to create a dynamic graphic download. To make it easier to create a downloadable file, we'll discard the simplistic turtle graphics package and use the Pillow package to create the image file. Many websites use Pillow to validate uploaded images and create thumbnails. It's an essential part of any site that uses images.

For more information on Pillow, see `https://pypi.python.org/pypi/Pillow/2.8.1`.

A web service must provide a resource in response to an HTTP request. A simple Flask-powered site will have an overall application object and a number of routes which map URLs (and possibly method names) to functions.

Here's a simple example:

```python
from flask import Flask, request
from PIL import Image, ImageDraw, ImageColor
import tempfile

spiral_app = Flask(__name__)

@spiral_app.route('/image/<spec>', methods=('GET',))
def image(spec):
    spec_uq= urllib.parse.unquote_plus(spec)
    spec_dict = urllib.parse.parse_qs(spec_uq)
    spiral_app.logger.info( 'image spec {0!r}'.format(spec_dict) )
    try:
        angle= float(spec_dict['angle'][0])
        incr= float(spec_dict['incr'][0])
        size= int(spec_dict['size'][0])
    except Exception as e:
        return make_response('URL {0} is invalid'.format(spec), 403)

    # Working dir should be under Apache Home.
    _, temp_name = tempfile.mkstemp('.png')

    im = Image.new('RGB', (400, 300), color=ImageColor.
getrgb('white'))
    pen= Pen(im)
    spiral(pen, angle=angle, incr=incr, size=size)
    im.save(temp_name, format='png')

    # Should redirect so that Apache serves the image.
    spiral_app.logger.debug( 'image file {0!r}'.format(temp_name) )
    with open(temp_name, 'rb' ) as image_file:
        data = image_file.read()
    return (data, 200, {'Content-Type':'image/png'})
```

This example shows three central features of Flask applications. This script defines a Flask instance. We've based the instance on the filename, which will be "__main__" for a main script, but will have the module name for an imported script. We've assigned that Flask container to a variable, spiral_app, for use throughout the module file.

A more complex Flask application may have a number of individual view functions in a package of submodules. Each of these will depend on the global Flask application.

Our image resource is created by the `image()` function. We provided a `route` decorator for this function that shows the URL path and the methods that work with this resource. There are a large number of methods defined for the HTTP protocol. Many RESTful web services focus on POST, GET, PUT, and DELETE because these match the idea of the **Create, Retrieve, Update, and Delete (CRUD)** rules commonly used to summarize database operations.

We've broken down the `image()` function into four separate pieces. First, we need to parse the URL. The `route` includes a placeholder, `<spec>`, which Flask parses and provides as a parameter to the function. This will be the URL-encoded parameter to describe the spiral. It might look like this:

```
http://127.0.0.1:5000/image/size=10&angle=65.0&incr=1.05
```

Once we've decoded the specification, we'll have a special multi-valued dictionary. This looks as if the input came from an HTML form. The structure will be a mapping from form field names to a list of values for each field. The object looks like this:

```
{'size': ['10'], 'angle': ['65.0'], 'incr': ['1.05']}
```

The `image()` function only uses one value from each item; each input must be converted to numeric values. We've collected all of the potential exceptions into a single `except` clause, obscuring the details of any incorrect input. We use the Flask `make_response()` function to build a response with an error message and a status code of 403 ("Forbidden"). A more sophisticated function would use the **Accept** header to formulate a response as JSON or XML, depending on the client's stated preference. We've left it as the default MIME type of text/plain.

The image is saved into a temporary file, created with the `tempfile.mkstemp()` function. In this case, we're going to save that temporary file from the Flask application. For a low-volume website, this is acceptable. For a higher-volume website, a Python application should never handle downloads. The file should be created in a directory where the Apache HTTPD server can download the image instead of a Python application.

The image construction uses a few Pillow-defined objects to define the drawing space. A customized class defines a `Pen` instance which parallels the `turtle.Turtle` class. Once the image has been constructed, it's saved with the given filename. Note that the Pillow package can save files in a wide variety of formats; we've used `.png` in this example.

The final section downloads the file. The comment notes that a high-volume website would redirect to a URL from which Apache would download the image file. This frees up the Flask server to handle another request.

Note that the local namespace in this function will have two copies of the image. The `im` variable will hold the entire, detailed image. The `data` variable will hold the compressed filesystem version of the image document. We could use `del im` to remove the image object; however, it is generally better to decompose this into two functions so that namespaces handle object removal for us.

We can run a demonstration version of this service with the following script:

```
if __name__ == '__main__':
    spiral_app.run(debug=True)
```

This allows us to work with a running web server on our desktop. We can then experiment with different implementation alternatives.

What's important about this example is that we can—very quickly—have a service running in our desktop environment. We can then explore and experiment with the user experience very easily. For example, since the image will be embedded in an HTML page, we want to design and debug the HTML, CSS, and JavaScript for that page. This whole development process is made easier when we have a simple, easily-tweaked web server.

Plugging into a MapReduce framework

For background on the Apache Hadoop server, see `https://hadoop.apache.org`. Here's the summary:

> *The Apache Hadoop software library is a framework that allows for the distributed processing of large datasets across clusters of computers using simple programming models. It is designed to scale up from single servers to thousands of machines, each offering local computation and storage.*

One part of the Hadoop distributed processing is the MapReduce module. This module allows us to decompose analysis of data into two complementary operations: map and reduce. These operations are distributed around the Hadoop cluster to be run concurrently. A map operation processes all of the rows of datasets that are scattered around the cluster. The outputs from map operations are then fed to reduce operations to be summarized.

The Hadoop streaming interface can be used by Python programmers. This involves a Hadoop "wrapper" that will present the data to a Python mapper program as the standard input file. The standard output from a mapper must be tab-delimited key-value pairs. These are sent to the reduce programs, again as standard input. For more information on packages that help Python programmers use Hadoop, see `http://blog.cloudera.com/blog/2013/01/a-guide-to-python-frameworks-for-hadoop/`.

One common example of MapReduce operations is creating a concordance of words found in books. The mapping operation will transform a giant text file into sequences of words found in the text file. The reduce operation will count the occurrences of each word, resulting in a final summary of words and their popularity. (For more information on how important this can be, visit the NLTK website: http://www. nltk.org.)

Practical problems may involve multiple mappings and multiple reductions. In many cases, the mappings will often seem trivial: they'll extract a key and a value from each row of source data. Rather than study Hadoop too much, we'll show how we can write and test mappers and reducers on our desktop.

Our goal is to have two programs, map.py and reduce.py, that can be combined into a stream like this:

```
cat some_file.dat | python3 map.py | sort | python3 reduce.py
```

This approach will simulate Hadoop streaming by supplying data to our map.py program and our reduce.py program. This will serve as a simple integration test for our map and reduce processing. For Windows, we would use the type command instead of the Linux cat program.

Let's look at some raw climate data from the US National Ocean and Atmospheric Administration's National Climatic Data Center. Refer to http://www.ncdc.noaa. gov/cdo-web/ for climate data online. We can request files with details such as snowfall for a given time period.

Our question is "Which months have snowfall at the Richmond, VA, airport?" The snowfall data attribute is named TSNW. It's in units of one-tenth of an inch, so our mapper needs to convert it to Decimal inches to be more useful.

We can write a map script that looks like this:

```
import csv
import sys
import datetime
from decimal import Decimal
if __name__ == "__main__":
    rdr = csv.DictReader(sys.stdin)
    wtr = csv.writer(sys.stdout, delimiter='\t', lineterminator='\n')
    for row in rdr:
        date = datetime.datetime.strptime(row['DATE'], "%Y%m%d").
date()
        if row['TSNW'] in ('0', '-9999', '9999'):
```

```
        continue # Zero or equipment error: reject
    wtr.writerow( [date.month, Decimal(row['TSNW'])/10] )
```

Because our input is in more or less standard CSV notation—with a heading—we can use a `csv.DictReader` object to parse the input. Each row of data is a `dict` object with keys defined by the first line of the CSV file. The output is more specialized: with Hadoop it must be a tab-delimited key and value, terminated with a newline character.

For each input dictionary object, we'll convert the date from text to a proper Python date so that we can reliably extract the month. We could do this by using `row['DATE'][4:6]`, but that seems opaque. The mapper includes a filter to reject months that have no snow, or have a domain-specific null value (9999 or -9999) instead of a measurement.

The output is a key and a value. Our key is the reported month; the value is the snowfall converted from one-tenth inch to inch measurements. We've used the `Decimal` class to avoid introducing floating-point approximations.

The reduce operation uses a `Counter` object to summarize the results produced by the mapper. For this example, the reduce looks like this:

```
import csv
import sys
from collections import Counter
from decimal import Decimal
if __name__ == "__main__":
    rdr= csv.DictReader(
        sys.stdin, fieldnames=("month","snowfall"),
        delimiter='\t', lineterminator='\n')
    counts = Counter()
    for line in rdr:
        counts[line['month']] += Decimal(line['snowfall'])
    print( counts )
```

The reduce reader matches the mapper's writer: they both use a delimiter of a tab and a line terminator of the newline character. This follows Hadoop's requirements for the data that flows from mappers to reducers. We've also created a `Counter` object to store our snowfall data.

For each line of input, we extract the inches of snowfall and accumulate those in the `Counter` object with a key of the month number. The final result will show the inches of snow for each month in the greater Richmond metropolitan area.

We can easily test and experiment with this on our desktop. We can execute a pipeline of mapper, sort, and reducer using either a shell script or perhaps a little wrapper program like this:

```
import subprocess
dataset = "526212.csv"
command = """cat {dataset} | python3 -m Chapter_15.map | sort |
    python3 -m Chapter_15.reduce"""
command = command.format_map(locals())
result= subprocess.check_output(command, shell=True)
for line in result.splitlines():
    print( line.decode("ASCII") )
```

We've created a command that will work on Mac OS X or Linux, and substituted a filename into that command. For Windows we can use `type` instead of `cat`; the Python program might be named `python` instead of `python3`. Otherwise, the shell pipeline should work fine in Windows.

We've used the `subprocess.check_output()` function to run this shell command and collect the output. This is a quick way to experiment with our Hadoop programs while avoiding the delays associated with using a busy Hadoop cluster.

This approach works well as long as we stick to elements of the libraries that are properly installed in the Hadoop environment. In some cases, our cluster might have Anaconda installed, giving us access to a wide variety of packages. When we want to use our own package—one that's not installed throughout the cluster—we'll need to provide the additional module to the Hadoop streaming command to be sure that our additional modules are downloaded to each node in the cluster, along with our mapper and reducer.

Summary

In this chapter, we've looked at several kinds of Python applications. While Python is used widely, we've picked a few areas of focus. We've looked at CLI applications capable of processing large volumes of data. The command-line interface is also present in other kinds of applications, making this a fundamental part of any program.

We've looked at GUI programs, using only the built-in `turtle` module. The GUI frameworks that are widely used involve downloads, installation, and more sophisticated programming that we could not illustrate in a single chapter. There are several popular choices; there's no consensus on a "best" package for GUI applications. Making a choice is difficult.

We've also looked at web applications, using the Flask module. This is also a separate download. In many cases, there are a number of related downloads that will become part of a web application. We might include Jinja2, WTForms, OAuth, SQLAlchemy, and Pillow, to expand the web server's libraries.

We've also looked at how we might leverage desktop Python to develop Hadoop applications. Rather than download and install Hadoop, we can create a processing pipeline that follows the Hadoop approach. We can write mappers and reducers using only desktop tools, allowing us to create reliable unit tests. This gives us the confidence that we'll get the expected results when running our applications on the Hadoop cluster with a complete set of data.

This isn't all, of course. Python can be used inside another application as the language for automating that application. A program can embed a Python interpreter which interacts with the overall application. For more information, see https://docs.python.org/2/extending/embedding.html.

We can imagine the universe of Python applications as a large body of water filled with islands, archipelagos, inlets, and estuaries. Chesapeake Bay on the US East Coast is an example. We've tried to show the principal features of this bay: the headlands, points, shallows, and coastlines. We've avoided the effects of currents, weather, and tides, so that we can focus on the essential features of the bay. Pragmatic navigation along a specific route requires more study of the area of interest: detailed navigation charts, pilot guides, and local knowledge from other mariners.

It's important to consider the extent of the Python universe. The distance to a destination can appear daunting. Our objective has been to show some principal waypoints that can help break a long voyage into shorter legs. If we isolate the legs of a long journey, we can solve each of them separately and build a larger solution from the pieces.

Index

Symbols

__call__() method 206
__init__() method 206
* notation
  using 133-135
** notation
  using 133-135
@property decorator 221
__slots__
  used, for saving storage 204
@staticmethod decorator 221
*tail assignment
  using 70, 71
__test__ variable 233

A

abstract base classes
  about 205
  callable class, writing 205, 206
acceptance test-driven development
    (ATDD) 235
Accept header 256
additional function annotations
  writing 142
add-on test libraries
  using 237
algorithms
  approaching, ways 159
alternative implementations
  designing 217
Anaconda project
  URL 33
and operator 104

application 209
argparse module 213
ASCII
  working with 64
assert statement
  about 81
  defining 92
assignment statement 67-69
attributes
  using 201, 202
augmented assignment statement 71, 72

B

bit-oriented operators
  using 27, 28
bits
  using 34, 35
Boolean data 82
Boolean expression 81
Boolean values
  using 34, 35
bool() function 82
break statement
  defining 116, 117
  executing 117, 118
built-in conversion functions
  complex() 46
  float() 46
  int() 46
  using 46, 47
built-in data types
  complex 25
  float 25
  int 25

Thank you for buying
Python Essentials

About Packt Publishing

Packt, pronounced 'packed', published its first book, *Mastering phpMyAdmin for Effective MySQL Management*, in April 2004, and subsequently continued to specialize in publishing highly focused books on specific technologies and solutions.

Our books and publications share the experiences of your fellow IT professionals in adapting and customizing today's systems, applications, and frameworks. Our solution-based books give you the knowledge and power to customize the software and technologies you're using to get the job done. Packt books are more specific and less general than the IT books you have seen in the past. Our unique business model allows us to bring you more focused information, giving you more of what you need to know, and less of what you don't.

Packt is a modern yet unique publishing company that focuses on producing quality, cutting-edge books for communities of developers, administrators, and newbies alike. For more information, please visit our website at www.packtpub.com.

About Packt Open Source

In 2010, Packt launched two new brands, Packt Open Source and Packt Enterprise, in order to continue its focus on specialization. This book is part of the Packt Open Source brand, home to books published on software built around open source licenses, and offering information to anybody from advanced developers to budding web designers. The Open Source brand also runs Packt's Open Source Royalty Scheme, by which Packt gives a royalty to each open source project about whose software a book is sold.

Writing for Packt

We welcome all inquiries from people who are interested in authoring. Book proposals should be sent to author@packtpub.com. If your book idea is still at an early stage and you would like to discuss it first before writing a formal book proposal, then please contact us; one of our commissioning editors will get in touch with you.

We're not just looking for published authors; if you have strong technical skills but no writing experience, our experienced editors can help you develop a writing career, or simply get some additional reward for your expertise.

Mastering Object-oriented Python

ISBN: 978-1-78328-097-1   Paperback: 634 pages

Grasp the intricacies of object-oriented programming in Python in order to efficiently build powerful real-world applications

1. Create applications with flexible logging, powerful configuration and command-line options, automated unit tests, and good documentation.

2. Use the Python special methods to integrate seamlessly with built-in features and the standard library.

3. Design classes to support object persistence in JSON, YAML, Pickle, CSV, XML, Shelve, and SQL.

Functional Python Programming

ISBN: 978-1-78439-699-2   Paperback: 360 pages

Create succinct and expressive implementations with functional programming in Python

1. Implement common functional programming design patterns and techniques in Python.

2. Learn how to choose between imperative and functional approaches based on expressiveness, clarity, and performance.

3. Apply functional Python to common Exploratory Data Analysis (EDA) programming problems.

Please check **www.PacktPub.com** for information on our titles